Get the eBook FREE!

(PDF, ePub, Kindle, and liveBook all included)

We believe that once you buy a book from us, you should be able to read it in any format we have available. To get electronic versions of this book at no additional cost to you, purchase and then register this book at the Manning website.

Go to https://www.manning.com/freebook and follow the instructions to complete your pBook registration.

That's it!
Thanks from Manning!

The Well-Grounded Python Developer

The Well-Grounded Python Developer

HOW THE PROS USE PYTHON AND FLASK

DOUG FARRELL

Foreword by MICHAEL KENNEDY

MANNING

SHELTER ISLAND

For online information and ordering of this and other Manning books, please visit www.manning.com. The publisher offers discounts on this book when ordered in quantity. For more information, please contact

    Special Sales Department
    Manning Publications Co.
    20 Baldwin Road
    PO Box 761
    Shelter Island, NY 11964
    Email: orders@manning.com

Manning Publications Co.
20 Baldwin Road
PO Box 761
Shelter Island, NY 11964

Development editor:	Christina Taylor
Technical development editor:	René van den Berg
Review editor:	Aleksandar Dragosavljević
Production editor:	Kathleen Rossland
Copyeditor:	Kristen Bettcher
Proofreader:	Michael Beady
Technical proofreader:	Mathijs Affourtit
Typesetter and cover designer:	Marija Tudor

ISBN 9781617297441
Printed in the United States of America

This book is dedicated to my partner and wife, Susan,
whose encouragement, patience, and
love makes all things possible.

brief contents

contents

foreword

We marvel at the modern creations of very experienced software developers. Instagram is a polished and beautiful experience, whereas YouTube dwarfs even the largest television audiences, and it still feels like you're the only user on the system. Both YouTube and Instagram have Python at their core.

When you first get started in programming, it's easy to look at the challenge ahead and see a towering mountain. Fortunately, you don't have to climb a mountain in a single bound, just as you don't have to become a confident Python developer all at once. Software development does not require you to be a genius. You don't need to be a mathematical wiz. Becoming a good software developer requires a strong sense of curiosity and a lot of persistence.

You don't have to take my word for it. Guido van Rossum, the inventor of Python, was interviewed for the *Sing for Science* podcast:

> *Host:* And you don't have to have a mathematical inclination?

> *Guido:* That's correct. Some sort of an inclination towards logical thinking and an attention to details is much more important than math.

So if programming is not centered on math, then what do you need to be successful? You need thousands of small and understandable building blocks. Like climbing a mountain with many small steps and lots of persistence, you build YouTube by solving thousands of small and easily understandable computer problems with a few lines of understandable code.

How do you discover these building blocks? You can bounce around the internet and programming tutorials, piecing them together yourself, or, like mountain climbing, you could hire a guide. Doug Farrell and this book of his are your guides.

Here, you will learn many building blocks. You will learn the importance of naming things clearly. The function `get_blog_post_by_id` doesn't need additional details to communicate its role, does it? You'll see how to group your code into reusable blocks with functions. You will build forms to display a UI on the web with Python and Flask. You'll use Python's SQLAlchemy database package to read and write data from a database without the need to understand SQL (the language of relational databases).

In the end, you'll have a practical and real-world application built out of these many building blocks. It'll be a fun journey, and the code will be a great resource to pull examples and ideas from as you grow in your software development career. With Doug and this book as your guides, you'll keep climbing and, before you know it, you'll be on the summit.

Michael Kennedy is a Python enthusiast and entrepreneur. He's the host of the Talk Python To Me *and* Python Bytes *podcasts. Michael founded Talk Python Training and is a Python Software Foundation Fellow based in Portland, Oregon.*

preface

I've worked at many interesting and varied jobs in my life and have been fortunate enough to be a software developer for almost 40 years. In that time, I've learned and worked with quite a few programming languages—Pascal, Fortran, C, C++, Visual Basic, PHP, Python, and JavaScript—and applied these languages to work in quite a few industries. Using all these languages and having these experiences taught me a great deal.

C taught me how to use—and certainly abuse—pointers and gave me a thirst to optimize my applications for speed. C++ taught me about object-oriented programming (OOP), a way of thinking in which I'm still firmly rooted. PHP was my first exposure to a scripting language, and it taught me that maybe it was okay not to manage everything, like memory, myself. PHP also brought with it my first dive into web development and the nascent ideas of browsers as an application platform.

It's been almost two decades since I discovered Python, and it has been my sweet spot for application development ever since. The language helped to crystalize the vague thoughts I had about development, the idea that there should be one obvious way to do things. Being able to use multiple concepts about development—like OOP, procedural, and functional programming—all in the same language is very valuable. A language can be relatively easy to learn and expressive, and yet seemingly have no ceiling on the kinds of problems it can be used to solve.

Because I was excited about Python, I wanted to promote it and encourage others to jump on board. This led me to give presentations and teach classes within the organizations where I worked. I also had the chance to teach Python at a STEM facility near my hometown to kids aged 8 to 16. It's a tossup which way the lessons were actually going, as I learned a lot from the kids in the class. Each class taught me more about how to present material in a more accessible way. It was apparent when something I was teaching was working or not by how hard I had to work to keep the kids from switching over to Minecraft on their laptops.

For the presentations and class work, I was writing my own Python material. I wanted to do more of this, which led to writing articles for RealPython.com. I wrote several well-received articles for the site, which was gratifying. Those articles were how I connected with Manning. An acquisitions editor reached out to me, and we talked about writing a Python book for them and what that would look like.

The result of those conversations is this book, which will help you along your journey to becoming a developer. Python is a wonderful, expressive, and enjoyable tool to bring with you. I've enjoyed the journey for a long time and am still doing so. That is my goal for the book, and I hope this book helps you reach your goals.

acknowledgments

I've worked hard to make this book an informative, as well as enjoyable, read. But if it is any of these things, it's because of the people who have contributed to its creation.

Many people at Manning Publishing helped bring this book into existence. The acquisitions editor who approached me to write a book, the production people who helped shape it, the reviewers who helped refine it, and my development editors who helped me every step of the way. They helped me navigate the many facets of writing and publishing a book, and I enjoyed many conversations with them that kept me on track through the process.

To all the reviewers: Alejandro Guerra Manzanares, Amanda Debler, Angelo Costa, Bernard Fuentes, Bhagvan Kommadi, Brandon Friar, Chad Miars, Christopher Kardell, Dan Sheikh, Danilo Abrignani, Deshuang Tang, Dhinakaran Venkat, Dirk Gomez, Eder Andres Avila Niño, Eli Mayost, Eric Chiang, Ernest Addae, Evyatar Kafkafi, Ezra Schroeder, Félix Moreno, Francisco Rivas, Frankie Thomas-Hockey, Ganesh Swaminathan, Garry Alan Offord, Gustavo Gomes, Hiroyuki Musha, James J. Byleckie, James Matlock, Janit Kumar Anjaria, Joaquin Beltran, John Guthrie, John Harbin, Johnny Hopkins, Jose Apablaza, Joseph Pachod, Joshua A. McAdams, Julien Pohie, Kamesh Ganesan, Katia Patkin, Keith Anthony, Kelum Prabath Senanayake, Kimberly Winston-Jackson, Koushik Vikram, Kup Sivam, Lee Harding, Leonardo Taccari, Lev Veyde, Lúcás Meier, Marc-Anthony Taylor, Marco Carnini, Marcus Geselle, Maria Ana, Michael Patin, Mike Baran, Mohana Krishna, Muhammad Sohaib Arif, NaveenKumar Namachivayam, Ninoslav Cerkez, Patrick Regan, Philip Best, Philip Patterson, Rahul Singh, Raul Murciano, Raymond Cheung, Richard Meinsen, Robert Kulagowski, Rodney Weis, Roman Zhuzha, Romell Ian De La Cruz, Samvid Mistry, Sandeep Dhameja, Sanjeev Kilarapu, Satej Kumar Sahu, Sergiu Raducu, Shankar Swamy, Stanley Anozie,

Stefan Turalski, Teddy Hagos, Vidhya Vinay, and Vitosh Doynov, your suggestions helped make this a better book.

I also want to thank Samantha Stone, a young editor I only know virtually. Paul Chayka, the executive director of Robotics & Beyond, a local STEM education center, introduced me to her. Samantha was a high school member of R&B who volunteered to review the book while it was in progress. She proved to have outstanding editorial skills, honest and forthright feedback, and a great source of clarity for what worked and didn't in my writing.

I'd also like to thank Carmine Mauriello. He and I have been friends for decades and colleagues a few times working for the same organizations. Almost from the get-go, he told me, "You should write a book." It's still unclear if this was just his kind way of trying to get me to stop talking, but Carm, I appreciate the encouragement all the same. Here, at long last, is that book.

I'd like to thank my mom and dad, both of whom were great writers in their own right. Mom encouraged (read that as arm-twisted) me to take a typing class in the age of the IBM Selectric Typewriter. That has proven to be one of the best skills I've ever learned. My dad was a great storyteller who taught me the value of writing simple declarative sentences. He was also the fastest typist I'd ever seen on an ancient Underwood mechanical typewriter.

Lastly, I would like to thank my wife, Susan, whose steady encouragement, unfailing patience, and most of all, love, has made all of this possible.

about this book

The Well-Grounded Python Developer exists to help beginning programmers bridge the gap to becoming developers. It does this in two ways—by presenting approaches to thinking about the development process in relation to larger projects, and by portraying how to do it using Python.

Who should read this book

This book does not teach Python; many other resources do that quite well. In fact, the reader should have some experience with Python and have a desire to go further with the language. If this feels like you, then I think this book has a lot to offer.

One of the goals of this book is to help you become a Pythonista. With that in mind, who is the intended reader of this book? I think there are broad categories of readers who will benefit from the material presented here.

The first type of reader is someone who knows the basics of Python programming—how to write loops and conditional statements and use variables to get things done. This reader has written utility programs that exist in a single file and knows how to run them from the command line. They might want to build more complex applications but don't understand how to do so. They could be thinking about writing a web server using Python and what technologies they'd have to know to do that. Essentially, this reader has a basic toolset, has hammered things together, and wants to build something more significant.

The second type is a developer in another language who is interested in broadening their skill set to include Python. This could be because Python is growing in popularity in both usage and interest, or it could be out of necessity for a project at their current job. They know how to get things done in the language they currently use and want to learn how to do similar work with Python in a Pythonic way.

xix

The third type could be someone involved with data science and big data analytics. Python is becoming one of the key players in this space, with many well-developed libraries serving the needs of this kind of work. This book won't get into the use of those libraries—that would be another book onto itself—but it will help readers involved in that space. Many who work in data science aren't necessarily software developers. Coding is a means to an end, a tool to help reach a goal. Learning to use that tool better and with greater expressiveness by becoming a Python developer will take coding out of the problem domain, giving them more room to focus on the task at hand.

How this book is organized: A road map

The book is divided into two sections, Groundwork and Fieldwork. Groundwork builds foundational information about the development process and manner of thinking using Python. Fieldwork builds on that foundation to build a web application with sophistication. Each of the two sections encompasses multiple chapters:

- Groundwork
  - *Chapter 1*—"Becoming a Pythonista" introduces concepts around thinking like a developer and reaching goals as such. It also introduces Python as not only a viable path to reach those goals but a powerful one.
  - *Chapter 2*—"That's a good name" introduces the importance of how developers name things and how powerful the concept of namespaces is.
  - *Chapter 3*—"The API: Let's talk" presents how developers and computers "speak" to each other: the contract between the two, what's passed as input, and what's expected as output. The chapter goes into detail about the design and implementation of good Python functions.
  - *Chapter 4*—"The object of conversation" presents object-oriented programming (OOP) with Python. This includes how to define classes and the uses of inheritance, polymorphism, and composition when implementing a class hierarchy.
  - *Chapter 5*—"Exceptional events" covers Python exceptions and how to handle them: when and where to catch exceptions and approaches to addressing them when the developer does catch them. It also talks about intentionally raising exceptions and creating custom exceptions.

- Fieldwork
  - *Chapter 6*—"Sharing with the internet" is the start of creating the demonstration web application that pulls together the groundwork of the previous chapters.
  - *Chapter 7*—"Doing it with style" sets the baseline for the style of the demonstration web application by introducing Bootstrap. It also introduces the steps necessary to implement and maintain a larger application by using Flask Blueprints and how the application is navigated and configured.

- *Chapter 8*—"Do I know you? Authentication" presents techniques to authenticate users of the application.
- *Chapter 9*—"What can you do? Authorization" presents authorization of users and what different kinds of authorization provide users with different capabilities. It also adds the ability to send emails from the application and how authentication adds security that can be used to protect parts of the application.
- *Chapter 10*—"Persistence is good: Databases" is something of a tangential chapter, as it discusses relational databases and how to design, implement, and query them. It also introduces SQLAlchemy as a tool to access database information using Python objects.
- *Chapter 11*—"I've got something to say" completes the demonstration web application to create a fully functioning blogging platform where users can view and create content, as well as comment on that content.
- *Chapter 12*—"Are we there yet?" is the final chapter of the book that wraps up what the users have learned and the world that awaits them for further learning.
  - Appendix
    - *Appendix*—"Your development environment" covers installing Python on various platforms, how to set up virtual environments, and why it's a good idea to do so. It also covers installing Visual Studio Code as an integrated development environment (IDE) to aid in the creation of Python code.

Depending on where you are in your Python journey will contribute to where you start in the book and what you find most valuable. If you are on the beginning part of the path, you'll benefit by reading the entire book. If you're further along, you can start with the Fieldwork section and continue from there.

About the code

This book includes examples of the source code from the GitHub repository that accompanies the book, both in complete, standalone listings and in the body of the text. The code is formatted in a `fixed-width font like this` to separate it from the formatting of the rest of the book. Some code is presented in **bold** to draw attention to it. This is usually accompanied by code annotations to explain the bolded code.

The code listings in the book have been reformatted to better fit the constraints of the book design. In addition, in many cases, the code comments that are part of the repository have been removed to save vertical space on the page and reduce visual clutter.

You can find executable snippets of code from the liveBook (online) version of this book at https://livebook.manning.com/book/the-well-grounded-python-developer. Complete source code for all examples in the book is available at the author's GitHub site at https://github.com/writeson/the-well-grounded-python-developer and from the Manning website at https://www.manning.com/books/the-well-grounded-python -developer.

liveBook discussion forum

Purchase of *The Well-Grounded Python Developer* includes free access to liveBook, Manning's online reading platform. Using liveBook's exclusive discussion features, you can attach comments to the book globally or to specific sections or paragraphs. It's a snap to make notes for yourself, ask and answer technical questions, and receive help from the author and other users. To access the forum, go to https://livebook.manning .com/book/the-well-grounded-python-developer/discussion. You can also learn more about Manning's forums and the rules of conduct at https://livebook.manning.com/ discussion.

Manning's commitment to our readers is to provide a venue where a meaningful dialogue between individual readers and between readers and the author can take place. It is not a commitment to any specific amount of participation on the part of the author, whose contribution to the forum remains voluntary (and unpaid). We suggest you try asking the author some challenging questions lest his interest stray! The forum and the archives of previous discussions will be accessible from the publisher's website as long as the book is in print.

about the author

DOUG FARRELL has been developing software since 1983, though his BS is in physics, and he has an AAS in commercial art—two obviously related fields. Doug is a self-taught programmer and has used quite a few languages over the years in a lot of industries: Pascal, Fortran, C/C++, PHP, Python, and JavaScript. He has been working with Python since 2000, and it's been his primary language since 2006.

Doug has written articles for RealPython.com. He has also taught at a STEM facility where a lot of his course material is used.

about the cover illustration

The figure on the cover of *The Well-Grounded Python Developer* is "Femme de l'Isle de Pathmos," or "Woman of Patmos Dodecanese Islands," taken from a collection by Jacques Grasset de Saint-Sauveur, published in 1788. Each illustration is finely drawn and colored by hand.

In those days, it was easy to identify where people lived and what their trade or station in life was just by their dress. Manning celebrates the inventiveness and initiative of the computer business with book covers based on the rich diversity of regional culture centuries ago, brought back to life by pictures from collections such as this one.

Becoming a Pythonista

Being a *developer* is an unusual pursuit. Developers spend time creating something out of nothing, and even then, it's hard to describe the things we've just created.

Ever tried explaining at a party what writing code is like? Even if you're a good enough storyteller to keep people from wandering off immediately, it's still challenging to reach the "aha" moment when someone might know what you're talking about. And it's not a failing on the listener's part. It's just objectively hard to describe being a developer.

Differences between programmers and developers

You may be wondering how a developer is different from a programmer:

- Programmers create working Python scripts. Developers build modules to construct larger applications.
- Programmers know Python well enough to create small applications. Developers know Python well enough to use it as one tool among many to build larger applications.
- Programmers solve problems using Python, whereas developers think about the big picture and where Python fits into that vision.
- Programmers know how to use the Python standard library, and developers know how to use third-party packages.
- Programmers write functioning code. Developers write consistently maintainable code.
- Programmers might not know coding conventions, whereas developers rely on conventions and idioms to speed up their development work.
- Programmers know that learning is a necessity. Developers embrace learning as a lifelong pursuit.

Computers are exceptionally static devices. Developing applications is a way for humans to express what we want a computer to do in a language we can read and write and the computer can understand. The trick is being exact enough to get the computer to do what's intended, rather than something else.

People can function in the world and achieve great things because we thrive in the inexactness of human communication. We obtain meaning from context, intention, inflection, and subtlety—all of the things that provide great richness to our communication. None of that is possible for a computer. Computers require an almost maddening exactness to function. The attention to minutiae to express that exactness, the patience to do so, and the ability to learn and stay open to new ideas are part and parcel of being a developer.

This book aims to build a foundation of skills and tools generally useful to developers. We'll use those tools to build standalone applications that demonstrate them.

Once your toolbelt has been expanded, you'll create a straightforward web application to get comfortable with the challenges it presents and then modify that application to incorporate new features. Each step will build on this knowledge to introduce one or more new abilities, techniques, modules, and solutions.

Python can transport you to wonderful places. You only need to take those first steps. With that in mind, let's get started.

1.1 *Commitment to learning*

Learning how to get better at technology and developing with Python is a valuable skill. Working to improve yourself as a Python developer has two benefits. The first is being able to take on larger projects with the confidence that you can complete them and create a working system. The second is the practice of learning. Being a lifetime learner isn't just a catchy educational phrase; it's the reality of being a software developer.

For example, during my career as a developer, I've worked in several languages— Fortran, Pascal, C/C++, PHP, and now Python and JavaScript. I learned some of these languages because they were being used where I was working. In other cases, the language was well suited to the task at hand. I once considered myself a strong C/C++ programmer and enjoyed working on the applications I wrote with it.

However, I don't have an interest in dusting off my C/C++ skills and doing that kind of coding again. Right now, for me, Python is the sweet spot as a language I want to use. It appeals to my desire to work in an object-oriented programming style but doesn't limit me to only that style. Python's syntax and grammar are clear and expressive enough that I can think about solutions in pseudocode that closely resembles Python code.

If software development is your vocation, or you want it to be, keep in mind that careers are long and changes happen continuously. Committing to learning new technologies and languages is the answer to both of those concerns. In this rapidly changing world, there is very little job security; the only real security is the skills you can bring to the table.

1.2   Reaching goals

This book has some goals, one of which—helping you become a stronger developer— is implied in the title, *The Well-Grounded Python Developer*. If you're reading this book, then I gather that's a goal you have as well.

1.2.1   Thinking like a developer

Learning a programming language means learning the syntax and grammar of that language: how to create variables, build loops, make decisions, and execute program statements. These are your basic tools, but thinking like a developer also means knowing how to combine those tools to create a useful program. The analogy goes much further toward building bigger and more powerful tools.

This process of seeing how to use smaller tools to build bigger ones is key to thinking like a developer. The steps of creating one thing by using other things eventually help you see the big picture. As you learn how to construct more powerful blocks of code, seeing the big picture as a developer means understanding the problem you're trying to solve and mentally traveling back and forth along the steps to implement a solution. From the smallest block of code to more extensive functionality, you'll be able to follow the path to success.

1.2.2   Building applications

In developer terms, an application is a complete program providing useful functionality and a user interface. An obvious one you know already is Microsoft Word, a big desktop application. Google's Gmail is a big web application. These are examples of large applications that provide many features with a great deal of functionality.

There are many smaller applications; for example, if you're familiar with the command line available on most computer systems, you may have used the `ping` command. This application is often employed to determine whether another computer on a network is responding to a `ping` request. Using `ping` is a simple troubleshooting test to see if the remote computer is running before digging further into any existing problems.

The ping application is pretty much on the other end of the spectrum from applications like Word or Gmail, but it is a complete application in its own right. It provides a useful function and has a user interface from the command line in a terminal window.

There are other blocks of code on which developers work, and these are code libraries. They provide useful functionality and have interfaces but, for the most part, are used by larger applications that want access to the library's functionality. The standard modules that come with Python, a feature commonly referred to as "batteries included," is an excellent example of library code. You'll be creating library modules to use in the applications we'll develop as we move forward through this book.

1.3   Using Python

For the most part, everything you've read up until now about thinking like a developer could apply to just about any programming language. What makes Python an excellent choice to pursue thinking like a developer? As I mentioned in the previous section, I believe Python provides a sweet spot for application development. Let's talk about why I think that, and hopefully you will come to feel the same way.

1.3.1   Programming paradigms

Most, if not all, of the languages in everyday use draw their abilities from other languages and programming paradigms. Python is a member of this club in good standing. If you've done any programming in Python, you know it's a flexible language that covers a lot of ground. Part of the flexibility of the language is the many ways in which you can work with it:

- The ability to code with control flow provided by loops, nested loops, conditional evaluation, and procedure calls makes Python a structured programming language.
- Python is a procedural language in that you can create functions (procedures), allowing you to generate blocks of code that can be reused in other parts of your program.
- You can code using class-based, object-oriented programming (OOP), which captures state information along with code that operates on that state.
- Python, though not strictly a functional language, provides features that allow you to program in that manner. Functions in Python are first-class objects and can be passed around like any other object. This feature is required by functional programming, and Python's provision of this feature is useful when working in that style.

- Event-driven programs, like a windowing GUI application—where events determine the program control flow—are entirely possible with Python.

Python can be brought to bear on any and all of these paradigms to solve programming problems and create applications.

1.3.2 Creating maintainable code

When you create an application, you expect it will be used, which means it will have a lifetime. During that lifetime, bugs that testing doesn't always reveal will manifest themselves in your code. Even if you're the only user of the application, a change in how you use it, or the environment in which you do so, could reveal problems you can resolve and improve. The PyTest module (https://docs.pytest.org/en/7.2.x/) is a powerful framework to help test the applications you develop.

If other people use your application, its requirements will change. Changing requirements mean changes will need to be made to the existing code to add new features.

Nothing in the software development world is more constant or happening faster than change. Program code is read more than it is written and what you write today will change over time. If you come back to your own code after a surprisingly short amount of time has passed, you will be amazed at how much you have to read your own work to return to the context in which it was created. If you work in a team and someone else in the team will be modifying your work, that person will bless or curse you based on how maintainable and readable your code is.

Writing maintainable code is a developer strength worth pursuing. Adopting a coding style and consistently using it goes a long way toward this goal. Using intelligent and meaningful variable names, function names, and class names is important. I'm a firm believer that no programming language, even Python, is completely self-documenting. Comments that clarify the intention of a section of code go a long way toward understanding the code's purpose and intent.

Another important aspect of writing maintainable code is making it flexible. It's difficult to anticipate how the functions and classes you create might be used later on in the development of an application.

A simplistic example would be a function performing some complex calculation, formatting the results, and then printing those formatted results to standard output. The future use of that function is severely limited to how it's currently implemented, including printing output. Very likely, it can't be reused for anything else because of this. If explaining what a function does has an "and" in the explanation, it should be implemented as two functions. Refactoring the example creates two functions—one that performs the complex calculation and returns the raw results and another that formats the results.

The second function that formats data can be used later in the application to format and output the results to a destination device. By leaving the formatting and output until it's needed, the output can be directed to any device—a display screen, a web page, a printer, or perhaps a response to an API call. The complex calculation function remains unchanged.

1.3.3　Performance

The run-time performance of any programming language is an often debated, highly charged, and complex topic. Python is often compared to other languages, like C and Java, regarding execution performance. Beyond blanket statements about this or that being faster, those comparisons often become more complicated.

What is being compared—CPU speed or memory speed? How is it being measured? Is the benchmark software optimized for one language but not the other? Does the benchmark make the most of efficient coding practices in both languages being compared?

At the risk of sounding flippant, I don't care very much about any of this. It's not that I don't care about performance (we'll get to that), but the argument about this language being faster than that language is not one worth engaging in.

Computers are well past the point in time when CPU cycles and memory access times are worth considering in any performance calculation. To steal a business idiom, *optimize your most expensive resource.*

You are the most expensive resource. And if you work for a company as a software developer, you are the most expensive resource connected to their computer resources. Optimizing your performance as a developer is paramount, and if you can transpose the big picture in your mind quickly into code that runs, you have become invaluable. If you can express an idea into code and get it up and running faster and improve time to market, that is a huge win. This is where Python shines.

All of this is not to say I don't care about performance. When I first got into programming, I was obsessed with speed and would go to great lengths to shave CPU cycles from my code. Along the way, I learned a lot about what's important and what's not.

The first thing you should do before beginning any optimization effort is to determine whether it's necessary at all. Is there a speed requirement your application needs to meet? If so, does a metric exist to measure your application, defining when it's fast enough? If the answers to these questions determine that your application is already fast enough, then you have struck upon the ultimate in terms of time spent optimizing—zero.

On the other hand, if it's determined that your application does need to be faster, then you need to take the second step. This second step is to profile the application to measure where it's spending time.

With this measurement in hand, you can apply the 90/10 rule of code optimization. The rule states that 90% of an application's execution time is spent in 10% of the code. This rule is a generalization to be sure, but it does provide a roadmap of where you should pursue optimization. Focusing on anything other than the 10% of code where the application spends most of its time is time poorly spent that won't improve the overall speed of your application.

Any optimization work needs to be done iteratively and in tandem with profiling. This tells you whether your optimization efforts are making improvements or not. It will also help you decide whether the improvements you've made are incremental or orders of magnitude better. Small gains in performance need to be balanced against the complexity of the code.

Lastly, know when to quit. With a target of what performance metric your application has to meet, you'll know when to stop optimizing and ship. Shipping is a feature that can't be overstated.

1.3.4   *The language community*

The most popular programming languages currently in use have large and active communities of people who are willing to share their experiences, problems, and expertise with others. Python has a particularly welcoming community with a minimum of flame wars or bullying. The community is a valuable resource for the newcomer to programming, as well as old hands who are working out new problems.

> **TIP**   Being a developer makes you part of a community, and the Python community is a particularly good one. Participate, contribute, listen, and add to that community. Everyone will be better for it, including yourself.

Very often, when working out Python puzzles, you will find that others have worked on similar puzzles before and published solutions. The Python Package Index (https://pypi.org/) is an invaluable resource when building applications and looking for libraries and modules to help that process along.

Beyond searching Google for Python help, here's a short list of useful Python resources:

- https://realpython.com—Real Python is an excellent source of tutorials about Python.
- https://realpython.com/podcasts/rpp/—A Python podcast hosted by Real Python.
- https://pythonbytes.fm—A Python podcast delivering interesting headlines and banter.
- https://talkpython.fm—The Talk Python To Me podcast has interviews with people and personalities in the community.
- https://pythonpodcast.com—Another good interview podcast.
- https://testandcode.com—Test and Code, a podcast about software testing and Python.
- https://www.pythonweekly.com—The sign-up page for a weekly Python newsletter containing links to useful articles and information.
- https://pycoders.com—The sign-up page for another great Python newsletter.

1.3.5   *Developer tooling*

As a developer, one of your goals is to get your thoughts and ideas from your mind and into a Python code file with as few impediments as possible. A good keyboard that works for you, proper lighting, a decent screen—all of these things contribute to the flow of the work you're trying to do. There are many good editors out there that recognize Python code and syntax highlight as you write, making it easier to find errors and keywords.

A good editor is an important tool, but beyond that, a good IDE—or integrated development environment—is even more so. An IDE is a big step up from an editor when productively writing code. Not only will it have a good editor with syntax highlighting, but it will have knowledge of the language itself. This gives you additional assistance when writing code, commonly called IntelliSense. IntelliSense provides a code completion aid interactively, refactoring existing code, symbolic name information and usage, and much more.

One last thing a good IDE should provide is a debugger. A debugger allows you to run a program interactively and set breakpoints. A breakpoint is a marker you can set on a program line where the code will stop running when it attempts to execute that line. While the program is paused, you can examine the variables that are within the current scope and see what the program is doing at that point. You can even modify the value of a variable, which will affect the execution from that point forward. You can single-step through the code from the breakpoint following the behavior of the program on a line-by-line basis. You'll be able to step into a function call and follow the behavior within it.

Being able to debug a program is a valuable tool and skill to have at your disposal. It goes far beyond inserting `print()` statements in your code to try to glean what's happening inside. Python has standalone debugging tools as well as mature and powerful IDEs available:

- Visual Studio Code by Microsoft is an advanced source code editor that has extensions making it a complete IDE for Python. It's available across Windows, Mac, and Linux platforms, which is a win if you work on multiple computers. It's also free to download and use and is the tool I used to develop the example code in this book.
- PyCharm is one of the suites of development tools provided by JetBrains and is a commercial Python IDE. It also has syntax highlighting, IntelliSense, and a powerful debugger, as well as tools to integrate with databases and source code control systems. It's a powerful tool for the development of Python code and applications and runs on Windows, Mac, and Linux.
- WingIDE is yet another powerful, commercial Python IDE with syntax highlighting and IntelliSense and an advanced debugger with features useful in data science work. This platform is also available for Windows, Mac, and Linux.

- The Python standard library comes with an interactive debugger called pdb. It provides features provided by the IDE debuggers listed previously but from a terminal window.

1.4   Selecting which Python version to use

The code in this book is based on Python version 3.10.3. If you are relatively new to Python, you might know there are two major versions of Python in existence—2.* and 3.*. The 3.* version has been around for a long time, since December 2008. It took a while for this version to gain traction with users because libraries and frameworks on which those users depended weren't compatible with this version, so they stayed with the 2.* version. The time when that was true is well behind us, and there is no legitimate reason to start new Python projects in anything other than the 3.* version.

From this point in time forward, the Python 3.* version will have newer features, the latest syntax, and more developer support. It also means important libraries and frameworks are dropping support for the 2.* version. This implies developing programs with Python 2.* will have to pin the use of those libraries and frameworks to older versions that will no longer get new features or bug fixes. This last item is particularly important to security concerns.

In addition, the Python 2.* version reached EOL (end of life) on January 1, 2020. This means that the core Python development team has stopped supporting that branch completely. This clean break by the core developers frees them from some compromises made to continue supporting 2.*.

Lastly, and I think this is very important, the Python community at large has moved to the 3.* version. This means that documentation, articles, books, and questions and answers on forums will leave the old version behind and focus more on the new version(s).

As a developer, this is an important problem: first, everything you need to know as a developer is too big to have in mind all at once. This makes finding relevant information of paramount importance. And second, the pace of change is ongoing and rapid, which makes trying to know everything an exercise in futility. It's much more useful as a developer to understand what you need and want to do and then be able to find how to do it. Hands down, this beats being a catalog of facts that become outdated almost as fast as you learn them.

1.5   Closing thoughts

I realize you might be feeling overwhelmed by the scope of becoming a developer. In some ways, you're looking up at the night sky and trying to take it all in. Trust me, I've been there.

My wish is that beginning to read this book gives you a small telescope to view that endless sky, narrow your field of view, and show you more details about where we're going. I hope this whets your appetite to take the next step in your development journey.

Summary

- Becoming a developer means broadening your view of the problem at hand and learning how the tools you use will interact to solve those larger problems.
- Python is an excellent choice of programming language to learn and work with as a developer. Making it a comfortable addition to your toolbelt is a skill multiplier.
- The Python language community is welcoming and helpful. Becoming a member of that community is a good step toward taking on your developer's journey.
- The adage "The poor workman blames his tools" is half the story; the rest is that a wise craftsman chooses their tools well. The Python developer space has a wealth of powerful tools from which to pick.

Part 1

Groundwork

You're prepared to become a Python developer, and you're about to take your first steps on that journey. The beginning of this book is about honing your Python skills and adding new ideas and behaviors to how you go about using Python.

In chapter 2, you'll gain a broader view of the importance of how to name things. You'll also see what namespaces are and why they're amazing and well-supported in Python.

Chapter 3 will introduce you to the application programmers interface, or API, which is where developers and computers connect. Object-oriented programming (OOP) is the subject of chapter 4. You'll learn how to use it in Python and how it can benefit your design and implementation process.

In chapter 5, you'll see how to handle exceptional events in your code, including generating exceptions of your own. Avoiding unwanted exceptions is important, but handling them properly when they happen is even more important. After this, you'll be ready to take your Python skills out for some fieldwork, where you'll pull together what you've learned to create a blogging web application.

That's a good name

The names that we give to items and concepts help us navigate the world and communicate with everyone else who shares it with us. The idea that names matter is even more important in the world of software development. Programming languages have keywords, grammar, and syntax that are generally a subset of a common, in-use language. In the case of Python, that language is English.

For programming languages, this means we use a prescribed set of keywords, grammar, and syntax to create programs that will ultimately run. Naming elements in those programs, however, is entirely within your control, as you can draw from the rich set of English words and phrases to name the items you create in a program. You can even use strings of nonsense characters if that suits you. But should you?

> *"There are only two hard things in Computer Science: cache invalidation and naming things."*

The quote is attributed to Phil Karlton, a programmer with Netscape, the developer of the first widely used web browser. Putting aside cache invalidation, you might be thinking, "What's so hard about naming things?" Let's find out.

2.1 Names

Back when I first started writing code, one of the systems I worked on was based on Pascal. It was the first language I knew that allowed almost unlimited choice when it came to naming variables in the programs. One of the other young guys on the team created two global variables to test for True and False. He named them `cool` and `uncool`. At the time, we both thought this was pretty funny and made for some laughs when writing conditional statements and testing function return values.

Over time, those variable names were all over the code, losing their humorous quality and becoming more challenging to consider and maintain. What was the meaning of `cool` and `uncool`? If you didn't know the actual value behind the symbol, were the meanings distinct or could they be more aligned with the English use of the words, which in many ways implied a range of meanings?

Naming something is a way for you and Python to share the identity of something. Usually, this means you want to identify a thing uniquely, so it's distinct from all the other named things in a program. For example, Social Security numbers in the United States are given to people so they can uniquely identify themselves within the usage context of the country. This unique string of numbers helps people obtain employment, do their taxes, buy insurance, and do all kinds of other activities that require a nationally unique identifier.

Does this mean a Social Security number is a good name for a unique thing? Not really. Unless you have access to the systems that use the number, it's entirely opaque. It conveys no information about the thing it's identifying.

Let's take this idea of unique names to another level. There are standardized identifiers called universally unique identifiers (UUIDs). A UUID is a sequence of characters that for all practical purposes is unique across the entire world. A sample UUID looks like this:

```
f566d4a9-6c93-4ee6-b3b3-3a1ffa95d2ae
```

You can use Python's built-in UUID module to create valid variable names based on UUID values:

```
import uuid
f"v_{uuid.uuid4().hex}"
```

This would generate a valid Python variable name like this:

```
v_676d673808d34cc2a2dc85e74d44d6a1
```

You can create variable names this way to uniquely identify everything in your applications. These variable names would be unique within your entire application and across the known world.

Naming variables this way would also be a completely unusable naming convention. The variable name conveys absolutely no information about the thing it identifies. A variable name like this is also very long to type, impossible to remember, and unwieldy to use.

2.1.1 Naming things

Naming things is not only about uniqueness but also about attaching information to named things. Trying to provide meaning to the name you assign, or as an indication of how the thing is used, adds meta information that's very useful when developing Python programs. For example, if you name a variable t versus total, you'd have to examine the context of the surrounding code to know what t is, whereas total has a meaning that provides an understanding of how the variable is used.

> **TIP** Creating useful variable names takes effort, but it's effort well spent as a developer. You'll find over time that variable names are difficult to change. This is because dependency on existing variables increases as an application is developed and used. Choosing good variable names avoids having to change a name down the road.

Based on the previous UUID example, the length of the name you give to something is also relevant to the effort of writing code. Programming does involve a lot of typing, which means the balance between meaning and brevity matters.

You're suddenly in a position where an entire language is your hunting ground for words and phrases to name things. Your goal is to find words that attach meta information and yet are short enough to not get in the way of writing, or reading, a line of program code. This constrains what you could or should do when naming things. Like a painter working from a limited palette of colors, you can choose to be frustrated or get imaginative within that constraint and build something with artfulness and creativity.

Many of the programs you'll write will include looping over a collection of things, counting things, and adding things together. Here's an example of code iterating through a two-dimensional table:

```
t = [[12, 11, 4], [3, 22, 105], [0, 47, 31]]
for i, r in enumerate(t):
    for j, it in enumerate(r):
        process_item(i, j, it)
```

This code is perfectly functional. The t variable consists of a Python list of lists, which represents a two-dimensional table. The process_item() function needs to know the row and column position of the item—the it variable—within the table to correctly process it. The variables t, i, j, r, and it are perfectly serviceable but give the reader no information about their intent.

You might be inclined to think it's not a big deal for this example code but imagine if there were many more lines of code between each invocation of the for loop. In that case, the declaration of the t, i, j, r, and it variables are visually separated from their use. The reader would probably have to go back and find the declaration to understand the intent of the variable. Keep in mind that the reader could be you six months after writing this code when the meaning and intent are not so fresh in your mind. Here's a better implementation of the code:

```
table = [[12, 11, 4], [3, 22, 105], [0, 47, 31]]
for row_index, row in enumerate(table):
    for column_index, item in enumerate(row):
        process_item(row_index, column_index, item)
```

The code has changed, so t is now table, i is row_index, j is column_index, r is row, and it is item. The variable names indicate what they contain and the meaning of their intended use. If the variable declarations are separated from their use by many lines of code, the reader can still quickly deduce what the variables mean and how to use them.

Another common operation in development is counting things and creating totals. Here are some simple examples:

```
total_employees = len(employees)
total_parttime_employees = len([
    employee for employee in employees if employee.part_time
])
total_managers = sum([
    employee for employee in employees if employee.manager
])
```

You can see a couple of pretty good naming conventions in the previous example. The name employees gives the variable meaning. The use of the plural employees indicates it's an iterable collection. It also shows that the collection has one or more things inside it that would represent an employee. The variable employee inside the list comprehension indicates it is a single item from within the employees collection.

The variables total_employees, total_parttime_employees, and total_managers indicate what they refer to by the use of total as part of their names. Each of them is a total count of something. The second part of each variable name indicates the thing being counted.

Besides numerical calculations, you'll often deal with things that have names already, like people within a company, community, or group. When you're gathering user input or searching for someone by name, having a useful variable name makes it much easier to think about the thing you're representing in code:

```
full_name = "John George Smith"
```

Depending on the purpose of the code you're writing, this might be a perfectly acceptable variable name to represent a person by name. Often, when working with people's names, you'll need more granularity and will want to represent a person's name in parts:

```
first_name = "John"
middle_name = "George"
last_name = "Smith"
```

These variable names also work well and, like `full_name`, give the variable names meaning about what they represent. Here's another variation:

```
fname = "John"
mname = "George"
lname = "Smith"
```

This version adopts a convention for how the variables are named. A convention like this means you're choosing a pattern to create the variable names of people. Using a convention means the reader has to know and understand the convention in use. The tradeoff in the previous example is less typing but still a clear meaning of the variable name. It also might be more visually appealing, as the variable names line up vertically in a monospaced editing font.

Adopting conventions is one technique for being more productive within the constraints of variable naming. If the shorthand naming convention is more visually appealing to you, this lends itself to recognizing patterns and identifying typos when visually parsing code.

> **TIP** Establishing conventions and habits based on those conventions helps reduce the cognitive load on you as a developer. You can think more about the problem you're trying to solve and less about what to name things.

2.1.2 *Naming experiment*

You may not remember, but in the early days of personal computers, they had tiny hard drives. Early operating systems also had no concept of directories or subdirectories; all the files on the hard drive existed in one global directory. Additionally, filenames were limited to eight characters, the period character (.), and a three-character extension, which was generally used to indicate what the file contained.

Because of this, bizarre and complex file-naming conventions were invented to maintain uniqueness and prevent filename collisions. These naming conventions came at the cost of logically meaningful filenames. An example of a possible resume file created in October 1995 would be something like this:

```
res1095.doc
```

The solution to this problem was adding support to the operating system for named subdirectories and removing the filename character-length limit. Everyone is familiar with this now, as you're able to create almost infinitely deep structures of directories and subdirectories.

EXPERIMENT

Here's a specification you've been asked to meet: the accounting department where you work requires all expense reports to have the same filename: `expenses.xlsx`. You need to create a directory structure where all your `expenses.xlsx` files can exist and not collide or overwrite each other to save and track these expense files.

The constraint is the requirement that all expense report files have a fixed filename. The implied constraint is that whatever directory structure you devise needs to work for as many expense reports as your work generates. The ability to create subdirectories is the tool you have to help solve this problem and keep the expense report files separated.

POSSIBLE SOLUTIONS

Any solution depends on how many expense reports you create to do your job. If you're working as a junior software developer, you might only travel a few times a year. In this case, you would only have to provide coarse granularity to keep your expenses.xlsx files separated. This simple structure gathers all the expense reports under a single root directory named expenses (figure 2.1). Each expense report exists in a directory named with the fully qualified date when the expense report was created. Using a date format of YYYY-MM-DD causes the directories to sort in a useful chronological order on many operating systems when displayed.

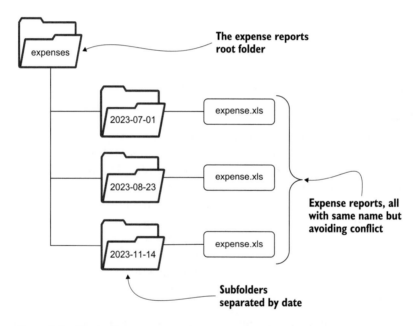

Figure 2.1   Simple directory structure to manage expense reports

However, if you're a sales engineer, you're most likely traveling all the time and possibly meeting multiple clients per day. This changes how you handle the constraint and requires your directory structure to support much more granularity to keep all the expenses.xlsx files separate. A possible solution for a sales engineer would be to use the year, month, day, and client name values as subdirectories. Doing this allows you to keep the expenses.xlsx files distinct even when visiting multiple clients per day. This creates a convention where each part of the path to a particular expenses.xlsx file has meaning as well as a value. Figure 2.2 illustrates this structure.

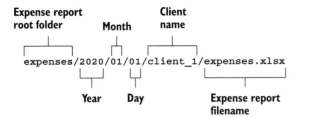

Figure 2.2 A more involved directory structure that provides more granular file separation

It might not be evident based on the previous experiment, but what you've created are variable names that have meaning and convention. Look at the directory path to a particular expense report. You've created namespaces, each one narrowing the scope of what it contains. Reading the path from left to right, you see that each segment of the path separated by the / character creates a new, narrower namespace within the context of the previous one (figure 2.3).

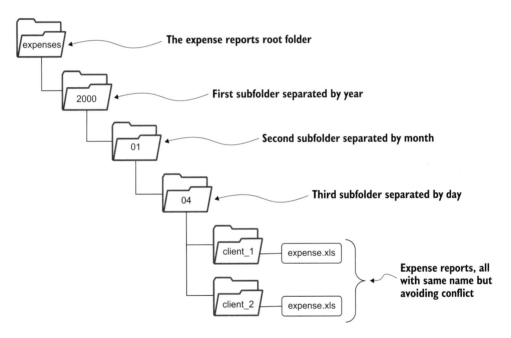

Figure 2.3 The directory path creates a hierarchy of namespaces.

Suppose you are the accountant who has mandated the file-naming convention for expense reports. As the accountant, you'll have to save all the expense reports that employees submit. You'd be under the same constraint as the employees who are generating the expense reports, but with the added complexity of keeping all the employee expense reports distinct and separated from each other.

Creating a directory structure to handle the added complexity could include higher-level abstractions of department and employee. Creating a directory structure providing this level of granularity to track and save all the employee expense reports is possible. Thinking about how to create the structure makes it clear that it's time for the accounting department to rethink the file-naming requirements and constraints and design a better system.

2.2   *Namespaces*

A namespace creates an abstraction containing other named things, including other namespaces. The name of the city or town where you live is an example. The city name provides a namespace containing all the people who live in that city. The city name may not be unique on its own, but within the context of the hierarchy it's in—county, state, and so on—it would be.

Going further, the streets and roads where people live all have names. The street and road names become a namespace within the city namespace. For example, there are many streets named "Main Street" throughout the United States. However, there is usually only one Main Street in each city.

This hierarchy of namespaces creates the convention of the United States mailing address. The full address for Janet Smith, working at the Empire State Building, might be something like this:

Janet Smith
Empire State Building, Suite 87A
20 W 34th Street
New York, New York 10001

By convention, the mailing address namespace scope gets narrower reading from bottom to top. A software developer might remove redundant information and represent this address like the previous directory experiments in a left-to-right form:

```
10001|20 W 34th Street|Empire State Building|Suite 87A|Janet Smith
```

Here the city and state have been removed because the zip code contains that information. The namespace fields have been delimited with the | character because that character doesn't appear in the address's text. Continuing from left to right, you come to the final leaf node, the person to which the address applies.

> **TIP**   The world is full of namespaces because it's a useful convention to help us organize information. That usefulness applies to information we want to organize in our Python applications.

Like the directory structure experiment, reading from left to right, the scope of information contained within each distinct namespace gets narrower. Also, like the directory structure hierarchy, the position of each namespace follows a convention that gives each meaning.

2.3 *Python namespaces*

The Python programming language provides the ability to create namespaces. Namespaces give you a great deal of power and control when handling the constraints of naming variables, giving them meaning, keeping them relatively short, and avoiding collisions. You do this by placing variable names in namespaces. Before you get to the point of creating namespaces of your own, let's look at the one provided by the language.

2.3.1 *Built-ins level*

When Python starts running an application, it creates a `builtins` namespace where `builtins` is the outermost namespace in Python and contains all of the functions you can access at any time. For example, the `print()` and `open()` functions exist in the `builtins` namespace.

You can see what's in the `builtins` namespace by entering this command at a Python interactive prompt:

```
>>> dir(__builtins__)
```

This command runs the `dir` (directory) command on the `__builtins__` object. You'll see all the exceptions and functions listed that are available everywhere in Python.

You might not have thought about functions like `print()`, `open()`, and others as existing in a namespace, and you don't have to to use them. The idea that they are in a namespace is useful as you learn more about creating your own namespaces and the scope of the objects within them.

There is something to keep in mind when working with the `builtins` namespace: it's entirely possible to overwrite an object in a namespace with something of your own. For example, you could define a function like this:

```
def open(…):
    # run some code here
```

Creating a function like this would be perfectly fine; however, the side effect of doing this is shadowing the `open()` function that's already defined in the `builtins` namespace. It might make perfect sense for the program you're writing to name your function `open()`, but shadowing Python's `open()` function, and making it inaccessible, is probably not what you intended.

You can handle this by creating your function as follows:

```
def my_own_open(…):
    # run some code here
```

The code works, but you've sacrificed brevity and simple meaning for uniqueness to avoid your function's name colliding with Python's `open()` function. Using a namespace provides a better solution.

2.3.2   *Module level*

The Python program file you create that starts your program running is considered the entry point for your program as a whole. When it starts, the objects in the `builtins` namespace are created and available anywhere in your Python programs. In Python, everything is an object—variables, functions, lists, dictionaries, classes—everything.

Anything you create and name is also an object in the main program file and has the potential to collide with and overwrite the objects in `builtins` and other things you create and name. You can, and should, avoid this.

Breaking up your program code into multiple files containing logically grouped functionality is a useful convention to adopt. Doing so has the following benefits:

- Keeps similar functionality together where it's easier to contemplate
- Prevents program files from becoming too long to edit and manage reasonably
- Creates namespaces

Each Python code file creates a namespace for your use. Let's say you create two functions named `add()` that have different behaviors, and you create a `main.py` file that looks like this:

```
def add(a, b):
    return a + b

def add(a, b):
    return f "{a} {b}"

print(add(12, 12))
print(add(12, 12))
```

When you run this program, it won't function the way you might think. There's no way to indicate in the code which `add()` function is being called in the `print (add(12, 12))` statement. When Python executes this code, it defines the first `add()` function and then immediately redefines it with the second, shadowing it and losing access to the first definition.

The behavior of the two functions is different; the first performs a mathematical addition on the two parameters, and the second performs a specialized `string` addition (concatenation) on the two parameters. However, as far as Python is concerned, the name of the function is the distinguishing feature. And because they are both defined in the same namespace, the second shadows the first and takes precedence.

To get both `add()` functions to exist, you need to create a namespace into which you can put one of the `add()` functions. To do this, create a `utility.py` file that looks like this:

```
def add(a, b):
    return f"{a} {b}"
```

Then change your `main.py` file to this:

```
import utility
```

```
def add(a, b):
    return a + b

print(add(12, 12))
print(utility.add(12, 12))
```

When you run the `main.py` file, you get the intended output of

```
24
12 12
```

Creating the `utility.py` file separates the two `add()` function definitions so they can both exist. In the `main.py` file, the import utility statement tells Python to pull all the objects in the `utility.py` file to a new namespace called `utility`.

Be aware that the namespace created by importing a file adds a namespace based on the base name of the file, which is the default behavior. You can override this default behavior in this way:

```
import utility as utils
```

This statement tells Python to pull all the objects in the `utility.py` file into a namespace called `utils`. Being able to alias the namespace specifically can be a useful feature if you want to import two modules with the same name but maintain a unique namespace for each.

It's also possible to mask a namespace when importing functionality. Using your current `main.py` example, it is done like this:

```
from utility import *

def add(a, b):
    return a + b

print(add(12, 12))
print(utility.add(12, 12))
```

The code tells Python to pull all the objects in the `utility.py` file into the current namespace. This program now has an error in it because the utility namespace no longer exists, so the `print(utility.add(12, 12))` statement doesn't work. Removing `utility` from the print statement makes the program work, but you're back to a variation of the original problem. The `add()` function defined in the `utility.py` file is shadowed by the `add()` function defined in the `main.py` file. For this reason, it's usually not a good idea to use the `from <filename> import *` form when importing files.

Being able to create namespaces based on files is useful, but Python's support goes further. By capitalizing on the filesystem directory structure, you can create namespace hierarchies. Just like the previous directory structure naming experiment, this gives you more tools to create meaning and scope for the hierarchies you create.

If you take your example a little further, you might decide to be more specific with the functionality you're creating. The `utility.add()` function is specific to string handling, so why not make that clearer?

Create a new directory called `utilities` in the same folder as your `main.py` file. Move the `utility.py` file to the `utilities` directory and rename it `strings.py`. You now have a directory hierarchy that looks like this:

```
utilities/strings.py
```

This adds meaning just like the directory structure experiment does; `utilities` indicates that everything under the directory is considered a utility.

One thing to keep in mind when creating directory hierarchies to contain functionality is the need to create an `__init__.py` file. This file has to exist in each directory to let Python know the directory contains functionality or the path to it. When the `__init__.py` file exists in a directory, that directory is a Python package.

Often the `__init__.py` file is empty, but it doesn't have to be. Any code inside the file is executed whenever the path containing it is part of an import statement.

Based on this, create an empty `__init__.py` file in your `utilities` directory. Once that's done, modify your `main.py` file like this:

```
from utilities import strings

def add(a, b):
    return a + b

print(add(12, 12))
print(strings.add(12, 12))
```

The `from utilities import strings` statement tells Python to navigate to the utilities package and pull all the objects from the `strings.py` file into the `strings` namespace. The `print(strings.add(12, 12))` line has been changed to use the `strings` namespace to access the `add()` functionality. Now the namespace plus function name combine to increase the clarity and intention of the `add` function.

When you create a Python file that you intend to import into other parts of your program, it's common to think of the file as a module. The module contains functionality that's useful to your program. This idea is very much like the "batteries included" statement that's often associated with Python. Python comes with a large selection of standard modules you can import and use in your programs.

If you've used any of Python's standard modules, like `sys`, you might notice those standard modules don't exist in the working directory of your program like the `strings.py` module you created previously. Python searches for modules you want to import through a list of paths, the working directory being first.

If you start a Python interpreter and at the prompt enter

```
>>> import sys
>>> sys.path
```

you'll see output that looks something like this:

```
['', '/Users/dfarrell/.pyenv/versions/3.8.0/lib/python37.zip', '/Users/
    dfarrell/.pyenv/versions/3.8.0/lib/python3.8', '/Users/dfarrell/.pyenv/
    versions/3.8.0/lib/python3.8/lib-dynload', '/Users/dfarrell/tmp/
    sys_path_test/.venv/lib/python3.8/site-packages']
```

The output is the list of paths Python will search through when it runs across an `import` or `from` statement in your code. The list shown here is specific to my Mac; the listing you see will most likely be different depending on whether you're using a Windows or Mac computer and whether you're running Python in a virtual environment.

The first element in the list is an empty string. Python will look in the current working directory for modules. This is how it found the `utilities` package and the `strings` module in that package.

It also means that if you create a module and name it identically to a Python system module, Python will find your package first and use it, ignoring the system package. When naming your packages and modules, keep this in mind.

In our short example, the `import sys` statement causes Python to search the earlier-mentioned list of paths. Because a `sys` module doesn't exist in your working directory, it looks in the other paths, where it does find the standard modules.

The list of paths is used when you install a package or module with the `pip` command. The `pip` command will install the package in one of the paths from the list. As mentioned previously, using Python virtual environments is recommended to prevent `pip` from installing into your computer system's version of Python.

2.3.3 *Function level*

There are other levels of namespace control available to you. When you create a Python function, you're creating a namespace for variable name creation. Another word used for this is *scope*. The functions you create exist in a module, either the main Python file of your program or separate module files.

The module file creates a namespace, and any functions you create in the module exist within that namespace. What does this mean? Take your `strings.py` module and make the following changes to it:

```
prefix = "added"

def add(a, b):
    return f"{prefix}: {a} {b}"
```

These changes create a variable named `prefix` at the module-level namespace and initialize it with the string `"added."`

If you run your main program, you'll see the output of the `strings.add(12, 12)` now outputs `added: 12 12`. When the `add()` function is executed, Python looks for the `prefix` variable inside the function namespace and, not finding one, looks at the module-level namespace. It finds the `prefix` variable in the module and uses it in the string formatting returned by the function.

Change the `strings.py` code again and make it look like this:

```
prefix = "added"

def add(a, b):
    prefix = "inside add function"
    return f"{prefix}: {a} {b}"
```

Inside the add() function, you've created a variable named prefix and initialized it to a different string. If you rerun your code, you'll see the output of the strings .add(12, 12) function outputs inside added: 12 12.

What's happening here is that Python now finds the prefix variable in the add() function's local namespace and uses it. Not only is the prefix variable defined inside the add() function's namespace, but it's also created in the function's scope. We'll talk about scope more in the next section.

2.3.4   *Namespace scope*

Names and namespaces are essential in your Python toolbox and are related to another tool as implied in the previous section. The scope of a variable is an important consideration when creating and using variables.

The scope of a variable relates to its accessibility and lifetime in a module—a Python file. In Python, a variable is created when a value is assigned to it:

```
prefix = "prefix"
```

This statement creates the variable prefix and assigns it the string value "prefix". The variable prefix also has a type of string, which Python determines at the time of assignment from the object being assigned—in this case, "prefix".

If the prefix variable was created in a function

```
def print_prefix():
    prefix = "prefix"
    print(prefix)
```

the prefix variable would be within the scope of the print_prefix() function and would exist only when that function is running. Any code outside of the function that tried to access the prefix variable would generate an exception.

Let's say you create a new module file named message.py that looks like this:

```
prefix = "prefix"

def my_message(text):
    new_message = f"{prefix}: {text}"
    return new_message
```

You created things that have different scopes and lifetimes. The prefix variable is in the global module scope. It is accessible anywhere within the message.py module. It also has the same lifetime as the module.

In this context, *lifetime* means from the point in the application where the module is imported to when the application is exited. It is possible to remove a module and reimport it, but in practice, this is rarely necessary.

If you use import message in your code, the prefix variable and my_message function are around for as long as the message module is. It is still within the message namespace and would be accessible to programs that import it like this:

```
import message
print(message.prefix)
print(message.my_message("Hello World"))
```

The variables defined inside the `my_message(text)` function have function-level scope. This means they are only accessible within the function, and their lifetime is from the point of their creation to the end of the function statements.

Because the `my_message(text)` function is contained within the module-level scope, the code within the function can access the `prefix` module variable. At the module scope, what's declared at that level is accessible—the `prefix` and `my_message` functions. The `my_message` function is part of the module-level (global) scope, but all the variables declared inside the function are not.

Inside the `my_message` function, the two variables `text` and `new_message` are accessible as they are in the local function scope but aren't accessible outside the function. The module variable `prefix` is in the global scope and is also accessible inside the function.

The previous program shows that the scope is nested. Inner scopes have access to outer scopes that enclose them, as demonstrated by the `my_message` function having access to the `prefix` variable. Outer scopes do not have access to the inner scopes they enclose. Figure 2.4 shows this scope nesting.

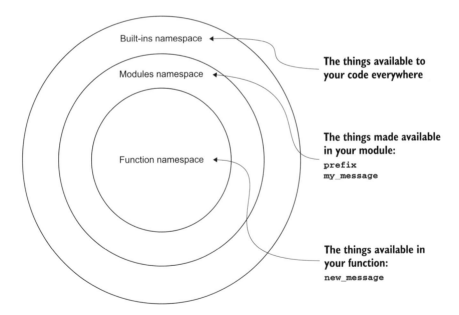

Figure 2.4   How the scopes nest inside one another and where in a scope a variable is visible

> ### Social namespaces
>
> Programming namespaces and scopes can be compared to the people we know who are from various parts of our lives. Let's say you have a friend named Mary, and you also work with someone named Mary. If you're with friends and someone mentions "Mary," you would most likely think about your friend; she is in your local scope.
>
> However, if someone says, "How's that person you work with doing; Mary I think her name is?" In that case, you would think of the Mary you work with because the context was changed by the question to the work module scope.

2.3.5   *Namespace experiment*

Using what you've learned about names and namespaces, try this experiment using the information provided to solve a problem. This problem is about using meaningful names and namespaces to solve an otherwise awkward development problem.

EXPERIMENT

You're the developer in charge of maintaining the software for an online community of users interested in similar things. The community wants the software to email them about upcoming events and to include noncommunity members who register to receive event emails. This latter group consists of potential new members who are interested but not yet committed to joining.

The software can send personalized emails to the mailing list of registered users, both members and nonmembers. When creating the personalized email, the current software calls a function get_name(person) to obtain the name to render into the email based on the person object passed to it.

The community wants to change how personalized email is rendered by creating a concept of "formal," "informal," and "casual" for the name. The email sent to non-members would always use the formal version. The email sent to members would base the name on the user's account settings and could use any of the three levels of formality. This becomes your requirement: make the logically named get_name (person) function return three different values for three different use cases.

POSSIBLE SOLUTION

One possible solution is to create three new versions of the get_name(person) function like this:

```
def get_name_formal(person):

def get_name_informal(person):

def get_name_casual(person):
```

This code is understandable and direct but is awkward to use in the rest of the application currently calling get_name(…). Using this approach requires you to modify every instance of a call to get_name(…) to be an if/elif/else conditional to call the correct function. You'd also have to make the conditional information that selects the right function available for those `if`/`elif`/`else` condition tests.

Another approach would be to change the `get_name(person)` function to take an additional parameter that indicates how to format the response. Something like this would work:

```
def get_name(person, tone: str):
```

In this example, the variable `tone` is a string theoretically set to `formal`, `informal`, or `casual`. The value of `tone` would be used to format the name in an expected manner.

This example would also work but is only a marginal improvement over the individually named functions. Choosing this method requires you to find and edit every instance where the `get_name(...)` function is called in the entire program and update it to include the new `tone` parameter. If the function is used in many places, this could become a maintenance headache.

The use of namespaces creates a workable solution that doesn't disrupt the other parts of the software. Rather than change the name signature of the `get_name(person)` function, or change its parameter list, you could use namespaces.

As a contrived example, here is a `main.py` program that simulates sending out an email to the community, before accounting for the required changes:

```
from utilities.names import get_name

# generate a community list of three of the same people
community = [{
        "title": "Mr.",
        "fname": "John",
        "lname": "Smith"
    } for x in range(3)
]
# iterate through the community sending emails
for person in community:
    # other code that calls get_name many times
    print(get_name(person))
```

The `get_name(person)` function from the `names.py` module might look like this:

```
def get_name(person):
    title = person.get("title", "")
    fname = person.get("fname", "")
    lname = person.get("lname", "")
    if title:
        name = f"{title} {fname} {lname}"
    else:
        name = f"{fname} {lname}"
    return name
```

This function looks at the `person` information and, depending on whether the person has a title value or not, formats the name accordingly and returns it. The `get_name(person)` function is the formal version and can be used as is.

The change requirements are to create a formal, informal, and casual greeting for the emails based on the tone determined by the account. You already have a formal version of the `get_name(person)` function and just need to create the informal and casual versions. Create a module file called `informal.py` in the utilities package directory that looks like this:

```
def get_name(person):
    fname = person.get("fname", "")
    lname = person.get("lname", "")
    name = f"{fname} {lname}"
    return name
```

This function concatenates the first and last name and leaves out the title. Create another module called `casual.py` in the utilities package directory that looks like this:

```
def get_name(person):
    fname = person.get("fname", "")
    name = f"{fname}"
    return name
```

This function returns the person's first name and nothing more.

Based on the change requirements, you also need to create a way to define the tone to use in the email based on the community members' account information. The information to examine is whether or not they are a member and, if they are a member, what the greeting setting is in the account.

For this experiment, you can create an `account.py` module in the `utilities` package directory. The `account.py` module contains the following code:

```
from random import choice

def get_tone(person):
    return choice(["formal", "informal", "casual"])
```

This code returns a randomly selected value from the list of tone strings—"formal", "informal", and "casual." In a real application, the tone would probably be retrieved from a database table containing information about the users.

Now you have everything you need to meet the requirements and change how the mailing list is processed. Here's an updated listing of the `main.py` program, showing how the namespaces you've created are used:

```
from utilities import names
from utilities import informal
from utilities import casual
from utilities import account

community = [{
        "title": "Mr.",
        "fname": "John",
        "lname": "Smith"
```

```
    } for x in range(3)
]

for person in community:
    tone = account.get_tone(person)
    if tone == "formal":
        get_name = names.get_name
    elif tone == "informal":
        get_name = informal.get_name
    elif tone == "casual":
        get_name = casual.get_name
    else:
        get_name = names.get_name

    # other code that calls get_name many times
    print(get_name(person))
```

This version of the main.py program imports the three new modules, informal, casual, and account. At the top of the community iteration, the tone is retrieved according to the person passed to the account.get_tone(person) function call. The tone variable is used in an if/elif/else set of statements to set the get_name variable.

Notice the get_name variable is set to the get_name function from a specific module depending on the value of the tone. The code sets the get_name variable to refer to a function; it does not call the function. Now that get_name is a function object, it can be used as a function in the print(get_name(person)) statement. The get_name(person) function call will get the right result because it refers to the desired module's get_name(person) function at each iteration when the tone variable is set.

All of this work up front to create the modules and the code within them was done to avoid losing a good logical name like the get_name function and allow it to be used unchanged anywhere else in the program. The work also prevents name conflicts through the use of namespaces.

Summary

- How we name things has an important and lasting effect on the way we think about the applications we're developing. It's well worth spending time thinking about the names we choose.
- Namespaces are a way to provide context for other things we name. Because a namespace is another thing we name to contain and give our applications structure, the same consideration applies to naming them.
- Namespaces create hierarchal structures, creating parent, child, and sibling relationships that help architect Python applications.
- Python has multiple means to create namespaces that help complex applications coexist and become simpler using convenient names without conflict.

The API: Let's talk 3

Communicating with people through the spoken and written word, gestures, expressions, and inflection is one of the cornerstones of our advancement as a species. Even across different languages and cultures, we can communicate with each other, perhaps with a bit more effort, but we can learn to convey meaning, intent, information, goals, and more.

The evolution of computers has also created many and varied ways for us to communicate with a computer, and it with us. Keyboards, mice, touchpads, voice, screens, printers, networks, motion sensors, and more are all devices that have different uses for providing communication between people and computers.

All these devices are examples of interfaces designed to convey information to and from a computer system. Keyboards provide a mechanical way for us to enter the written word into a system. A computer mouse provides one way to indicate gestures and events to a computer system. A display screen provides a way for the

32

computer to represent digital information so we can receive it. Speakers give a computer an interface to produce audio information.

All the complexities of capturing a keystroke, positioning the mouse pointer on the computer display, or generating a sound from a computer are simplified, hidden, and provided by the interface.

Interfaces exist to receive information, act on it, and send back results. The interfaces we've talked about so far are essential to computer users. As developers, we also use interfaces that exist at a deeper, and more abstract, level of computer systems.

The operating system of a computer provides hundreds, perhaps thousands, of interfaces that give access to all the services and functionality of which the computer is capable. Access to the filesystem, and ultimately the storage system, of a computer is provided to applications through an interface. If a computer is connected to a network, applications use interfaces to access those networks. If an application renders visual information, interfaces present that information onto the connected displays. These kinds of interfaces fall under the larger general category called application programming interfaces, or APIs.

3.1 *Starting a conversation*

A computer screen provides a level of abstraction between how the user sees things and how the computer represents things. A mouse provides a level of abstraction between our hand movements and button clicks to the computer that is translated as selections and events.

An API provides the same kinds of abstraction. However, it does so not between a person and a computer but between sections of programming code. All programs are composed of custom code, modules, and libraries of existing code. Even the most straightforward Python program performing a `print("Hello World")` is using standard library code provided with the Python language.

Having library code is a huge advantage that allows you to focus on what you're trying to accomplish rather than coding everything yourself. Imagine having to write a `print` function every time you start a new project or having to create something quite complex like network access.

Python is well-known for having "batteries included," meaning it comes with an extensive and powerful standard library of modules providing all kinds of functionality you can use and not have to create yourself. There's also a large selection of modules you can install from the Python Package Index (https://pypi.org/) that cover diverse and well-supported areas of interest.

> **TIP** Using existing library code and modules is a cornerstone of being a well-grounded developer. Existing code is often well-tested and used successfully in many applications. There is no sense in reinventing the wheel when a perfectly good wheel, or wheels, are readily available.

Because of these numerous modules, Python is sometimes called a "glue language" as it creates interesting ways to connect powerful libraries of code together. Thinking of Python as a glue language doesn't diminish its power but instead shows its versatility.

Python as a glue language is possible because of the API that the modules support, like calling `print("Hello World")`. This calls the `print` function, passing the literal string argument `"Hello World"`, abstracting the complexities of outputting text to a display. The API that a module supports makes it possible to use complex, sophisticated code in your programs.

3.1.1   *A contract between pieces of code*

Aside from the rather abstract discussion about what an API is, let's review what it is in practice. One way to think about it is to consider an API as a contract between your code and another piece of code whose functionality you want to use. Like a contract between people, it specifies if one party does this, then the other party does that.

In programming terms, this often means that when calling a function or method in a particular way, it performs some work and returns some information or both. In Python, when you create a function to be used elsewhere in your code, you've created an API. The name you give the function expresses some meaning about what the API does. The function's input arguments pass information to the API to specify the work to perform and the data to perform it on. If the function returns information, this is the output of the API.

This idea of passing information into a piece of code and getting information or an action out of it has existed in computer science for a long time and is known as the "black-box" model. The input a black box expects and the output it creates is understood well enough that knowing what goes on inside isn't necessary. Only the behavior needs to be known, not the implementation. The term *black box* comes from the idea that the internals of the invoked functionality are opaque and blocked from view, as illustrated by figure 3.1.

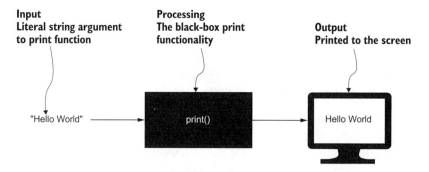

Figure 3.1   Representation of the black-box concept of functionality hiding

As a developer, you don't have to know about the internal implementation of the print() function. You only need to know that passing the function a string invokes its default behavior—printing that string to the screen.

A local API is a function or class you create or a module your code imports. The API is within the context of your program code and is accessed directly by calling the functions and class instance methods provided.

It's also possible to call an API that's hosted remotely—for example, connecting to a database server and accessing data. Here, the API is accessed over a network connection providing the transport mechanisms for your code to make calls to the remote API and for the API to respond. We'll get more into this in chapter 10, specifically about databases.

3.1.2 *What's passed as input*

When your code calls a function or method of an API, it's engaging in one part of the contract between your program and the functionality provided by the API. The input arguments are the information passed from the context of your program code to the context of the API through the parameters. In developer terms, arguments are the values passed to a function, and parameters are the names given to those arguments when the function is defined.

Python functions and methods support positional and keyword parameters. The order of the positional parameters and names of the keyword parameters are considerations when using and building an API. For example, Python's print function is most often used like this:

```
>>> msg = "Hello World"
>>> print(msg)
Hello World
```

When this function executes, it prints the string variable msg to the screen. The API provided by the print function is simple enough to understand; it takes the input argument and performs the work necessary to output it to the screen.

The complete API of the print function shows that it is a more versatile function. Here is the print function signature:

```
print(*objects, sep=' ', end='\n', file=sys.stdout, flush=False)
```

This signature indicates that the first parameter is a tuple of non-keyword parameters followed by additional keyword parameters with default values. The *objects parameter allows the caller to pass multiple, comma-separated values to the print function. This means

```
>>> print("Hello World")
Hello World
```

outputs the same thing to the display as

```
>>> print("Hello", "World")
Hello World
```

Calling the `print` function this way works because the function iterates through the `objects` tuple parameter, converting each to a string if necessary, and outputs each object to `sys.stdout` (the screen). Each output item is separated by the default separator string, a space character.

The `sep=' '` parameter provides the default space separator string and lets you change it to something else to separate the objects when they are output to the screen. The `end='\n'` parameter provides a carriage return as the default to end the output and lets you change how the output ends.

The `file=sys.stdout` parameter defines the default destination, called standard output, which is usually the screen. Changing this parameter lets you change that destination. The object you set the file parameter equal to must have a `write(string)` method for it to work as a file destination. If the object doesn't have a `write(string)` method, an `AttributeError` exception is raised when the `print` function is called. The `flush=False` parameter provides a way to forcibly push what's sent to the stream to the output destination rather than buffering it if set to `True`.

All of this tells us the `print` function API is well-designed and surprisingly powerful. The use of the initial non-keyword `*objects` tuple, followed by the keyword parameters with default values, lets you use the `print` function's most common use case. The rest of the functionality is there if needed but can be ignored otherwise.

Imagine if the `print` function was handled differently. A naïve API implementation might remove all the keyword parameters with default values and look something like this:

```
print(object)
```

A `print` function like this would satisfy the common use case but would start to fall apart beyond that. Suppose not long after this version is in use, you need to print more than one object at a time. One way to extend the simple implementation is to create additional `print` function variations:

```
print_two(object, object)
print_three(object, object, object)
```

What if additional requirements were placed on this naïve expansion of the API to have a different separator character, perhaps the pipe character (|)? Following the established simple variation pattern would lead to something like this:

```
print(object)
print_pipe_sep(object)
print_two(object, object)
print_two_pipe_sep(object, object)
print_three(object, object, object)
print_three_pipe_sep(object, object, object)
```

This solution doesn't scale well, and the code that uses this would have to change to use a different permutation of the API. The goal of this example is not to show the progression down an ill-conceived path of API development but to draw closer attention to the details of what makes Python's default `print` function a good API. There is work going on inside the `print` function to support the function signature and the use cases where it's applied.

This is one of the earmarks of a good API. It provides useful functionality that can be expanded upon without exposing the work involved in doing so. As a developer, you don't have to worry too much about how the `print` function works. You get to use it, knowing its functionality is well defined and contained.

> **TIP** Designing a good API takes work, especially if other developers will be using it. Everything you want an API to do should be part of the interface. If a developer has to use some internal part of the API to achieve a goal, then that API has become a problem. Any change to the API's internal functioning has the potential to break code that depends on the internal part that's being used.

When developing an API, how you define the input can dramatically influence its utility and future use.

3.1.3 *What's expected as output*

The other part of the contract provided by an API is its output. The output of a function consists of three parts:

- Return value
- Actions on the system, sometimes thought of as side effects
- Exceptions

RETURN VALUE

The most commonly considered output of a function is the return value—for example, this code:

```
>>> abs(-10)
10
```

The code looks like a mathematical expression, and that's very close to what it's modeled after. The input to the `abs` function is a number, and the output is the absolute value of that number.

A great deal of programming is creating and using functions that accept parameters, processing those parameters, and returning the results. Building an application is a process of orchestrating function calls and feeding the returned values into other functions until you arrive at the desired outcome.

Because everything in Python is an object, a function return value is also an object. This means you can build a function as part of your API that returns more than just a single scalar value, like the `abs` function.

One example commonly seen in Python is to return a tuple. Returning a tuple allows you to pass back more than one value to the calling function, which can then unpack the tuple into variables. Here's some code from `examples/CH_03/example_01.py`:

```
from typing import Tuple

def split_fullname(full_name: str) -> Tuple[str, str, str]:
    fname = mname = lname = ""
    parts = full_name.split()
    if len(parts) >= 1:
        fname = parts[0]
    if len(parts) >= 2:
        mname = parts[1]
    if len(parts) == 3:
        lname = parts[2]
    if not lname:
        mname, lname = (lname, mname)
    return (fname, mname, lname)

# use case
fname, mname, lname = split_fullname("John James Smith")
```

The split_fullname() function takes in a full name and returns the name parts, fname, mname, and lname. Even if the full_name parameter contains only one or two parts of a name, the function behaves correctly. If there are only two parameters, it assumes the second is the last name and sets mname to an empty string.

The use case shows how the tuple returned by the function can be unpacked into three variables. You can also assign the return value from split_fullname() to a single tuple variable, but it's often useful to unpack the returned tuple directly into waiting named variables.

ACTIONS ON THE SYSTEM

Many API functions perform work to transform data passed to them, create new data, or perform calculations based on the data passed. This new, or transformed, data is returned to the caller of the API for further processing.

API functions can also perform actions on the system it's running on. For example, if you are using an API that is part of a robot and call a function to rotate a motor attached to that robot, you'd expect the motor to start rotating.

The actions taken by API functions are what make applications useful. The ability to open, create, read, and write files; interact with networks; print documents; and control real-world devices are all actions an application can execute using API functionality.

An API function performing an action doesn't necessarily have to return any data to the caller if its primary purpose is to perform that action. That doesn't mean it can't return output data. The API function for the robot motor example could return a True or False value to indicate whether the motor is rotating.

EXCEPTIONS

Exceptions and how to handle them are a fact of life as a developer. Disk drives fail, networks can be unreliable, and any number of other unexpected behaviors can occur.

The API functionality you create can generate exceptions from operations, such as dividing by zero or raising exceptions, because the functionality created an unexpected or exceptional state. When creating an API function, one of your goals is to prevent exceptions when you can and handle them gracefully when you can't. For example, if your functionality is performing network IO and the network becomes unreliable, what can you do?

One possibility is to retry the operation several times with a gradually longer time-out between retries. If the network stabilizes within the retry attempt intervals, the function can continue and succeed. However, if the retries fail, a network exception is raised and passed upward to the caller. On the other hand, if a divide-by-zero exception is raised because of an input parameter, there's nothing you can do but let the exception bubble upward to a higher-level functionality that can handle it.

Handling an exception involves knowing whether you can do something about it. Never silence an exception without having a specific reason for doing so; this throws away information and makes an API untrustworthy.

Users of your API need to be aware of and prepared to handle the exceptions your API generates, as they do with any other exceptional condition when developing. Documenting your API is an excellent way to inform its users what exceptions they might expect. Exceptions are covered in more detail in chapter 5.

3.2   Function API

Functions provide the mechanism to interface with an API. In object-oriented programming (OOP), where you think about methods on an object, they are functions tied to that object instance. Let's spend some time talking about ideas you can put in place to create useful functions and, by extension, good APIs.

3.2.1   Naming

As we talked about in the previous chapter, names matter in development. How you name the functions you create goes a long way toward making sense of your API.

Function names should use meaningful words and use the `snake_case` format. There is no reason to shorten the name with abbreviations. Every modern code editor has autocompletion abilities, making typing the full name a one-time-only occurrence at the time of function definition.

Using domain-specific acronyms is also discouraged, as users who aren't familiar with the API domain would find the naming conventions confusing. For example, most people would recognize a variable name of `url` to mean a string containing the URL of a website. A variable name of `agtc`, an acronym used in genome research, would be less meaningful to many people.

The name indicates, or hints at, the use case of the function, what it returns, and what it accepts. Additionally, the documentation string (docstring) can elaborate further on the intended use. In Python, a function docstring is a triple, quoted string containing information about a function, and it immediately follows the function definition. When function name collisions are possible because the logical name choice is similar, or the same, use namespaces and separate the functionality into modules.

3.2.2   *Parameters*

When creating a function to provide an API for some functionality you want to encapsulate, you can think about the Python `print` function presented earlier. That seemingly simple function offers a surprising amount of functionality because of the interface definition and the way the encapsulated code is built. There are four ways to pass arguments to the functions you create.

POSITIONAL PARAMETERS

These are the most common forms of parameters used with functions, and they help define usability. Here is an example function definition with positional parameters:

```python
def full_name(fname, mname, lname):
    return f"{fname} {mname} {lname}"
```

The name of the function indicates what it returns, and the positional parameters `fname`, `mname`, and `lname` clarify what to expect as input and what order to expect from those parameters to be in. Calling the function with string literals looks like this:

```python
print(full_name("John", "James", "Smith"))
```

The code assigns the string literal arguments to the positional parameters in the same order created when the function was defined. It is possible to call the function using parameter names in this manner:

```python
print(full_name(fname="John", mname="James", lname="Smith"))
```

It's also possible to change the order of the parameters by calling the function and using keyword parameters:

```python
print(full_name(mname="James", lname="Smith", fname="John"))
```

Positional parameters are mandatory and must have a value assigned to them when calling the function. Otherwise, Python raises a `TypeError` exception.

KEYWORD PARAMETERS

Keyword parameters aren't mandatory when the function is called, as they have default values. Often these are used for optional parameters, allowing the function to operate with known default parameter values when the caller doesn't supply one. The `full_name` function defined previously can be altered to use keyword parameters like this:

```python
full_name(fname, mname=None, lname=None)
```

Now the function has one positional required parameter, `fname`, and two keyword parameters, `mname` and `lname`—each with a default value of `None`. The function makes `fname` the only mandatory parameter, implying the function operates correctly if `mname` and `lname` aren't provided by the caller. It's also possible to use the keyword parameters in a different order than defined by the function—for instance, calling the function in this manner:

```python
full_name("John", lname="Smith")
```

This code indicates that the function handles the case where fname and lname are supplied but mname is assigned the default value of None. When defining a function, once you create a parameter with a default value (keyword parameter), any parameter following it must also be a keyword parameter and have default values.

PARAMETER LIST

In the Python print function, the first parameter is of the form *objects. The *objects parameter is an example of passing a variable number of positional parameters to a function. The "*" character indicates that the parameter is expecting a variable number of arguments. The objects part is the name of the parameter.

Inside the print function, the objects parameter is a tuple containing all the remaining positional parameters in the function. A variable number of positional parameters is commonly named *args, but that's just a convention, not a requirement.

Modifying the full_name() function to use an argument list looks like this:

```
def full_name(fname, *names):
    return " ".join([fname, *names])
```

In this form, the full_name() function creates a temporary list of the fname parameter and the elements in the names to join them together, separated by a space character. This form is useful to pass multiple, similar arguments but can be confusing to the users of the function. The function will join any number of elements in the *names parameter tuple, which might not be your intention.

Defining the function in the original form where all the parameters have names is a better way to go in this case. From the Zen of Python, explicit is better than implicit.

> **TIP** You can view the Zen of Python by opening the Python REPL and entering:
>
> ```
> import this
> ```

Doing so prints out useful advice and idioms about Python programming.

KEYWORD PARAMETER DICTIONARY

The keyword parameter dictionary is akin to the parameter list; it's a way of wrapping up all keyword parameters into a single parameter for a function. You'll often see it defined as **kwargs, but again, this is only a convention. Changing the full_name() function to use this form looks like this:

```
def full_name(**kwargs):
    [CA]return f"{kwargs.get('fname', '')} {kwargs.get('mname', '')}
{kwargs('lname', '')}"
```

Internally, the full_name() function examines the kwargs dictionary looking for the keywords fname, mname, and lname. Without documentation, the user of this function would not know what to include as key-value pairs in the kwargs dictionary parameter.

The caller can also add other key-value pairs to the `kwargs` dictionary that possibly have no meaning to the `full_name()` function. Any extra key-value pairs are ignored by the `full_name()` function but could have meaning to functions it calls by passing the `kwargs` parameter along. Take care when using this form and do so intentionally.

PARAMETERS IN GENERAL

The ability to create proper function signatures includes being aware of patterns and consistency. Many APIs consist of multiple functions working together to accomplish something. This often means passing the same data into more than one function, so each function is aware of the state of the working data.

If you're processing data contained in a dictionary that's passed to multiple functions, it's a good idea to make the parameter position and the name representing the common data the same for all (or as many as possible) functions that work with it.

For example, make the dictionary the first parameter of the function, and all the additional parameters pass information about how to process the dictionary. The first parameter dictionary is the common, state data structure being passed between functions that act on that state data:

```
email_user(user_data, content, from)
populate_user_address(user_data, address, city, state, zipcode)
```

The `email_user` function gets the email address from the `user_data` structure and then generates an email with the `content` and `from` parameters and sends the email. The `popuplate_user_address` function adds address information to the existing `user_data` structure.

The same would apply to system resources passed to functions, file handles, database connections, and database cursors. If multiple functions need these resource objects, it helps make the API more readily understandable when the functions have a consistent signature.

A function that has many parameters starts to stretch our cognitive abilities and often indicates the function does too much and should be refactored into smaller functions, each with a single purpose. It's tempting to make a long list of function parameters into one using the keyword parameter ability of Python. Unless the dictionary passed as the `**kwargs` is documented, it just obscures what the function is expecting. It also sidesteps the original issue that perhaps the function needs to be refactored.

3.2.3   *Return value*

As you've seen, one-half of the API contract is what's returned by a function. In Python, even if you don't have a return statement in your function code, a value of `None` is returned automatically. If the function you create performs system actions (file IO, network activity, system-level changes), you can return a `True` or `False` to indicate the success or failure of the function.

3.2.4 *Single responsibility*

Strive to create functions that do only one thing; this is the single responsibility principle. Writing a useful function is already considerable work, especially if your goal is to make the function flexible through thoughtful input parameters and processing code. Trying to make it do two things can more than double the difficulty.

Here's a contrived example function from `examples/CH_03/example_02.py` that illustrates this concept:

```
def full_name_and_print(fname:str , mname: str, lname: str) -> None:
    """Concatenates the names together and prints them

    Arguments:
        fname {str} -- first name
        mname {str} -- middle name
        lname {str} -- last name
    """
    full_name = " ".join(name for name in [fname, mname, lname] if name)
    print(full_name)
```

This function concatenates the parameters to create the `full_name` variable and prints it to `sys.stdout`. The list comprehension inside `" ".join` is to ensure there is only a single space between the names should `mname` be left out when the function is called. This function is not as useful as it could be because it's trying to do too much.

It's not useful to other functions needing the full name because the full name isn't returned. Even if the full name was returned, any function calling this must expect the full name to be printed.

Also, the function is difficult to test because it doesn't return anything. To test this, you'd have to redirect `sys.stdout` in some way so a test could see the output, which could get messy quickly.

Here is a better version from `examples/CH_03/example_02.py`:

```
def full_name(fnameNone, mname=None, lname=None) -> str:
    """Concatenates the names together and returns the full name

    Arguments:
        fname {str} -- first name
        mname {str} -- middle name
        lname {str} -- last name

    Returns:
        str -- the full name with only a single space between names
    """
    full_name = " ".join(name for name in [fname, mname, lname] if name)
    return full_name
```

This version does only one thing: it creates the full name and returns it to the caller. Now the return value of the function can be used with the `print` function, included in a web page, added to a data structure, converted to a JSON document, and more. This function has also become easy to test because you can test the return value, and the same input arguments always produce the same output.

3.2.5   *Function length*

Related to the single responsibility principle is the length of the functions you write. It's difficult to keep too much context and detail in our heads at once. The longer a function gets, the more difficult it becomes to reason about and understand its behavior.

No hard-and-fast rule exists regarding the length of a function. A good rule of thumb is around 25 lines, but this is entirely dependent on your comfort level.

If you create a function that's too long to comprehend easily, it probably means the function is trying to do too much. The solution is to refactor it and break some of the functionality out into other functions.

When refactoring a function leads to multiple functions that work together on the same data, you can also create a class with the functions as the methods of that class. If you follow good naming practices and make the new functions handle only one task well, you'll create more readable code.

3.2.6   *Idempotence*

Though an ominous-sounding word, *idempotent* in developer terms indicates a function that always returns the same result when given the same input argument values. No matter how many times it's called, the same input yields the same output.

The output of the function isn't dependent on outside variables, events, or IO activity. For example, creating a function that uses the parameters along with the clock time to create the return value wouldn't be idempotent. The return value is dependent on when the function is called. Idempotent functions are easier to test because the behavior is predictable and can be accounted for in test code.

3.2.7   *Side effects*

Functions can create side effects that change things outside the scope of the function itself. They can modify global variables, print data to the screen, send information across a network, and do a whole host of other activities.

In your functions, the side effects should be intended—referred to previously as actions on the system. Unintended side effects need to be avoided. Modifying a global variable is something a function can do but should be thought about carefully as other, possibly surprising, functionality could be affected by those global modifications.

When opening a file, it's good practice to close it when done to avoid the possibility of corrupting the file. Database connections should be closed when unused so other parts of the system can access them. In general, it's good programming practice to clean up and release system resources as soon as your function or application is finished with them.

There is another side effect to be aware of when working with Python. Because arguments to functions are passed by reference, the function has the potential of altering variables outside of the function's scope. The example program `examples/CH_03/example_03.py` demonstrates this:

```
from copy import copy

def total(values: list, new_value: int) -> int:
    values.append(new_value)
    return sum(values)

def better_total(values: list, new_value: int) -> int:
    temp_list = copy(values)
    temp_list.append(new_value)
    return sum(temp_list)

values_1 = [1, 2, 3]
total_1 = total(values_1, 4)
print(f"values_1 has been modified: {values_1}")
print(f"total_1 is as expected: {total_1}")
print()
values_2 = [1, 2, 3]
total_2 = better_total(values_2, 4)
print(f"values_2 unchanged: {values_2}")
print(f"total_2 is as expected: {total_2}")
```

When this program runs, the following output is produced:

```
values_1 has been modified: [1, 2, 3, 4]
total_1 is as expected: 10

values_2 unchanged: [1, 2, 3]
total_2 is as expected: 10
```

Both the `total()` and `better_total()` functions return the same value, 10, but only `better_total()` is idempotent. The code in the `total()` function is changing the `values_1` list passed to it as an argument and exists outside of its scope.

This happens because of the way the sum is calculated. The `total()` function appends `new_value` directly to the `values` list parameter passed to it. Because parameters are passed by reference, the list variable `values_1` outside the function and the parameter variable `values` inside the function both reference the same list. When `new_value` is appended to the list, it's modifying the same list that `values_1` referenced.

The `better_total()` function makes a copy of the `values` parameter, creating a new list variable `temp_list` independent of the one referenced by the `values_2` list. Then it appends `new_value` to `temp_list` and returns the sum of `temp_list`. This leaves the `values_2` list variable untouched, which is the intended behavior. The `better_total()` function is idempotent because it returns the same results for a given set of inputs and has no side effects.

3.3   Documentation

Documentation is a necessary process when building and defining an API. Functions, and the modules of which they are a part, should have documentation that briefly describes the functionality of the module and the functions it contains. Modules should have docstrings at the top of the file describing the functionality that the module provides and possibly the exceptions that might be raised.

Functions and class methods should have docstrings that briefly describe what the function does, what the parameters are for, and what the expected return value is. The functions in the example programs shown previously include docstrings. Here's an example of a function with no documentation:

```
def get_uuid():
    return uuid4().hex
```

And here's the same function with a docstring:

```
def get_uuid():
    """Generate a shortened UUID4 value to use
    as the primary key for database records

    Returns:
        string: A shortened (no '-' characters) UUID4 value
    """
    return uuid4().hex
```

The functionality of the version with no docstring might be clear, but there's no indication of why the function exists or why the code would call it. The version with a docstring answers these questions.

You might hear people say documenting Python code is unnecessary because the code is so readable and therefore self-documenting. The readability part is genuine, but any reasonably complex piece of code can only benefit from documentation, helping the reader understand the intent.

Documenting code does take effort; however, modern code editors like VS Code make it easier to insert docstring templates. The template for the docstrings in the example programs was generated by hitting return at the end of the function definition, typing three double quotes ("""), and clicking return again.

> **TIP**   Most of the example code in this book doesn't include docstrings. My intent is not to ignore my own suggestions but to reduce the amount of code presented on these pages and save book real estate. The code in the accompanying repository does have docstrings.

Many tools extract and process Python docstrings as part of external documentation systems. Besides being a benefit to readers of the code, including the original author, there is another win. If you're at the Python prompt and type `help(<function name>)`, the built-in help system presents the docstring of the function for reference. This includes not only the built-in functions but those you create. The existence of a docstring makes this possible.

3.4   *Closing thoughts*

Creating a good API is important because ease of use is important. Users of your APIs, which include yourself, want to make use of the functionality provided, not struggle with how to get that functionality to work.

Creating useful APIs is challenging; there are a lot of moving parts and considerations. Well-named modules, functions, and classes with consistent, logical parameters and documentation help give an API good affordance or discoverability. Like many things, the work invested in creating something today pays rewards later when you're using that trusted tool.

Summary

- An API is a collection of structured interface touchpoints that an application can use to affect the code to which the API provides access. There are APIs around operating system code, around server code running locally or remotely, and around the modules you build to create functionality in your applications.
- An API is a contract that application software defines so other application software can interface with it consistently and predictably.
- Part of creating a good API is abstracting the implementation so the caller of the API can depend on the interface contract and not have to use the internal implementation to achieve their goals.
- Python has good support and tools to create APIs that are useful to your own applications and can be published for use by others.

The object of conversation 4

When having a conversation, particularly one with any complexity, it's helpful if everyone in the conversation has the same context. It would be difficult to have conversations if every time someone began a new sentence they had to present the full context of the conversation.

From the standpoint of software functions, the context is the current state of the information the functions are working with. In the previous chapter, we talked about creating function signatures where the data state is passed around to the function calls in consistent ways.

Utilizing function signatures is a useful and powerful way to conduct conversations between functions that work on stateful data. It becomes a little more complicated if the same functions are being passed multiple, distinct stateful data contexts. The data and the functions that work on that data are separate from each other, and it's up to the developer to keep them organized and connected. Python provides another layer of abstraction to reduce complexity by using the object-oriented programming model.

4.1 Object-oriented programming (OOP)

The ability to place functions into modules provides many opportunities for structuring an API. The type and order of the parameters passed to the functions that make up an API offer possibilities to make your API more discoverable and useful.

Using the concepts of single responsibility and keeping functions to manageable lengths makes it more likely your API will consist of multiple functions. Users of the API's functionality—which may itself call other API functions, further modifying the data or state—produce the result returned to the user.

Often, the data structures passed between functions are collection objects, lists, sets, and dictionaries. These objects are powerful, and taking advantage of what they offer is important in Python development. By themselves, data structures don't do anything, but the functions they are passed to know what to do with the data structures they receive as input.

Because everything in Python is an object, you can create interesting objects using OOP. One of the goals of creating objects is to encapsulate data and the methods that act on that data into one entity. Conceptually, you're making something with the functionality you designed and implemented. You can think about what you create as an object, or thing, that has behavior. Creating classes is how you design these objects, connecting data and functionality to them.

4.1.1 Class definition

Python provides OOP by defining classes that can be instantiated into actual objects when needed. Instantiation is the act of taking something from a definition (the class) to reality. You could say the blueprint for a house is the class definition, and building the house instantiates it.

Here's a simple class definition for a `Person` class from the `examples/CH_04/example_01` application code:

```
class Person:
    def __init__(self, fname: str, mname: str = None, lname: str = None):
        self.fname = fname
        self.mname = mname
        self.lname = lname

    def full_name(self) -> str:
        full_name = self.fname
        if self.mname is not None:
```

```
        full_name = f"{full_name} {self.mname}"
    if self.lname is not None:
        full_name = f"{full_name} {self.lname}"
    return full_name
```

This class definition creates a `Person` template containing a person's first, middle, and last names. It also provides the `full_name()` method to obtain the person's full name based on the information passed to the object by its initialing `__init__()` method. A function associated with a class is often referred to as a *method*. This is a convention to make a distinction between a module function and one that's part of a class. Creating and using an object instantiated from the `Person` class looks like this:

```
>>> p1 = Person("George", "James", "Smith")
print(p1.full_name())
```

The `self` parameter that is passed as the first parameter of every method of the `Person` class is the reference to the `Person` instance just created. In this way, your code can create as many `Person` instances as needed, and each will be distinct because the `self` value of each will reference a particular instance and the state attributes (data) it contains.

This class can be represented visually in UML (Unified Modeling Language) as well, as shown by figure 4.1. UML is a way to present the design of systems visually. It's not necessary to use UML diagrams when designing and building a system, but it can be useful to introduce abstract concepts that are difficult to present concisely with text documentation alone.

The UML diagram for the `Person` class shows the name of the class, the attributes it contains, and the methods it provides. The plus-sign character (+) in front of the attribute and method names indicates they are public. In Python, attributes and methods of a class are always public and have no notion of protected or private access.

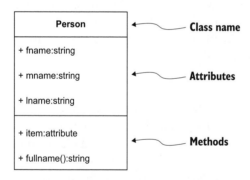

Figure 4.1   UML diagram of the `Person` class

Python's class design relies on the idea "We're all adults here," and the developers who use your classes will behave accordingly. Using plain attributes should be the default when designing your classes. You'll see later how class properties can gain control of how attributes are accessed and used. A simple use case for the `Person` class is presented in the `examples/CH_04/example_01` application:

```
def main():
    people = [
        Person("John", "George", "Smith"),
```

```
        Person("Bill", lname="Thompson"),
        Person("Sam", mname="Watson"),
        Person("Tom"),
    ]

    # Print out the full names of the people
    for person in people:
        print(person.full_name())
```

This code creates four instances of the `Person` class, each representing a different person and exercising all the variations of the constructor. The `for` loop iterates through the list of `Person` object instances and calls the `full_name()` method of each. Notice the `full_name()` method is not passed any state data; it uses the data attributes associated with the class instance. The `self` parameter of the `full_name()` method definition is what gives the method access to the individual attributes.

4.1.2 Drawing with class

The remaining examples you're going to build are object-oriented applications that animate some shapes on the screen.

> **TIP** Readers who have experience with OOP will probably recognize the analogy—a generic shape from which specific shapes, like rectangles and squares, are inherited. This analogy has been used to present object-oriented techniques for a long time and has become somewhat contrived. I acknowledge that, but I am using it anyway because it has advantages.

The concept of shapes is familiar enough outside of programming that readers can relate to them and to the idea that new shapes can be derived from them. Additionally, a program that moves shapes around on a computer screen is also familiar to most readers. The idea of moving shapes having speed and direction and staying within the boundaries of an onscreen window are well-known behaviors for computer-rendered graphics.

Because of this familiarity with shapes, the cognitive demand of learning about the object-oriented program can be focused on just that, not on any abstract quality of the object itself. For this reason, I'm asking you to bear with the contrived nature of the examples to see the larger picture. Each of the examples that follow expands upon the previous one to present the following concepts:

- *Inheritance*—Parent/child relationships between classes
- *Polymorphism*—Using an object as if it had multiple forms
- *Composition*—Giving attributes and behavior to a class through means other than inheritance

To create the drawing application, you'll be using the arcade module available in the Python Package Index (https://pypi.org/project/arcade/). This module provides the framework to build a drawing surface on the computer screen and draw and animate objects on that drawing surface.

The first thing to do is to define a class for a rectangle to draw on the screen. The UML diagram in figure 4.2 shows the attributes encapsulated in the class necessary to render a rectangle onscreen; x, y, width, and height define the position of the rectangle on the screen and the dimensions to use when drawing it.

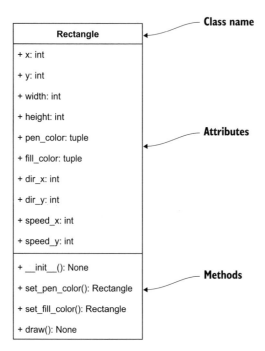

Figure 4.2   UML diagram for the Rectangle class

All of these attributes are initialized during the instantiation of a Rectangle object:

- pen_color, fill_color—Defines the colors used to outline the rectangle and fill it
- dir_x, dir_y—Defines the direction of movement relative to the screen's x and y axes; these are either 1 or –1
- speed_x, speed_y—Defines the speed at which the rectangle is moving in pixels per update

Figure 4.2 also includes the definition of three methods that the class supports:

- set_pen_color()—Provides a mechanism to set the pen color used to draw the Rectangle instance object
- set_fill_color()—Provides a mechanism to set the fill color used to fill a Rectangle instance object
- draw()—Draws a Rectangle object instance on the screen

This UML diagram is converted to a Python class definition in code. Here's the Rectangle class based on the previous diagram from the examples/CH_04/ example_02 application:

```python
class Rectangle:
    def __init__(
        self,
        x: int,
        y: int,
        width: int,
        height: int,
        pen_color: tuple = COLOR_PALETTE[0],
        fill_color: tuple = COLOR_PALETTE[1],
        dir_x: int = 1,
        dir_y: int = 1,
        speed_x: int = 1,
        speed_y: int = 1
    ):
        self.x = x
        self.y = y
        self.width = width
        self.height = height
        self.pen_color = pen_color
        self.fill_color = fill_color
        self.dir_x = 1 if dir_x > 0 else -1
        self.dir_y = 1 if dir_y > 0 else -1
        self.speed_x = speed_x
        self.speed_y = speed_y

    def set_pen_color(self, color: tuple) -> Rectangle:
        self.pen_color = color
        return self

    def set_fill_color(self, color: tuple) -> Rectangle:
        self.fill_color = color
        return self

    def draw(self):
        arcade.draw_xywh_rectangle_filled(
            self.x, self.y, self.width, self.height, self.fill_color
        )
        arcade.draw_xywh_rectangle_outline(
            self.x, self.y, self.width, self.height, self.pen_color, 3
        )
```

This class defines a simple Rectangle object. The object is initialized with the x and y coordinates, width and height, pen and fill colors, direction, and speed of motion of the rectangle. In the arcade module, the screen origin is in the lower-left corner, which is how most of us think about the x and y axes on paper, but it's different from many other screen-rendering tools.

TIP The 0, 0 origin location in the upper-left-hand corner of a drawing screen is there for historical reasons that involve how computer graphics were generated back in the day.

Modifying the values of the x and y attributes moves the Rectangle around the screen, as maintained by the arcade module and the instance of the Window class in the application. The Window class has two methods used to animate the objects on the screen: on_update() and on_draw(). The first updates the position of all the objects to render on the screen, and the second draws those updated objects on the screen. The on_update() method is called for every refresh iteration and is where the application modifies the position of the rectangles in the self.rectangles collection. The on_update() method looks like this:

```
def on_update(self, delta_time):
    for rectangle in self.rectangles:
        rectangle.x += rectangle.speed_x
        rectangle.y += rectangle.speed_y
```

This code iterates through the collection of rectangles and updates the position of each one by its x and y speed values, changing its position on the screen.

The updated rectangles are drawn on the screen by the Window instance method on_draw(), which looks like this:

```
def on_draw(self):
    # Clear the screen and start drawing
    arcade.start_render()

    # Draw the rectangles
    for rectangle in self.rectangles:
        rectangle.draw()
```

Every time the on_draw() method is called, the screen clears and the self .rectangles collection is iterated through, and each rectangle has its draw() method called.

The Rectangle class has behavior defined by the methods set_pen_color(), set_fill_color(), and draw(). These methods use and alter the state data encapsulated by the class definition. They provide the API you interact with when using the class. Using the methods abstracts away having to modify the state data directly.

Look at the set_pen_color() and set_fill_color() methods and you'll see they return self. Returning self can be useful for chaining methods of the class together into a series of operations. Here's an example from examples/CH_04/example_02.py using the Rectangle class. This code changes the pen and fill colors when the arcade schedule functionality code is called every second:

```
def change_colors(self, interval):
    for rectangle in self.rectangles:
        rectangle.set_pen_color(choice(COLOR_PALETTE)).set_fill_color(
            choice(COLOR_PALETTE)
        )
```

The change_colors() method of the Window instance is called by an arcade schedule function every second. It iterates through the collection of rectangles and calls the set_pen_color() and set_fill_color() in a chained manner to set random colors picked from the globally defined COLOR_PALETTE list.

When the examples/CH_04/example_02 application runs, it creates a window on the screen as shown in figure 4.3. The application animates a vertically aligned rectangle up and right at a 45-degree angle. It also changes the pen and fill colors of the rectangle every second the application runs.

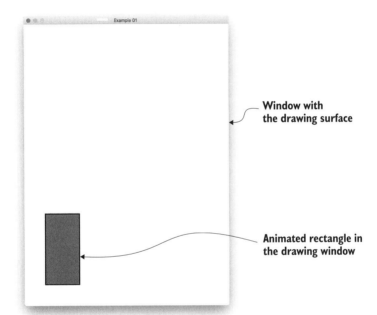

Window with
the drawing surface

Animated rectangle in
the drawing window

**Figure 4.3   Screenshot of
the rectangle on the
Window drawing surface**

PROPERTIES

As mentioned earlier, direct access to the attributes of a class should often be the default. The Rectangle example follows this practice. However, there are situations where you'll want more control over how the attributes of a class are used or changed.

The definition of the Rectangle class includes attributes for the x and y origin of the rectangle, which helps draw it in the window. That window has dimensions, and if you run the examples/CH_04/example_02 application long enough, you'll see the rectangle move off the screen.

Currently, the origin of a Rectangle instance is set to any integer value. No known screen has a resolution as large as the range of integer values, and none at all deal with negative numbers directly. The window declared in the application has a width range from 0 to 600 pixels and a height range from 0 to 800 pixels.

The boundaries of where `Rectangle` objects can be drawn should be constrained to within those window dimensions. Constraining the values of x and y means having code in place to limit the values that can be assigned to them. Your goal is to make the rectangle bounce around within the screen window.

If you're accustomed to other languages supporting OOP, you might be familiar with getters and setters. These are methods provided by the developer to control access to attributes of a class instance. These methods also give the developer a place to insert behavior when the attributes are retrieved or modified. The behavior you want to insert when setting or getting the x and y values is to limit the range of values to which those attributes can be set.

Adding getter and setter methods to the rectangle's x and y attributes could be done by defining methods like this:

```
def get_x(self):
def set_x(self, value):
def get_y(self):
def set_y(self, value):
```

Using these getter and setter functions also means changing the example code from

```
rectangle.x += 1
rectangle.y += 1
```

to this:

```
rectangle.set_x(rectangle.get_x() + 1)
rectangle.set_y(rectangle.get_y() + 1)
```

In my opinion, using getters and setters works but sacrifices readability when compared to the direct attribute access version/syntax. By using Python property decorators, you can control how class attributes are accessed and modified while still using the direct attribute access syntax. The `Rectangle` class can be modified to use property decorators offering this behavior. The updated portion of the `Rectangle` class from example program `examples/CH_04/example_03` is shown here:

```
class Rectangle:
    def __init__(
        self,
        x: int,
        y: int,
        width: int,
        height: int,
        pen_color: str = "BLACK",
        fill_color: str = "BLUE",
    ):
        self._x = x
        self._y = y
        self.width = width
        self.height = height
```

```
        self.pen_color = pen_color
        self.fill_color = fill_color

    @property
    def x(self):
        return self._x

    @x.setter
    def x(self, value: int):
        if self._x + value < 0:
            self._x = 0
        elif self._x + self._width + value > Screen.max_x:
            self._x = Screen.max_x - self._width
        else:
            self._x = value

    @property
    def y(self):
        return self._y

    @y.setter
    def y(self, value):
        if self._y + value < 0:
            self._y = 0
        elif self._y + self._height + value > Screen.max_y:
            self._y = Screen.max_y - self._height
        else:
            self._y = value
```

The first element to notice is that the attributes x and y are prefixed with a single underscore (_) character. Using the underscore this way is a convention to indicate the attribute should be considered private and not accessed directly. It doesn't enforce any notion of a private attribute, however.

The second element to notice is the new decorated methods in the class. For example, the two new methods for accessing the self._x attribute are as follows:

```
    @property
    def x(self):
        return self._x

    @x.setter
    def x(self, value):
        if not (0 < value < SCREEN_WIDTH - self.width):
            self.dir_x = -self.dir_x
        self._x += abs(self._x - value) * self.dir_x
```

The @property decorator over the first def x(self) function defines the getter functionality—in this case, just returning the value of self._x.

The @x.setter decorator over the second def x(self, value) function defines the setter functionality. Inside the function, self._x is constrained to within the screen x-axis minimum and maximum dimensions. If setting the value of `self._x` would place any part of the rectangle outside the screen area, the direction of travel is negated to start it moving in the opposite direction. Having these decorated methods in the `Rectangle` class means code like this works again:

```
rectangle.x += 1
```

The program statement appears to be setting the `Rectangle` instance x attribute directly, but the decorated methods are called instead. The += operation calls the getter method to retrieve the current value of `self._x`, adds 1 to that value, and uses the setter method to set `self._x` to that new value. If the resulting change places the rectangle outside of the screen dimensions, the direction of travel along the x-axis is reversed.

The beautiful part of this is you can define your classes using direct attribute access initially. If it becomes necessary to constrain or control access to an attribute, you can define getter and setter property methods. Existing code using your class doesn't have to change at all. From the point of view of the caller, the API of the class is the same.

Take note of another feature of using setter and getter decorated methods: you don't need to create both setter and getter decorated functions on attributes. You can create only a getter, which produces a read-only attribute. Likewise, you can create only a setter, which produces a write-only attribute. There is also an `@deleter` decorator to delete an attribute, but this feature is rarely used.

DECORATORS

Before moving on, let's talk about decorators. In Python, a decorator is a way to extend or modify the behavior of a function without changing the function itself. Decorating a function sounds confusing, but an example will help make the intent clear. As has been stated before, functions are objects in Python. This means functions can be passed to and returned from other functions as parameters like any other object.

The function defined here demonstrates the use of decorators:

```
from time import sleep

def complex_task(delay):
    sleep(delay)
    return "task done"
```

When the function is called, it uses the delay parameter to emulate some complex task that takes time to perform. It then returns the string `task done` when the function ends.

Suppose logging information about execution time is required, before and after this function is called, that includes the amount of time it takes to execute. This could be done by adding the logging information to the function itself, but that creates code maintenance issues, as every function to be timed would have to be updated if the timing code changes. You can instead create a decorator function to wrap `complex_task` with the desired new functionality. The decorator function looks like this:

```
def timing_decorator(func):
    def wrapper(delay):
```

```
        start_time = time()
        print("starting timing")
        result = func(delay)
        print(f"task elapsed time: {time() - start_time}")
        return result
    return wrapper
```

This code looks odd because the `timing_decorator` function defines another function inside itself called `wrapper`. The `timing_decorator` outer function also returns the `wrapper` inner function. This is perfectly fine Python syntax because functions are objects; the `wrapper` function is created and returned when the outer `timing_decorator` function is executed.

The `func` parameter of the `timing_decorator` is the function object being decorated. The `delay` parameter of the `wrapper` function is the parameter passed to the decorated function.

The code inside the `wrapper` function will execute, including calling the decorated `func` object. The following example will help clarify what's happening:

```
new_complex_task = timing_decorator(complex_task)
print(complex_task(1.5))
```

Here the `complex_task` function object is passed to the `timing_decorator` function. Notice there are no parentheses on `complex_task`; the function object itself is being passed, not the results of calling the function. The new variable `new_complex_task` is assigned the return value of `timing_decorator`, and because it returns the wrapper function, `new_complex_task` is a function object.

The print statement calls `new_complex_task`, passing it a delay value and printing the following information:

```
starting timing
task elapsed time: 1.6303961277008057
task done
```

This output shows the functionality added by `timing_decorator` and the original functionality of `complex_task` that is executed.

The example is interesting but not that useful, as every invocation of `complex_task` would have to be passed as a parameter to `timing_decorator` to obtain the additional timing functionality. Python supports a syntactic shortcut that makes this easier by adding `@timing_decorator` right before the definition of the `complex_task` function. This addition has the effect of "decorating" `complex_task` and creating a callable instance of the now-wrapped function. The code is shown here:

```
@timing_decorator
def complex_task(delay):
    sleep(delay)
    return "task done"

print(complex_task(1.5))
```

The `examples/CH_04/example_04` program demonstrates wrapping the task directly and using the decorator syntax, and when run, it produces this output:

```
starting timing
task elapsed time: 1.5009040832519531
task done

starting timing
task elapsed time: 1.5003101825714111
task done
```

The output shows `complex_task` running, but it also indicates that `@timing_decorated` has wrapped `complex_task` with additional functionality that is also running and generating log messages about the elapsed time. The `complex_task` code hasn't changed to provide this; the `wrapper` function inside `timing_decorator` does this work. The win here is that any function or method with the same signature as `complex_task` can be decorated with the `@timing_decorator` to generate timing information.

4.1.3   Inheritance

Being able to merge data and the behavior relevant to that data into classes gives you very expressive ways to structure your programs. When building classes, situations arise where functionality is common to more than one class. As a developer, it becomes part of our nature to follow the DRY (don't repeat yourself) principle. You can follow this principle when creating objects in Python by using inheritance.

> **TIP** As a developer, it pays not to repeat yourself, as repetition opens the door to introducing mistakes or differences in the code. If the code you use repeatedly is right, then it's right everywhere. If you repeat code, rewrite it; it can be right in some places and wrong elsewhere. This makes it hard to find and fix.

Like actual parents and their children, attributes and behaviors are inherited from the parent but aren't exact duplicates. When talking about OOP class design, the terms *parent* and *child* are used because the metaphor works well. The terms *base class* and *derived class* are also used to indicate the parent–child relationship.

You'll also see words like *superclass* used to refer to the parent and *subclass* to refer to the child. These are terms applied to the relationship between objects when talking about inheritance.

One of the reasons to use inheritance is to add attributes and behavior unique to the child, possibly modifying those inherited from the parent. It's also useful to derive multiple children from a parent class, each with its own set of unique attributes and behaviors but still imbued with characteristics from the parent. Creating an inheritance relationship between two classes in Python is performed like this:

```
class ParentClass:
    pass

class ChildClass(ParentClass):
    pass
```

The ParentClass definition creates a root-level class definition. The definition of the ChildClass includes the class inherited from inside the parentheses. In the example, it inherits from ParentClass. The pass statement in both class definitions is a nop (no operation) in Python and is necessary to make the class definitions syntactically correct but without functionality.

In the examples/CH_04/example_02 code, a Rectangle class was created with a position on the screen, a pen color to draw with, and a color to fill the rectangle. What if you wanted to create other shapes, like squares and circles? Each shape would have a position and dimension on the screen and a pen and fill color.

The direct approach would be to create complete, standalone Square and Circle class definitions and draw instances of each on the screen. Each class would have all of the attributes and methods of the Rectangle class but with a different draw() method to draw that unique shape. Creating separate classes for Square and Circle would work for the relatively small number of shapes involved but wouldn't scale well if many more shapes were required.

This presents an opportunity to use inheritance to gather the attributes and their associated behavior into a parent class you could call Shape. This Shape parent class would be used to collect the common attributes and methods in one place. Any shape drawn onscreen would be a child of the Shape parent.

You'll start by reproducing the functionality of the examples/CH_04/example_03 application by making use of inheritance. The examples that follow are from the examples/CH_04/example_04 application.

Figure 4.4 shows that the attributes and methods of the Rectangle class definition have moved to the Shape class, and the Rectangle now inherits from it. The Shape name in italics indicates it's abstract and shouldn't be instantiated directly. The draw() method is also in italic because it exists in the Shape definition but has no functionality of its own. The functionality must be provided by the child class—in this case, Rectangle.

Because the Shape class is essentially what the Rectangle was, the code isn't shown; instead, the updated Rectangle class is shown here:

```
class Rectangle(Shape):

    def draw(self):
        arcade.draw_xywh_rectangle_filled(
            self.x, self.y, self.width, self.height, self.fill_color
        )
        arcade.draw_xywh_rectangle_outline(
            self.x, self.y, self.width, self.height, self.pen_color, 3
        )
```

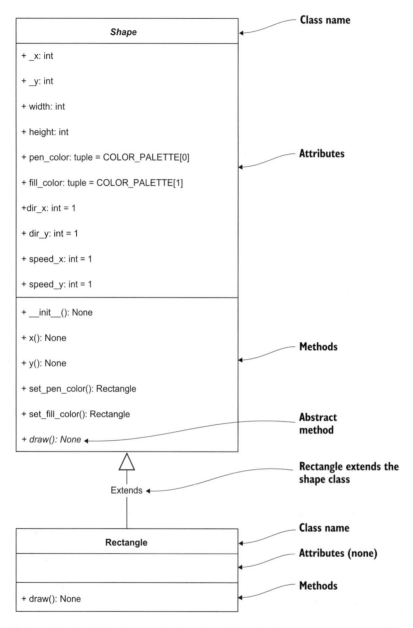

Figure 4.4   The UML diagram showing the relationship between the Shape and Rectangle classes

The first line of the Rectangle class has been modified to include Shape within parentheses. This is how the Rectangle class inherits from the Shape class.

The rectangle has been refactored to have only a unique `draw()` method to draw itself on the screen. The `draw()` method overrides the empty abstract method provided by the `Shape` class. Everything else is managed and maintained by the `Shape` class. Even the `__init__()` initializer has been removed because the initializer from the `Shape` class is sufficient.

It's reasonable to question the advantage of splitting the original `Rectangle` into two new classes, `Shape` and `Rectangle`. You'll see this in the next examples when `Square` and `Circle` shapes are added to the application. Figure 4.5 shows that running the application presents a screen exactly as seen previously—a single rectangle bouncing around the screen and changing colors.

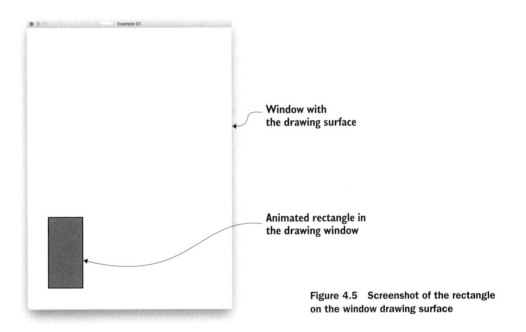

Window with
the drawing surface

Animated rectangle in
the drawing window

**Figure 4.5   Screenshot of the rectangle
on the window drawing surface**

MULTIPLE SHAPES

Now that you have an inheritance structure defined, you can use it to create multiple kinds of shapes with different attributes and behaviors. Adding a `Square` and a `Circle` class to the inheritance structure is straightforward. Each additional class inherits from a parent class providing common attributes and methods that are useful to the new child class.

Figure 4.6 shows a few interesting elements of the inheritance structure. Notice the `Square` class inherits from `Rectangle` instead of `Shape`. This is because a square is a special case of a rectangle with the height and width equal to each other.

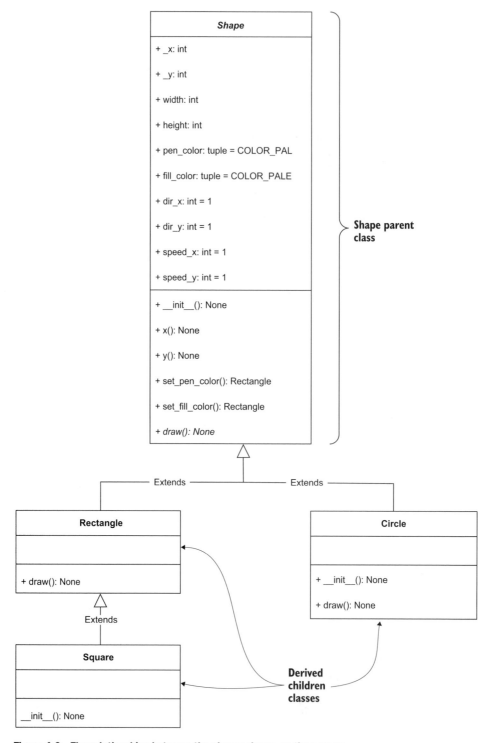

Figure 4.6 The relationships between the shapes drawn on the screen

This brings up a concept about inheritance and the relationships between objects. As just mentioned, a Square IS-A Rectangle, and a Rectangle IS-A Shape, which means a Square IS-A Shape as well. Here is the class definition code for the Square class:

```
class Square(Rectangle):

    def __init__(
        self,
        x: int,
        y: int,
        size: int,
        pen_color: tuple = COLOR_PALETTE[0],
        fill_color: tuple = COLOR_PALETTE[1],
        dir_x: int = 1,
        dir_y: int = 1,
        speed_x: int = 1,
        speed_y: int = 1,
    ):
        super().__init__(
            x, y,
            size,
            size,
            pen_color,
            fill_color,
            dir_x,
            dir_y,
            speed_x,
            speed_y
        )
```

The Square class has an __init__() method even though its parent class, the Rectangle class, doesn't. The Square provides this unique __init__() method because it only needs to get a single-dimension value—size—and not height and width. It then uses the parameters in the __init__() method when it makes a call to super().__init__(). Because the Rectangle class doesn't have an __init__() method, the super().__init__() calls the Shape class constructor, passing the size parameter for both height and width to set the attribute dimensions.

The super() method is how to explicitly call the __init__() method of the child's parent class. The Square class doesn't need to provide a draw() method, as the one inherited from the parent Rectangle class works fine but with the height and width attributes having the same value.

The Circle IS-A Shape because it inherits directly from the Shape class. The code that creates the Circle class is shown here:

```
class Circle(Shape):

    def __init__(
        self,
        x: int,
```

```
        y: int,
        radius: int,
        pen_color: tuple = COLOR_PALETTE[0],
        fill_color: tuple = COLOR_PALETTE[1],
        dir_x: int = 1,
        dir_y: int = 1,
        speed_x: int = 1,
        speed_y: int = 1,
    ):
        super().__init__(
            x,
            y,
            radius * 2,
            radius * 2,
            pen_color,
            fill_color,
            dir_x,
            dir_y,
            speed_x,
            speed_y,
        )

    def draw(self):
        radius = self.width / 2
        center_x = self.x + radius
        center_y = self.y + radius
        arcade.draw_circle_filled(
            center_x,
            center_y,
            radius,
            self.fill_color
        )
        arcade.draw_circle_outline(
            center_x,
            center_y,
            radius,
            self.pen_color,
            3
        )
```

Like the Square class, the Circle supplies its own __init__() method so the caller can provide a radius for the circle. The radius parameter is used in the super().__init__() call to set the height and width dimensions of the area that the circle will be drawn within. Unlike the Square class, the Circle class does provide a unique draw() method because it calls different drawing functions in the arcade module to draw itself onscreen. When the CH_04/example_05 application runs, it creates a window with three different shapes bouncing around within the window and changing colors. Initially, it looks similar to figure 4.7.

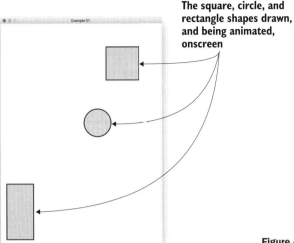

The square, circle, and
rectangle shapes drawn,
and being animated,
onscreen

Figure 4.7   All three shapes drawn onscreen

Object-oriented genealogies

Inheritance in OOP is a feature that allows you to create useful and powerful class hierarchies. Keep in mind that just like human genealogies, the descendants become less and less like the root parent class as you descend the tree.

Large hierarchies of classes can become complex to use and understand, and the root class functionality can become wholly obscured in distant child classes. In my work, I've never gone beyond three levels in any parent–child relationships in the class hierarchies I've built.

4.1.4   Polymorphism

Another feature of inheritance, called polymorphism, can be useful when creating class hierarchies. The word *polymorphism* means "many forms," and in relation to programming, it means calling a method of multiple objects by the same method name but getting different behavior depending on which instance of an object is used.

The examples/CH_04/example_05 application has already taken advantage of polymorphism when rendering the different shapes in the window. Each of the shapes in the program supports a draw() method. The Rectangle class provides a draw() method to render itself on the application screen. The Square class uses the inherited Rectangle draw() method but with a constraint on the height and width to create a Square. The Circle class provides its own draw() method to render itself. The Shape root parent class also provides an abstract draw() method that has no functionality.

Because the Rectangle, Square, and Circle classes all have an IS-A relationship with the Shape class, they all can be considered instances of Shape and use the methods provided by the class. This is what happens in the Display class when the on_update(), on_draw(), and change_colors() methods are called. The Display class has a collection of shapes in the self.shapes = [] list created in the __init__() method. For example, here is the code in the on_draw() method:

```
def on_draw(self):

    # Clear the screen and start drawing
    arcade.start_render()

    # Draw the rectangles
    for shape in self.shapes:
        shape.draw()
```

This code is called every time the system wants to draw the objects on the screen, which is approximately 60 times a second when using the arcade module. The code takes advantage of polymorphism to iterate through the list of shapes and call the draw() method of each one. It doesn't matter that each shape is different; they all support a draw() method, and all the shapes are rendered onscreen. Any number of different shapes could be derived from the Shape class, and so long as they support a draw() method that renders the shape on the screen, the mentioned loop would work.

Real-world objects shouldn't constrain object design

It is common to use analogies to real-world objects or concepts when writing about inheritance. The examples presented do exactly this, using the idea of shapes, rectangles, squares, and circles. Using concepts already familiar to you is a useful metaphor because they are things you know already. There are plenty of other new concepts presented when talking about inheritance; using familiar ideas reduces the cognitive load while learning.

However, this metaphor can get in the way of creating useful hierarchies of classes in your applications. Because we've been talking about things that have behavior like actual objects in the real world, it can color how you think about your class design. The objects you create from the classes you design don't have to model real-world objects. Many of the objects that are useful to model with classes have no analog in the real world, and adhering to the analogy too strictly can hinder the work you're trying to accomplish.

4.1.5   Composition

In the inheritance section, you saw the relationships between the Rectangle, Square, Circle, and Shape classes. These relationships allowed the child classes to inherit attributes and behavior from their parent class. This creates the idea that a Rectangle IS-A Shape, and a Square IS-A Rectangle, which also means a Square IS-A Shape as well.

These relationships also imply a certain similarity between attributes and behaviors of the parent classes and the child classes that inherit from them. But this isn't the only way to incorporate attributes and behavior into classes.

Look at the Shape class; it has two attributes for pen and fill color. These two attributes provide color to the shape and are distinguished from each other by their names. But they offer the same thing—a color, most likely from a palette of colors the system can create. This means the color is a common attribute within the Shape itself and is expressed twice.

It's possible with inheritance to handle this and add to the hierarchy in the examples by creating a Color class with pen and fill color attributes and then having the Shape class inherit from it. This would work, but the inheritance feels awkward. You can make a Shape have an IS-A relationship to a Color class in code, but logically it doesn't make sense. A shape is not a color, and it doesn't fit the mental IS-A model of an inheritance structure.

Instead of trying to force inheritance to provide the desired behavior, you can use composition. You've already been using composition when giving classes attributes that are integers and strings. You can take this further and create custom classes to be used as attributes, composing behavior into your own classes.

Creating a new class Color provides a consistent abstraction for color in the application. It has a class-level definition for the colors supported and has a mechanism to allow only defined colors to be set. The Color class is connected to the Shape class as a composite, indicated in figure 4.8 by the connecting line with the filled black-diamond symbol.

Here is what the Color class looks like from the examples/CH_04/example_06 application program:

```
@dataclass
class Color:
    PALETTE = [
        arcade.color.BLACK,
        arcade.color.LIGHT_GRAY,
        arcade.color.LIGHT_CRIMSON,
        arcade.color.LIGHT_BLUE,
        arcade.color.LIGHT_CORAL,
        arcade.color.LIGHT_CYAN,
        arcade.color.LIGHT_GREEN,
        arcade.color.LIGHT_YELLOW,
        arcade.color.LIGHT_PASTEL_PURPLE,
        arcade.color.LIGHT_SALMON,
        arcade.color.LIGHT_TAUPE,
        arcade.color.LIGHT_SLATE_GRAY,
    ]
    color: tuple = PALETTE[0]
    _color: tuple = field(init=False)

    @property
    def color(self) -> tuple:
        return self._color

    @color.setter
    def color(self, value: tuple) -> None:
        if value in Color.PALETTE:
            self._color = value
```

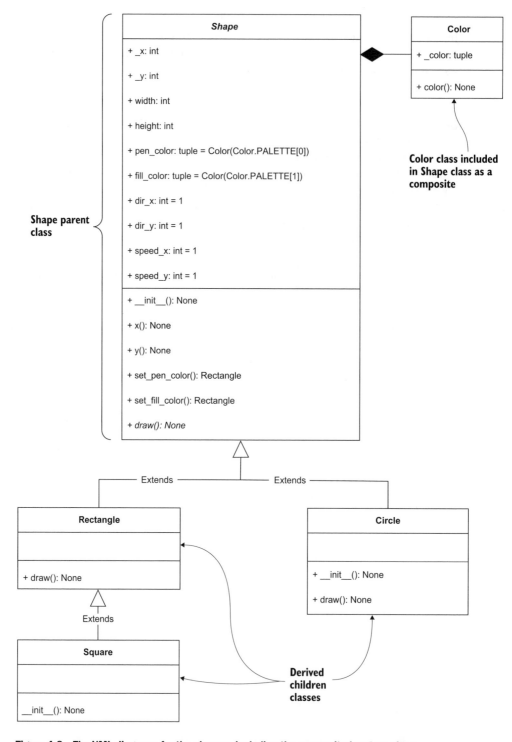

Figure 4.8   The UML diagrams for the classes, including the composited `Color` class

The `Color` class moves the allowable color list within the scope of the class and out of the global module namespace. It's also a Python data class, which can make defining simple classes that are mostly data easier to implement. The class provides getter and setter property decorators to make using the color within the class more straightforward.

The `Shape` class is modified to use the `Color` class for the pen and fill color attributes. The updated __init__() method for the class is shown here:

```
class Shape:

    def __init__(
        self,
        x: int,
        y: int,
        width: int,
        height: int,
        pen: Color = Color(),
        fill: Color = Color(),
        dir_x: int = 1,
        dir_y: int = 1,
        speed_x: int = 1,
        speed_y: int = 1,
    ):
        self._x = x
        self._y = y
        self.width = width
        self.height = height
        self.pen = Color(Color.PALETTE[0])
        self.fill = Color(Color.PALETTE[1])
        self.dir_x = 1 if dir_x > 0 else -1
        self.dir_y = 1 if dir_y > 0 else -1
        self.speed_x = speed_x
        self.speed_y = speed_y
```

The attribute names for pen and fill color have been simplified to just `pen` and `fill` because they are both `Color` class instances. The initial default values have been set to black for the pen and light gray for the fill colors. Adding the `Color` class to the `Shape` class this way creates a HAS-A relationship; a `Shape` class has `Color` attributes but isn't a color itself.

The `set_pen_color()` and `set_fll_color()` methods have also been modified to use the new `pen` and `fill` attributes. Setting a color for the pen now looks like this:

```
def set_pen_color(self, color: tuple) -> Rectangle:
    self.pen.color = color
    return self
```

Running the `examples/CH_04/example_06` application produces a screen exactly like you've seen before—three shapes bouncing around the window and changing colors every second. The use of composition gives you a way to add attributes and behavior to a class without having to create contrived inheritance hierarchies.

4.2 Closing thoughts

Creating classes and class hierarchies gives you a way to create code that's clean and well-controlled in its usage. Classes are another avenue to give your users an API into application functionality.

A class definition also can be used to create namespaces and control scope. A module provides a namespace, and classes defined within that module create more namespaces within it. The attributes and methods of a class are within the scope of instance objects created from the class.

You've moved closer to particular elements of the developer domain and are now using binoculars to gain more detailed views of those domains. We'll continue to scan useful and powerful domains for insights on our journey.

Summary

- OOP gives you the ability to encapsulate data together with the functionality that acts on that data. This gives objects "behaviors" that make thinking about how those objects react and interact with other objects a little easier.
- Python creates the structure of objects using class definitions. A class gives the object a look and feel; an instance of a class is the realization of a class in your code. Like a cookie cutter defines what a cookie is, the cookie is the instance of what the cookie cutter defines.
- Like namespaces, classes can create hierarchal structures by using inheritance from a parent class to a child class. A child class inherits attributes and features from its parent and can add new, unique features of its own.
- Using composition, attributes and functionality can be added to a class design without creating awkward or illogical inheritance structures.
- You've learned about classes, inheritance, and creating class hierarchies. Using classes is a powerful way to take advantage of code reuse and adhere to the DRY principle.
- By using composition, you can add additional attributes and features to definitions that don't come from inheritance and thus avoid awkward and illogical inheritance hierarchies.

Exceptional events 5

Developing software can lead you to think in a binary way—things are either on or off; they work or don't work; something is either true or false. However, the real world is far from binary; it is a sea of variety. The software you create for yourself, and others, lives in that world.

The real world is not black or white; it is an infinitely variable field stretching between those two extremes. Computer systems that run software lose power and fail. The networks connecting systems are slow, intermittent, or unreliable. The storage systems on which software depends to save information become full, unreliable, or fail. The users of your software make incorrect assumptions and enter wrong or misleading data.

In addition to the problematic world in which software runs, you will create bugs in the code you write. Software bugs are errors or failures, causing an application to produce unexpected results. Most software applications providing something useful are complex enough that bugs will creep in. These come from wrong assumptions on the part of the developer, oversights, and simple everyday mistakes.

This shouldn't discourage you as a developer but should broaden the way you think about creating software applications. The problems outlined previously can be managed and handled and are part of the challenge of becoming a developer. How you handle these challenges is dependent on the requirements of the application and its users.

If you're knocking together a quick program to solve a problem for yourself, creating something that might crash if given incorrect input is probably acceptable. On the other hand, if you're creating something hundreds, or thousands, of users will access, application crashes are far less acceptable. It will take longer to develop and build code to handle conditions that might arise. Figure 5.1 shows the relationship between three things related to the development of software applications.

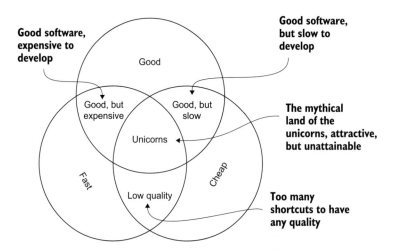

Figure 5.1   The Venn diagram of three aspects of the reality of developing software

Good in this context indicates that the software application quality is good and meets the requirements and user expectations, with a low occurrence of bugs. Fast and Cheap are a little harder to define because they relate to time and money, as the adage goes.

The intersection of Good and Cheap represents the time it takes to develop a software application and indicates that it can take more time to create. This can happen if an inexperienced developer, or a small team of developers, works for a relatively long time to create a good application.

The intersection of Good and Fast also represents time and indicates creating the application quickly, with good quality. This almost always entails more experienced developers who can create an application in a relatively short amount of time.

The intersection of Fast and Cheap involves making tradeoffs in quality to create the application quickly. An application created this way might be acceptable for a one-off utility application but generally should be avoided.

Only the intersection of two of the circles can ever be achieved, even though the diagram shows the intersection of all three circles. The intersection of all three circles is where magical unicorns live. Trying to find a path to the land of the unicorns will keep you from actually creating something useful.

A software application with good quality meets the needs of its users in a couple of ways. It provides the functionality intended and what the user expects, and it doesn't behave in unexpected ways if things go wrong.

As mentioned in the introduction to this chapter, in the real world, unexpected events happen all the time. Storage devices become full, networks disconnect, and users enter incorrect data, unintentionally or otherwise. Unexpected events can occur at any time and are handled in Python by an exception being raised.

5.1 Exceptions

Python handles unexpected events in running applications by raising exceptions. You can think of these as exceptional conditions occurring while an application runs, and they're not all necessarily errors.

If you've written any Python programs, you've seen exceptions raised. A simple math error in a program statement will raise an exception, as shown here:

```
>>> print(10/0)
Traceback (most recent call last):
  File "<stdin>", line 1, in <module>
ZeroDivisionError: division by zero
```

The exception `ZeroDivisionError` is raised by Python because the results of dividing a value of 10 by 0 are undefined. The exception `ZeroDivisionError` is a child, or subclass, of the base `Exception` class. The `Exception` class is the parent of most other exceptions that Python can raise.

In this way, the `Exception` class is precisely like how the `Shape` class is the parent of the `Rectangle` class in the previous chapter. A `ZeroDivisionError` exception is a more specific version of the more general base `Exception` class.

When an exception occurs in a program, Python will stop executing your program code and start working its way back up the call stack looking for an exception handler. The call stack is the series of function calls leading to the code that raised the exception. Python is looking for a handler to intercept the exception and do something with it. If no exception handler is found, Python exits the application and prints a stack trace.

The stack trace is a chronological listing descending from the root of the application down the call stack of functions that were called to reach the point in the code where the exception was raised. Each function listed in the stack trace also shows the line number in the module where the function in the stack trace is called. The stack trace continues until the last function is called, where the line number that raised the exception is displayed. The example program `examples/CH_05/example_01.py` demonstrates this:

```
def func_a():
    dividend = float(input("Enter a dividend value: "))
    divisor = float(input("Enter a divisor value: "))
    result = func_b(dividend, divisor)
    print(f"dividing {dividend} by {divisor} = {result}")


def func_b(dividend: float, divisor: float) -> float:
    return func_c(dividend, divisor)


def func_c(dividend: float, divisor: float) -> float:
    return dividend / divisor


func_a()
```

This program shows `func_a()` getting input from the user for the `dividend` and `divisor` and converting those input strings to floating-point values. It then calls `func_b()`, which calls `func_c()`, which performs the division operation on the two passed parameters. Running this program produces the following output for the values entered at the prompts:

```
Enter a dividend value: 12.2
Enter a divisor value: 0
Traceback (most recent call last):
  File "<path to code>/code/project/CH_05/example_01.py",
    line 20, in <module>
    func_a()
  File "<path to code>/code/project/CH_05/example_01.py",
    line 8, in func_a
    result = func_b(dividend, divisor)
  File "<path to code>/code/project/CH_05/example_01.py",
    line 13, in func_b
    return func_c(dividend, divisor)
  File "<path to code>/code/project/CH_05/example_01.py",
    line 17, in func_c
    return dividend / divisor
ZeroDivisionError: float division by zero
```

The code shows Python encountering an exception in `func_c()` when it tries to divide 12.2 by 0, then going back up the call stack to `func_b()` and up to `func_a()`, looking for a handler to intercept the exception. Because there isn't a handler, Python exits the program and prints the exception and stack trace that caused the application to crash.

> **TIP** I inserted <path to code> in the program output and stack trace above because the path to the code shown was relevant to my Mac and wouldn't be the same as what you would see running the code on your computer.

Another possible exception that the program can raise happens if the user enters a string at either of the two prompts that can't be converted to a floating-point value. Here is an example of running the program raising that exception:

```
Enter a dividend value: Python
Traceback (most recent call last):
  File "<path to code>/project/CH_05/example_01.py", line 20, in <module>
    func_a()
  File "<path to code>/code/project/CH_05/example_01.py", line 6, in func_a
    dividend = float(input("Enter a dividend value: "))
ValueError: could not convert string to float: 'Python'
```

In this example, the stack trace only shows `func_a()` because the `ValueError` exception was raised within that function when the program tried to convert the string `Python` to a floating-point value.

5.2 Handling exceptions

Handling exceptions in Python is done by using a `try` / `except` block in your program code:

```
try:
    # code that might raise an exception
except Exception as e:
    # code that executes if an exception occurs
else:
    # code that executes if no exception occurs (optional)
finally:
    # code that executes whether an exception occurs or not (optional)
```

The `try` statement begins a block of code that might raise an exception your program can handle. The `except Exception as e:` statement ends the block of code and is where an exception is intercepted and assigned to the e variable. The use of e is not required syntax, and the variable name e is just my convention.

Because of the `except Exception as e:` in the handler part of the block, the previous example will catch any exception raised by the code within the `try` / `except` block. The `else` and `finally` clauses of the `try` / `except` block are optional and used less often in practice.

5.2.1 Handling an exception if the code can do something about it

When thinking about exceptions, it's easy to get into a frame of mind to handle them everywhere they might occur. Depending on where in the program the exception occurs, this might be a logical choice.

Often, exceptions happen within the context of a function where the code is acting on the arguments passed to it. At this point, the scope of work the code is performing is narrow, and the broader context of what the program is trying to accomplish is at a higher level.

> **TIP** If you're using the concept of "single responsibility," then it is likely that the function has little context of the bigger picture that the application is creating.

When an exception occurs in a function, the exception handler can make reasonable choices within the context of the function. The handler might be able to retry the operation for a fixed number of attempts before letting the exception flow upward in the call stack to a higher context. It could make assumptions based on the exception and correct or change the state of data to make the code continue without raising an exception.

5.2.2   *Allowing exceptions to flow upward in your programs*

Unless the code where the exception occurs can do something useful about the exception, it's better to let the exception flow upward through the call stack to a higher level of context. At higher levels of context, decisions can be made about how to handle the exception. The higher-level context might be the point where choices about retrying operations are made. At the higher levels of context, more information might be available about what the program is trying to accomplish and what alternative paths can be taken. At this point, you can decide what information to present to the user so they can make choices about how to proceed.

The program should also log the exception and the stack trace associated with it, so the application developers have information about the path taken that generated the exception. This is incredibly useful information to have when debugging an application and trying to resolve problems.

Where in the code to log exceptions depends partly on whether the exception was handled or not. If the exception was handled, it may not be necessary to log information about it. However, it might be useful to output a log message, not as an error but at the information level to make it visible.

It's also possible that an exception is fatal to the program and nothing can be done other than logging the exception stack trace and exiting the program. Exiting an application is an entirely reasonable course of action for some applications, such as utility programs and command-line tools.

5.2.3   *Informing the user*

Keeping the application user informed about the status of an application and the events occurring in it is also useful. An exception handler in the right context of the application flow can inform the user to take steps toward corrective action, allowing the application to retry an action and succeed. The type of exception, and the message attached to it, can help generate an informative message to present to the user.

5.2.4   *Never silence an exception*

It's possible to handle an exception and silence it. Silencing an exception is shown in these two examples:

```
try:
    # some code that might raise an exception
except:
    pass
```

```
try:
    # some code that might raise an exception
except Exception:
    pass
```

The first example catches all exceptions, including system and keyboard events like CTRL-C to exit a program, which generates the exception `KeyboardInterrupt`. This is a system exception and not necessarily an error, just an exceptional event. The second example catches a narrower scope of exceptions, many of which can be considered error conditions, but it's still far too wide a net.

Worse than catching too broad a class of exceptions, the previous code lets the exception pass silently. It doesn't inform the user or log the exception stack trace. The user is deprived of information about why the application is malfunctioning, and the developer isn't given any information about what the exception is or where it's occurring.

The presence of either of these blocks of code is an indication of a low-quality application. Trying to find the source of the problem where this pattern of code exists in an application is frustrating and time-consuming.

EXAMPLE 1 IMPROVED

The following example code acts on the previous discussion to show when to allow exceptions to flow upward in the call stack and when an exception handler can be used to try and correct the situation that caused the exception. The program `examples/CH_05/example_01.py` can be improved to handle exceptions and provide a better user experience. The program `examples/CH_05/example_02.py` demonstrates this improvement:

```
def func_a():
    dividend = float(input("Enter a dividend value: "))
    divisor = float(input("Enter a divisor value: "))
    result = func_b(dividend, divisor)
    print(f"dividing {dividend} by {divisor} = {result}")

def func_b(dividend: float, divisor: float) -> float:
    return func_c(dividend, divisor)

def func_c(dividend: float, divisor: float) -> float:
    return dividend / divisor

successful = False
while not successful:
    try:
        func_a()
    except ZeroDivisionError as e:
        print(f"The divisor can't be a zero value, error:", e)
    except ValueError as e:
        print(
            f"The dividend and divisor must be a string that represents a
            ➡ number, error:",
            e,
        )
    else:
        successful = True
```

```
    finally:
        if successful:
            print("Thanks for running the program")
        else:
            print("Try entering a dividend and divisor again")
```

In this example, the functions `func_a()`, `func_b()`, and `func_c()` are unchanged and don't catch exceptions. They follow the pattern of letting exceptions flow upward through the stack to a higher-level context.

That higher-level context is `func_a()`. Now there is a while loop around the function that will keep trying `func_a()` until it can complete successfully.

Within the while loop, there is an exception handler catching two exceptions, `ZeroDivisionError` and `ValueError`. Both of these handlers prompt the user with information about what went wrong and provide advice about how to proceed.

The `else` clause of the handler only executes if `func_a()` runs successfully without raising an exception. When this happens, it sets the `successful` variable to `True`, signaling the enclosing while loop to exit.

The `finally` clause takes advantage of the state of the `successful` variable to either indicate the program is done or encourage the user to try again. Running this program with possible input from the user looks like this:

```
Enter a dividend value: Python
The dividend and divisor must be a string that represents a number, error:
    could not convert string to float: 'Python'
Try entering a dividend and divisor again
Enter a dividend value: 12.2
Enter a divisor value: 0
The divisor can't be a zero value, error: float division by zero
Try entering a dividend and divisor again
Enter a dividend value: 12.2
Enter a divisor value: 3.4
dividing 12.2 by 3.4 = 3.5882352941176467
Thanks for running the program
```

This program follows most of the recommendations to handle exceptions:

- Allows the exceptions that can't be handled locally to flow upward to a higher context
- Handles an exception if the code can do something useful about it
- Informs the user about the problem and suggests a solution
- Doesn't silence an exception

The program doesn't log the exception and the stack trace, as this would be distracting information for the user given the simplicity of this program. This program handled the exception as part of its expected program flow, which makes logging the exception information unnecessary.

That's not to say the information couldn't be added to the handlers for `Zero-DivisionError` and `ValueError` if it were deemed useful. Logging an exception can be handled by using Python's logging module in the following manner:

```
import logging
logger = logging.getLogger(__name__)
logger.setLevel(logging.DEBUG)
ch = logging.StreamHandler()
ch.setLevel(logging.DEBUG)
formatter = logging.Formatter(
    '%(asctime)s - %(name)s - %(levelname)s - %(message)s'
)
ch.setFormatter(formatter)
logger.addHandler(ch)

try:
    x = 10 / 0
except Exception as e:
    logger.error("something bad happened")
```

This code imports the `logging` module and creates a simple `logger` instance named after the module in which the instance is created. It then sets the terminal as the output of log messages, creates a formatter for what messages should look like, and adds the handler to the logger instance. Configuring a logger more fully will be part of later chapter examples when we start building the MyBlog web application.

Calling `logger.error()` inside the exception handler will print the message. That message will be formatted and look like this:

```
2022-07-23 18:50:29,803 - __main__ - ERROR - something bad happened
```

The output includes a timestamp when the exception occurred, the module name, the error level, and the message. In the previous example, the __main__ name exists because the example was run as a standalone application.

If the code was imported into a larger application as a module, __main__ would be replaced with the name of the module. In a larger application, this information is useful to narrow down the area where the exception occurred.

In this simple example, the output of the logger is directed to `stdout`, which is the console, or screen for most users. Most use cases of loggers are directed to log files, or log aggregator systems, to keep logging information from interfering with any output the program is producing for the user.

The introduction to this section states an exception should never be silenced, which is predominantly the right way to handle exceptions. There are situations where the developer's knowledge about the code would make silencing an exception acceptable if taken with forethought. The recommendations listed previously still hold, however.

5.3   Raising an exception

In Python, you can raise exceptions programmatically in your code. Raising an exception might seem like an odd thing to do since most of the time an exception equates to errors. However, raising an exception is a useful way to handle conditions within your programs that you decide are exceptional and not necessarily programmatic errors.

As an example, suppose you're writing a quiz application that provides calculations based on user input. One of the calculation functions only works if a user-entered parameter is greater than 0 and less than or equal to 100. The code should define a range of values acceptable to the function.

Because integers in Python have a large range, your program code will need to limit the user input to within the range 0 < value ≤ 100. Restricting the range is easy enough to do at the point of use in the function, but what should the function do if the range is violated?

Most likely the function should do nothing, as it doesn't have the context to do anything useful if the range restriction is violated. Keeping in mind the idea of letting exceptions flow upward to where they can be handled, raising an exception can be useful. Here is one way to handle the range restriction in the function:

```python
def range_check_user_input(value):
    if not 0 < value <= 100:
        raise ValueError("value range exceeded", value)
    # additional functionality
```

At the very top of the function, a conditional statement checks if the value parameter is not within the acceptable range, and if not, a ValueError exception is raised. If the parameter is within range, the function continues normally.

The code delegated the responsibility for handling the out-of-range ValueError exception up the call stack to the calling function. The calling function most likely does have the context necessary to handle the exception, perhaps by prompting the user to enter the value parameter again.

Handling the ValueError exception in the calling function might look like this:

```python
def get_data_from_user():
    # initialization and gather user input
    try:
        range_check_user_input(value)
    except ValueError as e:
        print(e)
        # restart code to get user input
```

The get_data_from_user() function calls the range_check_user_input() function inside a try / except block that handles a ValueError exception, prints the error out for the user, and restarts the process to get data from the user.

5.4   *Creating your own exceptions*

Python allows you to create custom exception classes your code can raise. Creating a custom exception might seem unnecessary since Python has a rich set of exception classes already defined. There are a couple of good reasons to create custom exceptions:

- Exception namespace creation
- Exception filtering

In the previous section, the ValueError was raised by the range_check_
user_input() function, so an exception handler at a higher level in the
get_data_from_user() function can intercept and address it. But suppose the
range_check_user_input() function raised an unrelated ValueError later in the
function. The exception would flow upward through the stack to the calling function
and be caught by the exception handler in get_data_from_user().

At that point, what should the get_data_from_user() function do? The code
can't assume the correct behavior is to show the error to the user and restart the process of gathering data, because the range check isn't the only possible source of the
exception.

One option is to examine the exception arguments by looking at the e.args attribute tuple. Then the code can make choices within the exception handler to determine the source of the exception. This solution is brittle since it depends on the
arguments passed at the point where ValueError was raised, and those might
change sometime later.

A better design is to create an exception specific to the needs of the program, narrowing the scope of the exceptions to handle. You can create a custom exception handler in the module that defines the range_check_user_input() function like this:

```
class OutsideRangeException(Exception):
    pass

def range_check_user_input(value):
    if not 0 < value <= 100:
        raise OutsideRangeException("value range exceeded", value)
    # additional functionality
```

This code creates a new exception class named OutsideRangeException that inherits from the parent Exception class. This new exception class is used in the range_
check_user_input() function and raised if the value parameter is outside the
defined range of acceptable values. Now the abbreviated program code looks like this:

```
class OutsideRangeException(Exception):
    pass

def get_data_from_user ():
    # initialization and gather user input
    try:
        calculated_result = calculate(value)
    except OutsideRangeException as e:
        print(e)
        # restart code to gather user input

def range_check_user_input (value):
    if not 0 < value <= 100:
        raise OutsideRangeException("value range exceeded", value)
    # additional functionality
```

If the parameter value is outside the acceptable range, the get_data_from_
user() function can catch that specific custom exception and handle it. If any other

exception is raised by the `range_check_user_input()` function, that exception will flow upward to a handler catching that specific exception (or just the base class `Exception`). A complete example program using the logging module that demonstrates this is shown here with comments removed for brevity:

```python
import math
import logging

logger = logging.getLogger(__file__)

class OutsideRangeException(Exception):
    pass

def range_check_user_input(value: int) -> float:
    if not 0 < value <= 100:
        raise OutsideRangeException("range exceeded", value)
    return value

def get_data_from_user():
    successful = False
    while not successful:
        value = input(
            "Please enter an integer greater than 0 and less than "
            "or equal to 100: "
        )

        try:
            value = int(value)
        except ValueError as e:
            logger.exception("Something happened", e)
            print(e)
            continue
        try:
            result = range_check_user_input(value)
        except OutsideRangeException as e:
            logger.exception("value outside of range", e)
            print(
                "Entered value outside of acceptable range,"
                " please re-enter a valid number"
            )
            continue
        print(f"value within range = {result}")
        successful = True

def main():
    get_data_from_user()

if __name__ == "__main__":
    main()
```

5.5   *Closing thoughts*

Understanding how to handle and use exceptions is essential to a developer. They are the events our programs receive from the real world about the things happening to our programs and the result of the actions our programs take.

A goal of development is to create something useful in the world. Exceptions and how we handle them are tools allowing you to develop successful programs that will be used and well-received in that world.

Exceptions and exception handling are another slice of the developer's world. Looking at them closely and gaining an understanding of their details allows you to use exceptions well as we examine other aspects of developing applications.

Summary

- The world is full of events—some expected, some unexpected. Applications are also subject to expected and unexpected events, which manifest themselves as exceptions. Exceptions, and how they're handled in an application, are part of the developer's life.
- Exceptions in Python are handled by introducing try/except blocks of code in our applications. These try/except blocks give us a way to catch exceptions and address them, if necessary.
- Where to catch an exception in an application is often decided by where in the code the context exists to do something useful about the exceptional event.
- Generating exceptions is not always about errors. An exception is neither good nor bad; it's just an event. They can be useful for signaling an event to other parts of an application that might be relevant to the design of your applications.

Part 2

Fieldwork

With the groundwork skills under your belt, you'll be ready to embark on a path that will rely on those skills. In this part, you'll be taking a step-by-step approach to build a functional and nice-looking blogging application.

The first step is chapter 6, where you'll create a web application using the Flask framework. You'll see how using Jinja2 templates can greatly simplify your work.

Chapter 7 is all about applying style to your first application and refactoring it to make expanding it a manageable task.

Chapter 8 presents an introduction to authentication. This allows you to grant access to users who want to use your web application, a big part of which is creating pages in your web application to register new users.

In chapter 9, we take authentication further by connecting it with authorization. Authorization is all about defining what a registered user can do with a web application, which protects them, other users, and the application itself.

Chapter 10 explores what can be done with databases and how useful they are to persist data over time. You'll also learn about what an ORM (object-relational mapper) is and how it dovetails nicely with Python, as well as how you access databases.

Finally, chapter 11 pulls all the fieldwork steps together to build the main functionality of the web application, creating blog content and allowing users to comment on it. By the time you finish chapter 11, you'll be well-stocked with powerful Python tools and ready to take on any number of new projects!

Sharing with the internet

We've covered a lot of material in the previous chapters about being a developer. Now we're going to put that knowledge to work. Choosing an application to create is tricky because the possibilities are nearly endless. The project you'll be creating is a small but well-featured blogging platform we'll be referring to as MyBlog. The MyBlog application will be available as a web-based Python application.

The MyBlog web application will provide tools with which users can join the blogging community and create blog posts. Registered users can post content using markdown for styling what they write. All users will be able to view the posted content, and registered users will be able to comment on it. Administrative users will be able to mark any content or comments active/inactive as they see fit. Registered users will be able to mark any content they've created as active/inactive.

6.1   *Sharing your work*

The MyBlog web application is a way to not only share your thoughts, and the thoughts of the application's users, but to share your work. The application serves a particular purpose with a host of features. The work involved to pull together the technologies to create the MyBlog features is a skill worth showing off.

6.1.1   *Web application advantages*

The project choice to create a web application is based on a few considerations. First and foremost, creating a useful web application builds on the topics covered in previous chapters quite well. Pulling together the topics of development tools, naming and namespaces, API use and creation, and class design will play into the big picture of the application.

Other types of applications also offer some of these opportunities to express what you've learned but can be challenging to share with others. For example, creating a desktop GUI application offers interesting challenges for a developer. However, distributing a GUI application for widespread use can be difficult. It's certainly possible to do so with Python, but the steps necessary are outside of the scope of this book.

A web server has some advantages in terms of distributing an application. The web server itself and the features and services are centrally located and are not running on the many varied computer environments that users have. Having the server centralized like this means that changes and updates to the application happen in one place. Restarting the server, or pushing changes out interactively, makes the changes and updates available immediately to all users.

Another advantage of a web server–based application is making a user interface available. A web application takes advantage of something installed on just about every computer in existence, a web browser. Modern web browsers provide a powerful platform on which to build user interfaces. Data can be formatted and presented in almost infinite ways. Images and multimedia are also well supported. Users can interact with applications hosted on browsers using interface elements like buttons, lists, drop-down lists, and forms.

6.1.2   *Web application challenges*

This isn't to say using a web browser as an application platform isn't without challenges. Creating a web application means you'll be working in multiple technical domains. Along with Python, you'll be creating HTML, CSS, and JavaScript code files. Additionally, desktop-based applications offer more direct access to the computer hardware and the tremendous computing power personal computers bring to bear.

However, with continuing advancements in browsers, new and expanding web technologies, and ever-increasing internet speed that's widely available, the performance gap between desktop and web-based applications is narrowing. In addition, web-based systems have grown to have widespread acceptance as a method of delivering applications. This acceptance makes creating them a valid path for both personal and professional development.

TIP It can't be overstated how important and valuable web development skills are. As more and more users migrate from desktop devices to mobile ones that take advantage of the ubiquity of the internet, this will only become more valuable.

There are existing blogging platforms available to use or download that you can run on your own. The MyBlog application won't be in competition with them, as its purpose is a useful teaching framework that gives the example code direction and goals.

What the application offers isn't groundbreaking features or technology; blogging software is well understood. This is one of MyBlog's advantages, already knowing what a blog application is intended to supply. The goal isn't to create a cutting-edge blog but to see the big picture of the application's intent and think like a developer to pull the necessary parts together and paint that picture into existence.

6.2 Servers

The MyBlog web application is a subset of what a server application in general provides. One definition of a server is an application running on a computer, or computers, providing functionality to other applications across a network. This arrangement of multiple applications accessing the functionality of a central server is known as the client-server model.

As you build out the MyBlog application, you'll be running it on your local computer, essentially turning it into a server. The software running on a computer is what makes it a server, not the computer hardware configuration. Commercial server hardware items are built to optimize the access that the server software needs to run well but are otherwise just computers.

We all use social networks and work with the programs that run on our desktop or mobile devices. Those tools are client applications using the functionality of many servers. If you play any multiplayer games, the game applications use a server's functionality to coordinate all the players' actions in the game. Figure 6.1 shows many kinds of devices connecting to a server across a network.

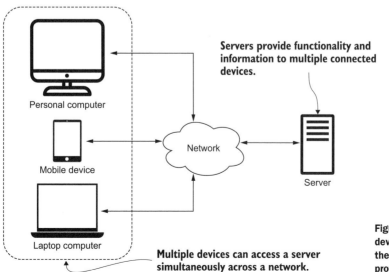

Figure 6.1 Multiple devices connecting to the functionality provided by a server

6.2.1 *Request-response model*

One common server implementation is the request-response model. The client application makes a request to the server, which processes the request and returns a response. In this kind of application, the server takes no action unless requested to do so.

In a web application, the client browser makes an HTTP request to the server for a response. The response is very often a stream of text representing an HTML page. When the client browser receives the response, it will render the HTML to the browser window. Depending on the HTML code that creates the page, it might also make additional requests to the server for information like CSS (Cascading Style Sheet) and JavaScript files.

Figure 6.2 represents a simplified view of the request-response communication occurring between a client and server over time. Initially, the client makes a request to the server, which might need to retrieve data from a database to compose the response. When the response is created, it is transmitted back to the client.

In this example, the response is an HTML page the client application will render in the browser window. Figure 6.2 shows the back-and-forth communication to render the HTML page. Part of the HTML code includes links to CSS and JavaScript files that

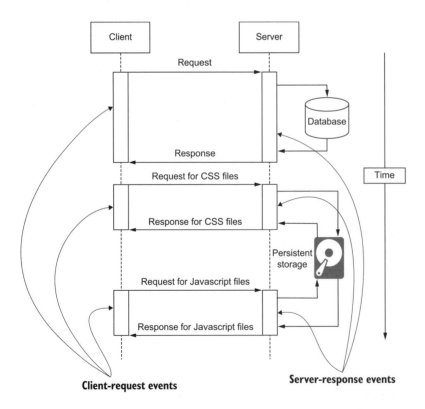

Figure 6.2   Client and web server interaction event flow to construct a web page

generate additional requests to the server. The server retrieves the requested files from the server's hard disk and sends them as a response to the client. The request-response model is the primary means that the MyBlog web application will use to get data from the server and build and present the application information to the users.

6.3   Web servers

A web server is an application responding to HTTP requests from a client application. A web browser is a client application that makes requests to the web server and interprets the responses and displays them on the screen. Often what's sent to the client's web browser are HTML documents the browser interprets and renders as web pages. HTML documents are the content the client requested.

There are many other interactions between a client's browser and a web server. The browser can request that the server send pictures and audio and video content, even downloading other applications to the client's computer.

HTML documents can contain links to CSS and JavaScript files. When the HTML received is rendered by the web browser, the embedded links to those files generate additional HTTP requests to the web server. The web server responds by sending the requested content.

> **TIP**   Modern web applications make many requests to one or more servers to provide the content and render the experience that the user expects from the web application.

CSS files contain styling information applied to the content in the HTML document displayed on the screen. The CSS code modifies a web page's look and feel and is the presentation layer of the HTML's content.

JavaScript files contain code that runs in the client's browser. Once downloaded, the web browser will start to execute the JavaScript code. This code can be connected to onscreen button clicks and updates to the display, and just about any action the user can make on a web page can be handled by JavaScript code.

JavaScript code can also make HTTP requests to web servers for text and data. These requests can be initiated by user actions or programmatically and can change and update web pages dynamically.

HTTP REQUESTS

The HTTP protocol definition is not the intent of this book and is beyond its scope, but some basic information is useful. Here is an example HTTP request to a web server:

```
1 GET /path_part/index.html HTTP/1.1
2 Host: fictional_website.com:80
3 Accept: text/html, */*
4 <CR-LF>
```

The line numbers in this example are not part of the request but were added to reference the lines in the explanation of the protocol:

1 `GET /path_part/index.html HTTP/1.1`—This is the start of the request to the web server. The word `GET` indicates the HTTP method to use—in this case, to retrieve the document located at `/path_part/index.html` using HTTP protocol version 1.1.

2 `Host: fictional_website.com:80`—Indicates the domain, suffix, and port number where the request is sent. The port number (80) is optional and, if absent, defaults to 80.

   – The domain suffix is the text name of the server hosting the website. This name is translated by a DNS (domain name server) to an IP address so the network protocol can direct the request to the right server on the internet.

   – The suffix comes from a list of suffixes that help manage and differentiate domains on the internet. You're probably already familiar with suffixes like ".com" and ".net," but there are many others. This makes "myserver.com" and "myserver.net" two distinct names.

   – Ethernet network cards can support 65,353 logical ports, with those from 0 to 1023 reserved for well-known ports used by common applications. For example, web servers commonly use port 80, which is why it's the default if not specified in the URL. However, a server, including web servers, can run on any port in the range that's not already in use.

3 `Accept: text/html, */*`—This header information is optional. In this example, it indicates to the server the kinds of responses the client can accept. There can be many headers, each containing additional information from the client that can be useful to the web server.

4 `<CR-LF>`—Indicates carriage return/line feed characters or a blank line, which is a required part of the HTTP protocol that ends the list of headers and tells the server to start processing the request.

When I was first getting into web development, it surprised me that the small amount of text shown here, and broken out in figure 6.3, was literally what was sent across the network to the server. The first two lines of the request create a URL, or uniform resource locator, which uniquely identifies what the client is requesting.

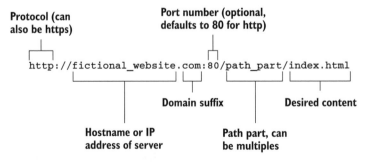

Figure 6.3   The fully formed URL uniquely identifies the resource to retrieve.

The server receives this request and takes one of the following steps:

- Maps the request to a file in the server's control and returns it to the client
- Maps the request to a handler (program code) and returns the output of the handler to the client
- Determines that the request can't be answered and returns an error message

The use of the slash character (/) is very much like the slash used as the path separator for directories and files on a file system. This pattern is a useful way to present a logical path hierarchy of the resources and content originating at the root domain `fictional_website.com`.

By allowing for multipart paths, a logical hierarchy is created. The hierarchy can be navigated by a browser application to access different parts of the web server. The endpoint of a URL can be an actual file resource the web server provides, but it doesn't have to be. The logical path created can have no relation to the actual file path to a resource on the server's file system.

6.4   Flask

You're going to build the MyBlog application using Flask, a lightweight web application framework for Python. Flask provides the mechanisms and plumbing necessary for Python to be used as a web application server to create useful applications that perform and scale well. Flask includes the ability to answer HTTP requests for URL resources and connect those requests to Python code that dynamically builds the response.

Flask (https://flask.palletsprojects.com/en/2.1.x/) is not part of the standard library modules that come with Python but is available as a third-party module hosted by the Python Package Index (https://pypi.org/). Like other modules available to Python, this makes it installable using the pip utility.

6.4.1   Why Flask?

Python is in the fortunate position of being popular as a language to build web applications. Because of this, many tools and frameworks exist that Python can use to create web applications, Flask being one of them. There's also Django, Bottle, Pyramid, Turbogears, CherryPy, and more. All the frameworks are useful; some have a more particular use case than others, some are faster than others, and some are more specialized for creating certain kinds of web applications and services.

Flask lives in the middle ground and is popular because it's small and has a minimal initial learning curve and is suitable as your skills and needs develop. Many modules are available that integrate with Flask that you'll use as the MyBlog application grows. These modules will give the MyBlog application access to databases, authentication, authorization, and form creation. Part of the beauty of Flask is not having to learn or use these expanded capabilities until they're needed and you're ready to create new features with them.

TIP   As a developer myself, I've worked with some of the other web application frameworks available to Python. Flask is the one I've used the most and with which I am most familiar. I chose to use Flask because I can write about it knowing that I can present Flask to your best advantage and not miss details I might otherwise miss if I were to choose a framework less familiar to me.

6.4.2   *Your first web server*

Now that you know where you're headed, let's get started. The first server comes right from the Flask website quick-start example and is as good as anywhere to begin learning Flask. This is the classic `"Hello World"` example program expressed as a web application. The code for the server is available in the repository as `examples/CH_06/examples/01/app.py`:

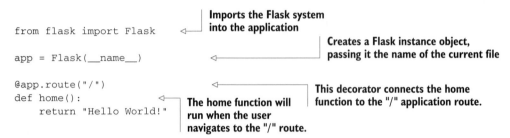

After running the install steps for the chapter examples and starting your Python virtual environment, the application is run by opening a terminal window and navigating to the `examples/CH_06/examples/01` directory. Enter the following command for Mac and Linux:

```
export FLASK_ENV=development
export FLASK_APP=app.py
```

For Windows users, enter the command:

```
set FLASK_ENV=development
set FLASK_APP=app.py
```

Once done, enter the command `flask run`, and the application will output the following text to the terminal window:

```
* Serving Flask app "app.py" (lazy loading)
* Environment: development
* Debug mode: on
* Running on http://127.0.0.1:5000/ (Press CTRL+C to quit)
* Restarting with stat
* Debugger is active!
* Debugger PIN: 325-409-845
```

These messages might look ominous, but they are just informing you that the web server is running in development mode, which isn't suitable for production. Production in this context means running the web server so it's publicly available. The

Flask built-in development server isn't optimized or secure enough to be used out in the wild.

You'll also notice the line that informs you that to stop the application you'll need to press the CTRL-C keys. Also notice that the terminal cursor doesn't return, because the flask run command is running the app instance in an infinite loop, waiting to receive and process requests.

A server is intended to run long term and, in fact, would never stop unless instructed to do so. The server you've just started is in an idle state waiting to receive and process HTTP requests. The Flask development server defaults to running at IP address 127.0.0.1 on port 5000.

The IP address 127.0.0.1 is known as localhost and is the loopback interface of your computer's network interface. This means you can create servers on this address and access them even if you don't have a network card installed on your computer. The port value of 5000 is just an unused port number out of the 65,535 available on network interfaces. Both values can be configured, but the defaults are fine for now.

To interact with the server, you need to open a web browser on your computer and navigate to http://127.0.0.1:5000 as the URL and click enter. The browser will respond by printing "Hello World!" in the content window. You'll also see a log message in the terminal window where the server is running indicating the request was received and processed correctly, as specified by the 200 at the end of the log message. The 200 value is the HTTP status code for "OK," which means the request was handled successfully.

CONNECTING ROUTES

One of the important things to notice about the application is how Python code is connected to a valid URL route to which the server will respond. The @app.route ("/") line of code is a decorator provided by the Flask app instance and applied to the home() Python function. The decorator is how the home() function is registered with Flask and connected to the URL "/" route and will be called when a user browses to http:127.0.0.1:5000. Because the route is defined, the server will respond to the results of running the home() function, returning the "Hello World" string.

SERVING FOREVER

Once the server is running, it will continue responding to requests until it's stopped, essentially running forever while waiting for HTTP requests. There is no explicit loop in the application code, so how is the server running forever? The loop is part of the functionality in the Flask app instance. When the flask run command is invoked at the terminal command line, it looks for an object named app and, if found, starts the server event loop.

The event loop is where the server waits for events to process. The events are the data showing up on the network socket at port 5000. For a web server, the events are HTTP requests arriving on the network port that the server is monitoring. Unlike what you might think of as an infinite loop in application code, the server is idle while waiting for events and uses very little CPU time.

UNDEFINED ROUTES

If you go back to the browser and modify the URL to `http://127.0.0.1:5000/something` and click the enter key, the browser will respond with a `Not Found` error. Looking at the log messages in the terminal window, you'll see a message that the request was received, but the server responded with a 404 status code. The HTTP protocol status code 404 essentially equates to `Page Not Found`.

This makes sense if you look at your web server application code. At the moment, the only URL supported is the home route `"/"`; there is nothing defined to handle the `/something` route. The server didn't crash because it didn't have the route defined; instead, the server handled it as an error and informed the user about the error through the browser.

The ability to handle errors and continue to function is an important part of the server's design and implementation. As you develop the MyBlog application, you'll use the errors handled and returned by the Flask server to help determine where problems exist in the application and where to resolve them.

6.4.3   *Serving content*

Getting your first web server coded and running is a big step. There's a remarkable amount of functionality implemented and executed by the very small amount of code in `app.py`. The `home()` function shows how you can map a URL to Python code that the web server will support. You can add new functions and map them to additional routes, and the web server will provide additional URLs to which the browser can navigate.

To create a proper web page, you can replace the `"Hello World!"` string returned by the `home()` function with a string containing HTML code. By doing this, the browser will receive the HTML and render it in the browser window.

However, useful and well-designed web pages are created with HTML code that can be hundreds, even thousands, of lines of code. Embedding strings of HTML code directly into your web server will make it difficult to maintain and does not take advantage of features available to you through Flask. It's better to keep HTML content and Python code separated and build HTML pages as distinct files, which is what we'll do next.

DYNAMIC CONTENT

The content served to the browser by the `home()` function is the string `"Hello World!"`, which is returned to the browser every time the page is accessed or refreshed. Because `home()` is a Python function, it could have returned anything, including information and data that is generated dynamically. The function could have returned the result of the `random()` function, and the browser would have rendered a random value every time the page was accessed. The `home()` function could have returned the results of a calculation, the data retrieved from a database, or the return value of some other HTTP web-based service.

Creating and returning dynamic information is one of the cornerstones of creating useful web applications, the MyBlog project being one of them. How do you merge dynamic information with HTML content that can be meaningfully rendered by browsers?

Flask includes access to a template language called Jinja2. A template can be thought of as a document that has placeholders for additional information. This template will be combined with data to produce a completed end-result document. Here's an example using Python f-string formatting to illustrate the idea:

```
name = "Joe"
result = f"My name is {name}"
print(result)
My name is Joe
```

Here the variable `name` is set to the string `"Joe"`, and the Python format string `f"My name is {name}"` acts as the template. The `result` variable is created and then printed, and `My name is Joe` is the output. Python's f-string formatting is like a small templating language; it takes in data in the form of the `name` variable and creates the resulting string output. Jinja2 works much like this as well.

> **TIP**   Keep in mind that once the server delivers content to the browser, there is no connection between them. For the MyBlog application, any dynamic content generated by the server has to be injected into the HTML content before it's delivered to the browser.

By using a templating language, you can place your HTML code in a separate template file and then have Jinja2 substitute your dynamic information and data into the right places in that template.

USING A TEMPLATE LANGUAGE

Let's modify the previous web server code to use Jinja2 templates and pass dynamic data to the template to render in the browser window. The following modified code is found in `examples/CH_06/examples/02/app.py`:

```
from flask import Flask, render_template          ◁─────────    Imports the Flask function
from datetime import datetime   ◁──┐                            render_template to use Jinja2
                                    │  Imports the datetime
                                    │  functionality to
app = Flask(__name__)               │  generate dynamic data    Uses the render_template
                                                                function to connect the
                                                                index.html template file
@app.route("/")                                                 with the now data element
def home():
    return render_template("index.html", now=datetime.now())      ◁──────
```

The first parameter to the `render_template` function is the string `index.html`, which is the filename of a template file containing Jinja2 template instructions. Everything else passed to `render_template` is a named parameter. In the example, the named parameter is `now`, and it will be assigned the value returned by the code `datetime.now()`, the current timestamp.

By default, Flask initially searches for template files in a directory called `templates`. The template directory should exist in the same directory as the `app.py` file, so create that now.

Inside the `templates` directory, you'll need to create a file named `index.html`. In the example application, the `index.html` file looks like this:

```
<!DOCTYPE html>
<html>

<head>
    <!-- Required meta tags -->
    <meta charset="utf-8">
    <meta
    ➡name="viewport"
    ➡content="width=device-width, initial-scale=1, shrink-to-fit=no"
    ➡
    <title>Your First Web Server</title>
</head>

<body>
    <h1>Current time: {{now}}</h1>          ◁──┐  Inserts the current datetime in the
</body>                                          {{now}} Jinja output expression

</html>
```

HTML 5 boilerplate code

The HTML 5 code here presents a complete web page that the browser can render in its window. The interesting thing in the file is the `<h1>` headline tag inside the body of the document:

```
<h1>Current time: {{now}}</h1>
```

The `{{now}}` part of the line is Jinja2 template syntax and will be replaced by the value of the `render_template` parameter `now`, which has a value of the current timestamp.

The `render_template` function uses the Jinja2 templating engine to parse the template file and substitute elements that follow the Jinja2 syntax rules with data. Jinja2 is also capable of doing much more processing than just substitution, and we'll get to that shortly. Once you've created the `index.html` file, the directory structure should look something like this:

```
├── app.py
└── templates
     └── index.html
```

If you run the `app.py` file and navigate to the URL, the browser will render the output of the handler shown in figure 6.4. Every time the page is refreshed, the timestamp will update. This demonstrates that the `home()` function is running and the `index.html` template is being rendered with a new `datetime.now()` value every time the page is refreshed.

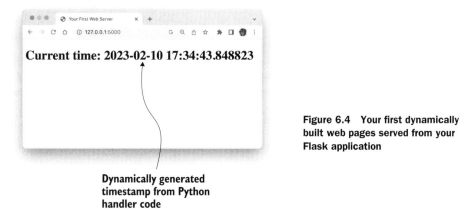

Figure 6.4   Your first dynamically built web pages served from your Flask application

Dynamically generated timestamp from Python handler code

6.4.4   More Jinja2 features

The previous example is a functioning web application, but it only shows off a small portion of what Jinja2 can do. Let's expand on the example web application to demonstrate more capabilities of Flask and Jinja2 that you can use in the MyBlog project.

The updated web application will have a banner and a sticky footer. A sticky footer is information on a web page that "sticks" to the bottom of the page even if there is whitespace between it and the rest of the page content above it.

Figure 6.5 is a screenshot showing the current time as it does now and a page-visits counter that will increment every time the page is refreshed. There will also be a list of

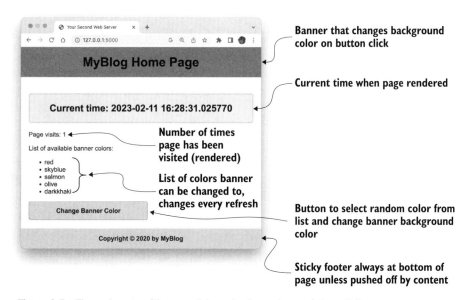

Banner that changes background color on button click

Current time when page rendered

Number of times page has been visited (rendered)

List of colors banner can be changed to, changes every refresh

Button to select random color from list and change banner background color

Sticky footer always at bottom of page unless pushed off by content

Figure 6.5   The web page with more style and color and some interactivity

different colors for the banner and a button that will change the banner background color randomly. The application supplies extra functionality to provide the random list of colors and the page-visits counter. The server also provides styling information to the browser in the form of CSS files and client-side (browser) interactivity as a JavaScript file.

The ability of the page-visits counter is provided by a Python class using a class-level variable. By using a class variable, the state of the page count is accessible by any instance of the class. Any change to the variable is visible to any instance that uses it. The `PageVisit` class has a simple purpose and interface:

```python
class PageVisit:
    COUNT = 0

    def counts(self):
        PageVisit.COUNT += 1
        return PageVisit.COUNT
```

The `PageVisit` class maintains the availability of the class variable `COUNT` for all instances of the class. It also provides the `counts()` method to increment the value of `COUNT` and return it to the caller. Every invocation of the `counts()` method will increment the `COUNT` value by one. The `PageVisit` class exists because the web server can handle many users at once who might be making requests for the page, and a consistent value of `COUNT` has to be maintained across all of them.

> **TIP** The `PageVisit` class works for this use case because there is only a single instance of the web server running. All requests the server handles would each have an instance of `PageVisit`, but they would all reference the same `COUNT` class-level variable. This wouldn't work if multiple web servers were running, as the `COUNT` class-level variable would no longer be shared across those multiple web server instances.

The list of banner background colors is used by both the template file that renders the HTML of the page and the JavaScript functionality that changes the banner background colors on button clicks. Therefore, the colors list has to be made available to the template and the JavaScript engine running on the browser.

To manage the list of colors, the class `BannerColors` is created. This class encapsulates the primary list of colors as a class-level variable and provides a method generating a random subset of those colors as a list to use. Like `PageVisit`, the class `BannerColors` has a simple purpose and interface:

```python
class BannerColors:
    COLORS = [
        "lightcoral", "salmon", "red", "firebrick", "pink",
        "gold", "yellow", "khaki", "darkkhaki", "violet",
        "blue", "purple", "indigo", "greenyellow", "lime",
        "green", "olive", "darkcyan", "aqua", "skyblue",
        "tan", "sienna", "gray", "silver"
    ]
```

```
def get_colors(self):
    return sample(BannerColors.COLORS, 5)
```

The BannerColors class maintains the class variable COLORS as a list of valid CSS color name strings. This creates the palette of banner colors that can be displayed on the page. The get_colors() method returns a random subset of five of those colors as a list using the Random module and its sample function from the Python standard library. Every time get_colors() is invoked, it returns a random subset of colors as a list from the COLORS class-variable list. The PageVisit and BannerColors classes are added to the app.py file in the examples/CH_06/examples/03 directory and integrated into the home() function that renders the web page:

```
@app.route("/")
def home():
    banner_colors = BannerColors().get_colors()
    return render_template("index.html", data={
        "now": datetime.now(),
        "page_visit": PageVisit(),
        "banner_colors": {
            "display": banner_colors,
            "js": json.dumps(banner_colors)
        }
    })
```

Gets a random list of five colors and assigns it to the variable banner_colors

Creates a dictionary of information to pass to the template as the data-named variable

The BannerColors class is instantiated right away, and the get_colors() method is called, storing the results in the variable banner_colors. This variable is used later to create the data that is passed to the template for rendering.

The render_template function is called with the name of the template to render, index.html, and the data variable. The data variable is a dictionary containing key/value pairs to pass information used in the template:

- now—The value returned by datetime.now()
- page_visit—An instance of the PageVisit class
- banner_colors—Another dictionary
- display—The previous create banner_colors list variable
- js—The result of JSON stringifying the banner_colors list

The banner_colors dictionary inside the data dictionary contains two variations of the banner_colors list variable. You'll see how this is used when we review the updated index.html template.

All the work to this point adds functionality to the home operation that's run when a user browses to the home page of the application. This functionality passes new data to the index.html template and is rendered as a complete HTML page by Jinja2.

TEMPLATE INHERITANCE

Before we review the updated index.html template, take a look at the screenshot of the web application presented earlier in figure 6.5. The page has a banner and a footer section. Very often these kinds of visual and informative features are common to every page of a web application. HTML boilerplate code is also common to every page.

Based on the "don't repeat yourself" principle (DRY), it would be useful to pull the common elements of an HTML page together rather than copying those pieces to every page. Even worse would be maintaining all those copies of the common elements as the web application changes and evolves. The Jinja2 templating engine provides for this using template inheritance, which is conceptually similar to class inheritance in Python.

Before using template inheritance, you'll need to expand the directory structure of the web application. Because you're going to be serving static CSS and JavaScript files to the application, those files need to live somewhere that the web server can access them. By default, Flask looks for static files in a directory named `static`, a sibling of the `templates` directory.

Create the `static` directory at the same level as the `templates` directory. To help keep the `static` directory organized, create `CSS` and `JS` subdirectories to place the CSS and JavaScript files into. These files will give the web application its presentation and interactivity. Your directory structure should look like this:

```
├── app.py
├── static
│   ├── css
│   └── js
└── templates
    └── index.html
```

PARENT TEMPLATE

Copy the `index.html` file to create a new file named `base.html` in the `templates` directory. This is now the parent template containing all the common features presented on the web pages of the application. Modify the new `base.html` template file to look like this:

```html
<!DOCTYPE html>
<html>
<head>
    {% block head %}
    <!-- Required meta tags -->
    <meta charset="utf-8">
    <meta name="viewport" content="width=device-width,
    ➥initial-scale=1, shrink-to-fit=no">
    <title>Your Second Web Server</title>
    {% block styles %}
    <link
    ➥    rel="stylesheet"
    ➥    type="text/css"
    ➥    href="{{ url_for('static', filename='css/myblog.css') }}"
    ➥ >
    {% endblock %}
    {% endblock %}
</head>
```

Creates an inner template section named styles, which will be referred to by child templates to insert CSS file references

Creates a template section named head, which will be referred to by child templates

```
<body>
    <div id="header">
        <h1>MyBlog Home Page</h1>
    </div>
    <div id="content">
        {% block content %}{% endblock %}
    </div>
    <div id="footer">
        {% block footer %}
        <h4>&copy; Copyright 2020 by MyBlog</h4>
        {% endblock %}
    </div>
</body>

{% block scripts %}{% endblock %}

</html>
```

Creates an empty template section named content, which contains the content of the page and is provided by the child templates

Creates a template section named footer, which can be referred to by child templates

Creates an empty template section named scripts, which child templates can use to insert JavaScript file references

This template includes HTML code you've seen before mixed with Jinja2 template code. The template code that begins with `{% block head %}` and ends with `{% endblock %}` creates a template section named `head` that can be referenced in a child template by referring to the block name. Blocks like this can even be referenced from other files.

The block named `styles` contains a stylesheet link. Inside the `href` portion of the link is another Jinja2 template construct, `{{url_for('static', filename ='css/blog.css')}}`. This expression substitution is executing the Python `url_for` function.

It's generally a bad idea to hardcode URL paths within a web application, and the `url_for` function helps avoid this. By passing a known URL endpoint as the first parameter and the relative file path as the second, the function can create a URL to the desired file that's valid for the Flask application. When the template is rendered, a valid URL to the `blog.css` file will exist in the stylesheet link rendered by the browser.

The empty block sections named `content` and `scripts`, respectively, create references that will be used by the `index.html` file, inheriting from the `base.html` template. The `index.html` file will use the references to inject content into the page and include a page-specific JavaScript file named `index.js` containing client-side interactivity code.

CHILD TEMPLATE

Now that you have a base template, it's time to inherit from it by modifying the `index.html` template:

```
{% extends "base.html" %}

{% block content %}
<h2>Current time: {{ data["now"] }}</h2>
<p>Page visits: {{ data["page_visit"].counts() }}</p>
<p>List of available banner colors:</p>
<ul>
```

Makes this child template inherit from the base.html parent template

Creates the content to render to the page, which will replace the empty content block in the parent template

```
    {%
        for banner_color in
        data["banner_colors"]["display"]
        %}
    <li>{{ banner_color }}</li>
    {% endfor %}
</ul>
<div id="color-change">
    <button class="change-banner-color">
        Change Banner Color
    </button>
</div>
{% endblock %}
```

Creates the content to render to the page, which will replace the empty content block in the parent template

```
{% block styles %}
{{ super() }}
<link
    rel="stylesheet"
        type="text/css"
        href="{{ url_for(
            'static', filename='css/index.css'
            ) }}">
{% endblock %}
```

Adds specific CSS style information for this child template to the styles block. The {{ super() }} expression calls the parent styles block first and then adds the content of this block.

```
{% block scripts %}
{{ super() }}
<script>
    const banner_colors =
        {{ data["banner_colors"]["js"]| safe }};
</script>
<script
        src="{{ url_for(
            'static', filename='js/index.js') }}"
></script>
{% endblock %}
```

Adds specific JavaScript file references for this child template to the scripts block. The {{ super() }} expression calls the parent styles block first and then adds the content of this block.

Like Python classes, the child template references the parent template to inherit from by referring to it in the template code on the first line. The `{% extends base.html%}` template code informs Jinja2 that `index.html` is inheriting from `base.html`. The template engine knows how to find the `base.html` template file in the same way that it found the `index.html` template, by looking in the `templates` directory.

The content provided by the `index.html` file begins with the `{% block content%}` start marker and ends with the `{% endblock %}` marker. When the complete page is rendered by Jinja2, the content will be placed on the HTML page at the position of the content block reference in the `base.html` parent template file.

The data that is passed to the template by the `render_template` function is used inside the content section. The `{{data["now"]}}` Jinja2 expression gets the current timestamp. The `{{data["page_visit"].counts()}}` expression gets the Page-Visit instance and calls its `counts()` method to obtain the current page-visit counts.

The Jinja2 language provides a mechanism to create repeating data in the rendered template by using a `for` loop. Mimicking Python, the loop construct is a

For-In loop iterating over the contents of the iterable data["banner_colors"]["display"] list. Each item in the list is used to create an HTML list element with the code <li>{{banner_color}}</li>. The for loop ends with the {% endfor %} marker.

The block named styles refers to the same block in the base.html template. Recall that the stylesheet block in the parent template wasn't empty; it had a stylesheet link to pull presentation information common to all web pages. The {{super()}} expression renders the parent stylesheet block before including the information defined in the child index.html template.

The block named scripts handles a couple of functions. It uses the {{super()}} expression to render anything defined by the parent template, which is nothing currently. It then builds some JavaScript code directly to define a variable called banner_colors, which is initialized with the JSON formatted string of banner colors supplied by {{data["banner_colors"]["js"] | safe}}. The | safe part of the syntax prevents Jinja2 from translating symbols that could be dangerous. It's not necessary here because the data is coming from the application itself but is good to keep in mind.

If the data had been supplied in a form by a user, the data could contain information that might be an XSS attack. An XSS attack can be JavaScript inserted into the data that was entered by a user, which could cause your site to take unintentional actions. Lastly, a script tag referencing an external JavaScript file using the same url_for() mechanism to create a valid relative URL for the web application is included.

PRESENTATION

The presentation of the web page is controlled by the index.css file, which contains CSS code that applies style information to the HTML elements created by the Flask render_template function as presented by the browser. There are two CSS files connected to the application—myblog.css and index.css. The myblog.css file applies to the parent template file base.html:

```css
html, body {
    height: 100%;
}

body {
    display: flex;
    flex-direction: column;
    margin: 0px;
    font-family: Arial, Helvetica, sans-serif;
}

#header h1 {
    margin: 0px;
    background-color: darkcyan;
    height: 75px;
    text-align: center;
    line-height: 75px;
}
```

```
#content {
    flex: 1 0 auto;
    margin: 20px;
}

#content h2 {
    border: 3px solid lightgray;
    border-radius: 5px;
    padding: 20px;
    text-align: center;
    background-color: bisque;
}

#footer {
    flex-shrink: 0;
}

#footer h4 {
    margin: 0px;
    background-color: lightgrey;
    height: 50px;
    text-align: center;
    line-height: 50px;
}
```

Though this book isn't about CSS, it's worth reviewing some of the previous code to get a feel for how CSS code affects the presentation of a web page. Keep in mind that the spacing and indentation of the CSS code is a convention for readability and is not part of the required syntax.

CSS code is about using and creating selectors to attach specific style information to HTML elements so the browser can render the HTML elements with the intended look and feel. For example, the code #content h2 {...} attaches style rules to the HTML header <h2> element contained in the <div id="content"> element. This selector narrows where the style will be applied on the page; in this case, only the <h2> tag within the <div id="content"> tag will have a rounded border with an internal padding of 20 pixels. The header text will be centered and have a background color of bisque. The rest of the selectors apply style rules to other parts of the base.html page.

These styles will be applied to every page that inherits from the base.html parent template. The index.css file applies rules to the index.html child template page:

```
#color-change button {
    background-color: lightgrey;
    border-radius: 5px;
    border: 1px solid grey;
    display: inline-block;
    cursor: pointer;
    color: black;
    font-family: Arial;
    font-size: 16px;
    font-weight: bold;
    padding: 13px 69px;
```

```
    text-decoration: none;
    text-shadow: 0px 0px 0px lightskyblue;
}

#color-change button:hover {
    background-color: darkgrey;
}

#color-change button:active {
    position: relative;
    top: 1px;
}
```

The selectors in this code apply styles to HTML elements that are created by the index.html page, essentially giving some style and CSS interactivity to the color-change button.

INTERACTIVITY

This book isn't about JavaScript, and its use will be kept to a minimum, but most of the interesting web applications will include some JavaScript code. Once the HTML page is built by the server, it is sent to the browser as a response. The browser will then render the HTML visually in the browser window. It will also parse and compile the JavaScript sent in the response and pulled from the external file:

```
window.addEventListener('load', function (event) {          Waits for the page to be
    let banner = document.querySelector(                     loaded before executing
            "#header h1"                Gets a reference to   the nested code
        );                              the banner element
    window.addEventListener(
            'click', function (event) {  Adds a click event handler for the
        // is this the click event       banner color-changing button
            we're looking for?
        if (event.target.matches(
                '.change-banner-color'
            )) {                         Checks to see if the click event
            let color = banner_colors[    originated from the button
                Math.floor(
                    Math.random() *
                    banner_colors.length)  Selects a random color from
                ];                          the banner_colors list
            banner.style.backgroundColor = color;   Changes the banner
        }                                            background color
    })
});
```

This is vanilla JavaScript code (no frameworks like jQuery involved) that adds an action if the displayed button is clicked. The code creates an anonymous function to run when the page is finished loading. The anonymous function creates a reference to the banner element and then adds another anonymous function to listen for the click event.

Inside the click event handler, a conditional statement checks if the event was generated by the button to change banner color. If so, a random color is selected from the `banner_colors` list and is used to change the background color of the banner.

6.5   *Running the web server*

The updated app exists in `examples/CH_06/examples/03`:

```
├── app.py
├── static
│   ├── css
│   │   ├── index.css
│   │   └── myblog.css
│   └── js
│       └── index.js
└── templates
    ├── base.html
    └── index.html
```

In the terminal, move to the directory and set the environment variable `FLASK_APP` to point to your application by entering the following in your command line for Mac and Linux:

```
export FLASK_ENV=development
export FLASK_APP=app.py
```

And this for Windows users:

```
set FLASK_ENV=development
set FLASK_APP=app.py
```

Run the web server by entering `flask run` at the terminal command line. You should see the server start up, and then you can navigate to `http:127.0.0.1:5000` to see the application.

When you run the web application with the `flask run` command, the server starts and runs with the Flask built-in web server. The built-in web server is suitable for development and experimentation, but it is not suitable for production.

For production, you'll need to use a production-ready WSGI server, which stands for Web Server Gateway Interface. A WSGI server is an application that provides a simple calling convention to forward requests from a web server to a Python web application. The web server built into Flask is a WSGI server that provides this calling convention for development purposes.

The WSGI standard exists to abstract away the complexities of interfacing your Python web application with a web server and the world. As long as you're building your application to the WSGI interface standard—which Flask and just about all other Python web frameworks do—your application can provide request-response handling accessible through the internet.

Two of the most common production-grade WSGI servers are uWSGI and Gunicorn. The uWSGI application is a popular, high-performance application written in C/C++. Gunicorn, short for Green Unicorn, is also a high-performance WSGI-compliant web server application. Both are production-ready.

6.5.1 *Gunicorn*

To run your application using Gunicorn, you need to install it using the following command from your Python virtual environment:

```
pip install gunicorn
```

In one of the example application directories, enter this command while in the terminal:

```
gunicorn -w 4 app:app
```

This tells Gunicorn to start four worker instances of your application, which it finds with the `app:app` part of the command. The first part is the name of the Python file, `app.py`, and the second part, `:app`, refers to the Flask application instance created within the application by the `app = Flask(__name__)` part of the code.

Running multiple instances of the application with Gunicorn workers allows your application to scale up to handle hundreds, even thousands, of requests per second. The number of requests per second that the application can handle depends upon the workload each request makes on the application and how much time it takes before a response is generated.

According to the Gunicorn documentation, the recommended number of workers for an application running on a single production server is (2 × number_of_CPU cores) + 1. The formula is loosely based on the idea that for any given CPU core, one worker will be performing IO (input/output) operations, and the other worker will be performing CPU operations.

6.5.2 *Commercial hosting*

When you want to make your web application available for public use, you need to do so using a hosting service. There are many services available to host your application. They will offer options like Apache or Nginx for web serving and uWSGI and Gunicorn for WSGI interfacing with your Python-based web application. It's also possible to deploy your application using Docker containers.

> **TIP** Inside a Docker container, you would run a WSGI-compliant web server to interface with your contained Python application. You would connect to this WSGI-compliant web server (uWSGI, Gunicorn, and so on) by the host of the Docker container.

I'm sure there are more options and configurations than I've listed here. The choice depends on you, your goals for the application, and the cost of those choices.

Because of the wide array of options available and combinations afforded by those options, I'm not going to spend time defining how to deploy a Flask-based Python application to specific examples. My reasons are twofold:

- It's unlikely I would hit upon a combination of choices that would suit your deployment use case perfectly.
- Deploying an application is a topic worthy of its own book and doesn't directly contribute to becoming a well-grounded Python developer.

6.6   *Closing thoughts*

The next chapter will begin to build the groundwork for the MyBlog application, which will grow throughout the book to become fully featured. Along the way, you'll learn how to handle the development of a larger application and how to integrate it with a persistent database. What you've learned so far can make the project manageable to build and enjoyable to achieve.

You've brought ideas from your field of view into focus and can now see the direction to take and some of what we'll learn along the way. We'll continue along this path to consider development items in detail as we look at them more closely.

Summary

- Much of the internet world is available because of servers and, in particular, web servers. Knowing how to create server-based applications is a cornerstone skill of a well-grounded developer.

- The Flask web application development framework is one of many such frameworks available to Python developers. It's well-suited as the teaching framework to create the MyBlog web application that we'll create as we move through the rest of the chapters in this book.

- The Jinja2 template system included with Flask is a powerful way to create web pages that have common elements mixed with dynamically created ones. The content of dynamic elements in a template can come from any source—including databases, computations, and other servers. Almost anything you can access with your Python programs can be injected into a template through a dynamic element.

- Jinja2 templates allow for inheritance, which means that a template containing common elements used throughout a website can be inherited from page-specific templates. Using this inheritance significantly lowers the workload for building a dynamic web application.

Doing it with style

Creating a web application pulls together many concepts and technologies. To create an engaging application, it's necessary to think about the look and feel, or style. For a web application, this is largely provided by using CSS styling applied to the HTML content.

Integrating good styling practices raises the bar of complexity an application encapsulates. To help maintain growing complexity, it's necessary to think about project structure and the use of namespaces. Project structure and namespaces help the project grow and scale in a way that keeps the complexity manageable. This chapter lays the foundation for the MyBlog application so that it can grow and evolve in a way that will help you maintain clarity about the goals of the application and stay ahead of the complexity curve.

7.1 Application styling

Creating an application with interesting and useful features is necessary to keep users actively engaged in any application. The feature set is essential, but it's not the only thing needed to capture and keep users' attention. The way your application looks is a critical factor in what your users will expect in a modern computer system.

Look at any popular cell phone app and you'll know this is true. The best apps have both useful feature sets and an engaging visual experience for their users. Even apps with compelling features will be hard pressed to find users willing to accept and use them if the app looks clunky and unpolished.

The browser's CSS styling code controls a web application's visual look to determine how to render the HTML code to the screen. The first web application from chapter 6 used simple, hand-crafted CSS code to apply a distinct look and feel. Continuing to hand-code CSS styles for the MyBlog application is possible but has the following drawbacks:

- It takes effort to create appealing CSS styles.
- As an application grows, it becomes challenging to maintain style consistency across an entire application.
- Normalizing styles for consistent rendering across multiple browsers is tricky.
- Phones and tablets are becoming the primary interface between an application and your users; making a web application responsive to those devices is vital.

7.1.1 Creating appealing styles

The first web application from chapter 6 had a single page with relatively simple styles applied to it that consisted of two files—`myblog.css` and `index.css`—each of which was about a page of text long. Continuing to create custom styles leads to many CSS files containing hundreds of lines of code. It becomes apparent very quickly that this is additional hard work.

7.1.2 Styling consistency

A web application with even moderate complexity will have multiple pages associated with it that users will navigate around. Making sure the buttons, lists, panels, and other visual elements look the same across all pages is important to the cohesive picture you're trying to paint across the entire application.

Giving those visual elements the same style, even in different use cases within the application, is challenging. Maintaining that consistent style as your application scales upward with more features and pages compounds that challenge.

7.1.3 Normalizing styles

Like myself, you probably use a single web browser most of the time. Even if you use one at home and another at work, you might be unaware of the importance of styling consistency and the need to normalize styles across browsers. When you're building an application and generating HTML code without any styles applied to it, the browser will render the HTML using its default styles.

Each browser applies its default style to headers, paragraphs, fonts, and spacing between elements. If you could suppress the CSS style when navigating to web applications that you're familiar with, you'd see how the pages are rendered with the browser's default style. If you were to do the same thing using multiple browsers like Chrome, Firefox, Safari, Edge, and others across multiple operating systems, you'd see the pages rendered differently between those browsers—sometimes subtly, sometimes dramatically. Giving any web application you create a consistent look across the different browsers and operating systems means creating CSS code to override those browsers' default styling.

7.1.4   *Responsive design*

We've already talked about the advantages of providing application features using web browsers as the platform to deliver the experience. One of the implications is that web browsers are everywhere—on mobile phones, tablets, laptops, and desktops. They are even integrated into cars and household appliances. These devices can and do have varied presentation capabilities, including screen size, screen resolution, speed, and accessibility.

Because the internet is widely available, your web application can run on any of these devices that can access its URL. Attempting to style your application for all of these devices is impossible; there are just too many of them. Also, new ones with new capabilities are continually being introduced.

Because it is impossible to code for so many devices, it's necessary to use responsive design principles. Responsive design means using fluid, proportion-based grids; media queries; and flexible images. Using these tools creates a design layout that automatically adjusts to the screen size of the device. The Bootstrap framework provides much of what's needed to create a web application that uses responsive design ideas and implementations.

7.2   *Integrating Bootstrap*

I wouldn't present the styling speedbumps involved in developing the MyBlog web application without proposing a solution. The solution I've chosen is the Bootstrap CSS framework created by Twitter (https://getbootstrap.com/). The Bootstrap framework addresses the problems raised previously, frees you from solving many styling concerns, and lets you focus on the application design and implementation.

Adopting Bootstrap relieves you from having to create the CSS style code that creates the MyBlog presentation. Using Bootstrap gives the MyBlog application an attractive, consistent user interface; normalizes that interface across browsers and operating systems; and resolves many responsive design problems. The use of Bootstrap means you'll still need to add CSS class names to the MyBlog web application's HTML elements, but the reduction in the amount of custom CSS code required is well worth it.

Using Bootstrap to style your web-based applications also means your applications will have a Bootstrap "look" to them. This "look" can be advantageous because the visual presentation is attractive, well known, and understood. The choice to use Bootstrap is a good one because this book focuses on becoming an accomplished Python developer, with some web page design skills. Using Bootstrap doesn't exclude you from completely customizing your design, and it provides an excellent jumping-off point if you want to pursue the possibilities offered by customizing your application design.

> **Bootstrap version**
>
> The MyBlog application uses Bootstrap version 5. Version 5 focuses more on modern browsers, making the CSS code more future friendly, more straightforward to implement, and possibly faster to render.
>
> This version also drops any dependency on the jQuery JavaScript library and instead uses straight JavaScript. There is absolutely nothing wrong with jQuery; it's a powerful library to access and manipulate HTML elements. However, since its creation, browser support for JavaScript has become much more consistent and powerful, making dependence on jQuery a choice rather than a necessity.

7.2.1   *The previous example, now with Bootstrap*

The last example web application in chapter 6 used hand-coded CSS for styling. Figure 7.1 presents a refresher on that page before getting started on making changes.

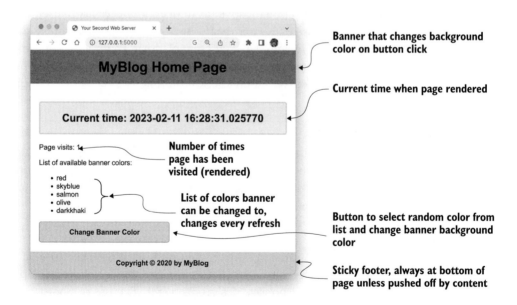

Figure 7.1   A look at the web page from chapter 6, figure 6.5, before we start making changes

Your initial goal is to replace all of the hand-coded CSS style information with that supplied by Bootstrap. It will be the same application with the same content and functionality but styled entirely with Bootstrap CSS-style classes. Figure 7.2 presents the destination that the upcoming changes will create.

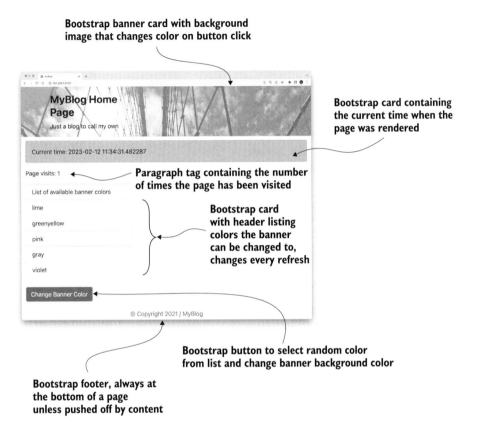

Bootstrap banner card with background image that changes color on button click

Bootstrap card containing the current time when the page was rendered

Paragraph tag containing the number of times the page has been visited

Bootstrap card with header listing colors the banner can be changed to, changes every refresh

Bootstrap button to select random color from list and change banner background color

Bootstrap footer, always at the bottom of a page unless pushed off by content

Figure 7.2   The page goal to achieve by replacing the custom CSS with `Bootstrap styling`

The first step on your way to replacing the hand-coded CSS styles with Bootstrap is making the Bootstrap framework available to the MyBlog web application. Rather than download the Bootstrap framework and copy the necessary files into your `static/css` and `static/js` directories, you're going to access the files directly from a CDN (content delivery network). Using a CDN to access Bootstrap relieves you from having to copy files for this chapter and the chapters to come. It also relieves Flask from having to serve the files, as the CDN will handle that. The MyBlog application will use the https://www.jsdelivr.com/ CDN and is the delivery mechanism recommended on the Bootstrap home page.

BASE.HTML

You're changing the style of the application only, so the app.py file doesn't need to change. Because Bootstrap will be used for all of the MyBlog pages, you'll add it to the base.html template, making it available to any template that inherits from it. You'll also need to update the hand-coded style information in the template file with Bootstrap style classes as follows:

```
<!DOCTYPE html>
<html lang="en">
<head>
  <meta charset="UTF-8">
  <meta name="viewport" content="width=device-width, initial-scale=1.0">
  <title>MyBlog</title>
  {% block styles %}
  <style>
    :root {
        --background-url: url({{url_for("static",
   filename= "images/myblog_banner_50.png")}});
    }
  </style>
  <link
        rel="stylesheet"
   href="https://cdn.jsdelivr.net/npm/bootstrap@5.0.2/
   dist/css/bootstrap.min.css" integrity="sha384-
   EVSTQN3/azprG1Anm3QDgpJLIm9Nao0Yz1ztcQTwFspd
   3yD65VohhpuuCOmLASjC" crossorigin="anonymous">
  <link
        rel="stylesheet"
        href="https://cdn.jsdelivr.net/npm/
            bootstrap-icons@1.8.1/font/
            bootstrap-icons.css"
        >
  <link
        rel="stylesheet"
        type="text/css"
        href="{{ url_for(
            'static',
            filename='css/base.css'
            ) }}"/
        >
  {% endblock styles %}
</head>
<body class="d-flex flex-column h-100">
  <div class="banner card">
    <div class="card-body">
      <div class="col-md-4 offset-md-1">
        <h2 class="card-title fw-bold">
            MyBlog Home Page
        </h2>
        <p class="card-text">
            Just a blog to call my own
        </p>
      </div>
    </div>
  </div>
```

Creates the CSS variable background-URL referencing the banner image, applied here because it uses url_for() in a template processed by Jinja2

Includes the Bootstrap-minimized CSS files from the CDN

Creates the banner section content and its styles

```
<main class="flex-shrink-0">
   {% block content %}{% endblock %}
</main>
<footer
      class="footer fixed-bottom py-1 bg-light"
   >
   <div class="container text-center">
      <span class="text-muted">
             &copy; Copyright 2021 / MyBlog
         </span>
   </div>
</footer>
{% block scripts %}
<script
      src="{{ url_for(
          'static',
          filename='js/bootstrap.bundle.min.js'
      ) }}">
   </script>
   {% endblock %}
</body>
</html>
```

Creates the content section enclosing style, which is provided by child templates

Creates the Bootstrap footer that sticks to the bottom of the page

Includes the Bootstrap-bundled, minimized JavaScript code

The template code creates the content and style basis of the MyBlog application. Every template that inherits from the base.html template will have these content and style elements. The base.html template gives a foundation for the look and feel of the entire application as well as eases the work of doing so.

BASE.CSS

The base.html template has its own base.css file that overrides some of the Bootstrap styling for the banner. It also has a CSS media query as follows that makes the application responsive in a specific way for smaller devices:

```
.banner.card {
    border: 0;
    border-radius: 0;
    background-clip: none;
}
```

Modifies the Bootstrap card style to remove the border, make the radius 0, and remove the background image clipping

```
.banner {
  display: none;
}
```

Sets the default visibility of the banner to none, or invisible

```
@media (min-width: 768px) {
  .banner {
    display: block;
    background: var(--background-url)
    no-repeat center center / cover;
  }
}
```

Uses a CSS media query to override the .banner setting to be visible if the screen size is greater than 768 pixels

The interesting part of the base.css file is the .banner and @media sections. The first sets the .banner display value to none, preventing it from being rendered to the display. The @media section takes advantage of the cascading nature of CSS to affect how the banner is displayed. In CSS, the last defined style overrides any previously defined style. The @media section acts as a conditional statement in the CSS. If the screen size is greater than 768 pixels, then set the display value to block, meaning it will be rendered to the display. The background portion defines how to display the background image and gets that image from the CSS variable background-url defined in the base.html template.

If the screen size is less than 768 pixels, the initial .banner definition of none stands, and the banner image isn't rendered to the display. The @media query gives MyBlog control over displaying the banner image, giving small-screen devices more display real estate to show MyBlog content. You'll see an example of how the media query affects the display after going over the changes to the index.html file.

INDEX.HTML

As before, the index.html file holds the content of the home page. The content is the same, but like the base.html file, the styling information is updated to use Bootstrap. Here's the updated index.html file:

```
{% extends "base.html" %}

{% block content %}
    <div class="container-fluid">
        <div
            class="card bg-warning mb-3
            font-weight-bold"
            style="margin-top: 10px;"
        >
            <div class="card-body">
                Current time: {{ data["now"] }}
            </div>
        </div>
        <p>
            Page visits: {{
                data["page_visit"].counts()
            }}
        </p>
        <div class="card" style="width: 18rem;">
            <div class="card-header">
                List of available banner colors
            </div>
            <ul
                class="list-group list-group-flush"
            >
                {% for banner_color in
                    data["banner_colors"]
                %}
                    <li
                        class="list-group-item">
                            {{ banner_color }}
                    </li>
                {% endfor %}
```

Creates the home page content, styled using a Bootstrap responsive container and card

```
            </ul>
        </div>
        <br />
        <button
➡           id="change-banner-color"
➡           type="button"
➡           class="btn btn-primary"
➡        >
            Change Banner Color
        </button>
    </div>
{% endblock %}

{% block scripts %}
    {{ super() }}
    <script>
        const banner_colors = {{ data["banner_colors"] | tojson | safe }};
    </script>
    <script src="{{ url_for('static', filename='js/index.js') }}"></script>
{% endblock %}
```

Creates the home page content, styled using a Bootstrap responsive container and card

Converts the template parameter data["banner_colors"] to JSON so it can be used by the page's JavaScript

The home-page content changes are all about styling the content presentation and not about the content itself. When the changes are complete, the directory structure should look like `examples/CH_07/examples/01`:

```
.
├── app.py
├── static
│   ├── css
│   │   └── base.css
│   ├── images
│   │   ├── myblog_banner.png
│   │   └── myblog_banner_50.png
│   └── js
│       └── index.js
└── templates
    ├── base.html
    └── index.html
```

From that directory, execute the following commands from a Mac or Linux terminal:

```
export FLASK_ENV=development
export FLASK_APP=app.py
flask run
```

Or as follows for a Windows system terminal:

```
set FLASK_ENV=development
set FLASK_APP=app.py
flask run
```

The MyBlog web server will run, and you can navigate with your browser to `127.0.0.1:5000` and see the application.

The application shows the modified banner containing the image at the top of the display. It also shows the Bootstrap sticky footer at the bottom of the page. These elements come from the `base.html` template and will be present on every page that inherits from it.

The current timestamp is displayed in a Bootstrap card, and the list of available colors is contained in another card. Additionally, the button that changes the color of the banner background is styled as a Bootstrap button.

The display banner is rendered if the browser screen size is greater than 768 pixels, which is most likely correct for a desktop or laptop computer. This is what's presented in figure 7.3. If you resize the browser window to be narrower, eventually you'll cross the 768-pixel boundary and the web application display will change. Figure 7.4 shows the updated page. The absence of the banner text and image demonstrates the conditional implied by the `@media` query in the `base.css` file. The conditional becomes false, and the initial definition of the `.banner` CSS class becomes active, setting the display value to `none`. Using the media query gives the web application more vertical screen real estate for smaller devices like tablets and mobile phones.

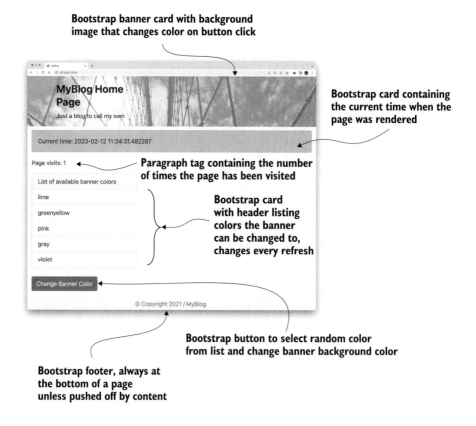

Figure 7.3   The page displayed after incorporating Bootstrap styling

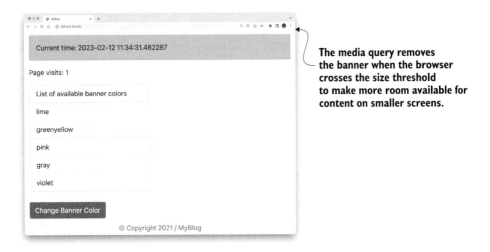

The media query removes
the banner when the browser
crosses the size threshold
to make more room available for
content on smaller screens.

Figure 7.4   Changing the browser size activates the media query to remove the banner.

7.3   *Helping MyBlog grow*

At this point in the development, the MyBlog app has expanded on the basic Flask example application often found in Flask documentation. Everything we've added extends what this basic example can do with the addition of functionality and styling and the use of Jinja2 templates. Continuing to extend the capabilities of the code we've written so far is possible, but doing so would hinder developing a fully featured and extensible application.

All new functionality would have to be included in the app.py file as a long list of functions decorated with @app.route(...) to connect that functionality to the Flask application. Doing so breaks the concept of single responsibility and makes naming the web application URL endpoint function handlers awkward.

The mental demand of working in many technical domains in a single large file would be even harder. The app.py file would contain all of the parts necessary for a full-featured blogging application—authentication, authorization, database access, user management, and creating and presenting the blogging content.

You've seen how to break up functionality along logical or complex boundaries by using modules to create namespaces and create namespace containers for functionality. The same approach will be used in the MyBlog application. However, one thing that needs attention to make that possible as you move forward is the Flask app instance.

7.3.1   *The Flask app instance*

In the current version of the app.py program file, the Flask module is imported and the Flask application instance variable app is created directly. Creating the Flask app instance in the root application file works fine for a sample application whose purpose is to build a working example web server quickly.

Why is this structure a problem when you want to use modules to namespace functionality in the web application? Because any feature or functionality you'd want to add to the web application with a URL endpoint function like `hello_world()` will need access to the app instance variable.

With the current MyBlog application setup, creating modules to contain features and functionality becomes difficult because those modules will need access to the app instance. The current structure is illustrated in figure 7.5. That presents a problem. The `app.py` code could import modules to access additional functionality, but those same modules would need access to the app instance. If those modules import the app instance from `app.py` to gain access, a circular reference problem is created that Python won't allow. Adding features and functionality to the current implementation of MyBlog leads to a structure that's difficult to scale upward.

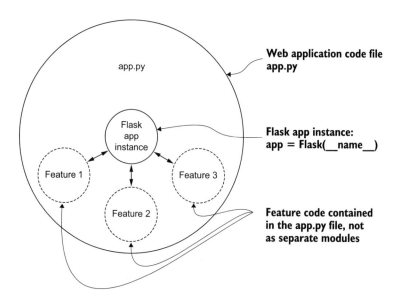

Figure 7.5   The application code structure where features are contained in the `app.py` file

RESOLVING THE APP INSTANCE PROBLEM

To resolve the problem of modules accessing the Flask app instance, you'll need to change the application's structure. The Flask app instance is the central hub around which the features of a Flask-based application revolve. Besides the `@app.route(…)` functionality seen so far, more functionality and features will need access to the app instance, as presented in later chapters.

Given the central role of the app instance, how do you gain access to it when needed? You'll be following a two-step process to resolve the problem: putting the bulk of the application code into a Python package and creating a factory function to instantiate the Flask app instance.

The use and creation of packages were presented in earlier chapters and used to create module namespaces. As a refresher, creating a package means creating a directory and adding an __init__.py file to the directory. The existence of this file lets Python import modules from the package. Adding packages can continue to any reasonable depth by creating packages within packages to create meaningful namespace hierarchies.

In earlier chapters, the __init__.py file needs only exist to make a directory a Python package. Part of the activity of importing a module from a package also includes executing any Python code in the __init__.py file. The __init__.py file in many packages doesn't contain code, but Python code can be added to it.

Any module in the package automatically has access to the code and variables in the package __init__.py file, and the __init__.py file has access to the package's sibling modules. Packages will be useful when creating the application factory function to create the Flask app instance.

MYBLOG RESTRUCTURING

You're at an excellent point to restructure the file layout of the MyBlog application to create a meaningful hierarchy. Having an intentional file structure helps use the files contained in the directory structure that are related and useful to your projects.

The first thing to do is rename the app.py file to myblog.py. Then create a directory named app, which is the root package directory for the MyBlog application. Move the static and templates directories into the app directory.

Inside the app directory, create an __init__.py file, which turns the app directory into a Python package. The directory structure should now look like this:

```
├── app
│   ├── __init__.py
│   ├── static
│   │   ├── css
│   │   │   └── base.css
│   │   ├── images
│   │   │   ├── myblog_banner.png
│   │   │   └── myblog_banner_50.png
│   │   └── js
│   │       └── index.js
│   └── templates
│       ├── base.html
│       └── index.html
└── myblog.py
```

APPLICATION FACTORY

The renamed myblog.py file creates the Flask app instance directly and then uses it to connect URL endpoints to functionality. Our goal is to get more control over creating the app instance and make using it with external modules easier. To do this, you're

going to implement an application factory function called `create_app()` inside the
app package `__init__.py` file. Edit the `app/__init__.py` file and add this code:

```
from flask import Flask, render_template
from datetime import datetime
from random import sample

class PageVisit:
    COUNT = 0
    def counts(self):
        PageVisit.COUNT += 1
        return PageVisit.COUNT

class BannerColors:
    COLORS = [
        "lightcoral", "salmon", "red", "firebrick", "pink",
        "gold", "yellow", "khaki", "darkkhaki", "violet",
        "blue", "purple", "indigo", "greenyellow", "lime",
        "green", "olive", "darkcyan", "aqua", "skyblue",
        "tan", "sienna", "gray", "silver"
    ]
    def get_colors(self):
        return sample(BannerColors.COLORS, 5)

def create_app():
    app = Flask(__name__)

    with app.app_context():

        @app.route("/")
        def home():
            return render_template("index.html", data={
                "now": datetime.now(),
                "page_visit": PageVisit(),
                "banner_colors": BannerColors().get_colors()
            })

        return app
```

**The support classes used
by the home() function**

**Creates the Flask app instance inside the
application factory create_app() function**

**Begins a context manager to
initialize the rest of the app**

**Returns the app
instance to the caller**

This code is basically everything in the `myblog.py` file placed inside the app package
`__init__.py` file. Because this replicates almost all of the code in `myblog.py`, this
file needs to be updated to this:

```
from app import create_app

app = create_app()
```

All that `myblog.py` does now is import the application factory `create_app` and then
call it to create the Flask app instance. Change your working directory to `examples/`
`CH_07/examples/02` and execute the commands to run the application from a Mac
or Linux terminal:

```
export FLASK_ENV=development
export FLASK_APP=app.py
flask run
```

Or for a Windows system terminal:

```
set FLASK_ENV=development
set FLASK_APP=app.py
flask run
```

Navigating to 127.0.0.1:5000 in your browser will show the same application view as before but using the new MyBlog application structure. Figure 7.6 shows the application page and its functionality.

The next step is to move the home() function to an external module where other features can be added. To do this, you'll make use of the Flask Blueprints capability.

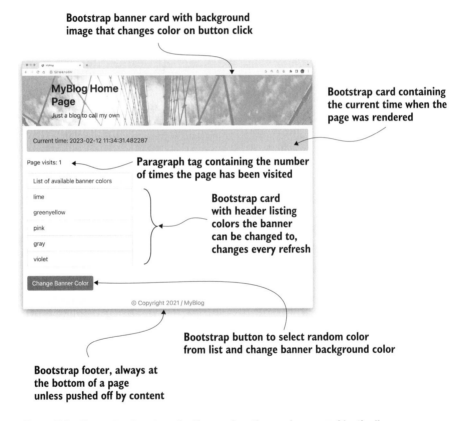

Figure 7.6   The restructured application renders the previous page identically.

7.4   Namespaces

Any interesting application will have many features that necessitate interaction between those features, which adds complexity. The MyBlog web application is no different and will acquire functionality focused on particular application parts. Rather than roll all the other functional areas of code into one big Python file, it's better to break the work into modules so you can work in one functional domain at a time.

Just like you've seen in previous chapters where Python packages and modules contain high-level namespaces, the same idea will be applied here. In a web application, this separation of concerns includes creating modules for the URL endpoints that provide functionality and are to be placed into namespaces. The Flask framework implements namespaces through Blueprints.

7.4.1 Flask Blueprints

In the MyBlog application, when the `@app.route("/")` decorator is applied to a function, the function is registered with the server so it will be called when the URL endpoint path `"/"` is accessed by a browser. As the decorator's name implies, the `"/"` URL path parameter passed in is an application route being defined.

The `@app.route` decorator lets you connect a URL route to the Flask application so it can process a request for the route with the decorated function. All of the URL routes could be handled this way, but in a larger application, this becomes unwieldy. The Flask web framework provides a feature called Blueprints to implement separate modules that service URL endpoints or routes.

Flask Blueprints lets you separate specific functionality into modules. A Blueprint is useful when creating logically distinct features like authentication, authorization, and other parts of a web application. In chapter 8, you'll be adding user authentication to the MyBlog application. Authentication secures access to almost all other pages and features the MyBlog application provided to users.

Getting authentication working and contained in one place is valuable, but this functionality could be used in an entirely different web application with little trouble once complete. You could make almost any functionality you've created available to other projects by placing the Blueprint in a shared library for all your application projects to use. You could also put it in a repository like GitHub, where a team of developers could access it.

7.4.2 Add Blueprints to MyBlog

The MyBlog application creates the app instance inside the application factory `create_app()` function in the app package. The home page is also contained in the `create_app()` function. A little later in this chapter, you're going to add an about page to the application. Let's create a namespace for the home page and the future about page where they both can live. We'll call that namespace `intro`, as the home and about page will be introductory to the MyBlog application.

To do this, you'll create an intro package within the app package. As a first step, create an `intro` subdirectory within the `app` directory. In that subdirectory, create an empty `__init__.py` file, which makes the `intro` directory a Python package.

THE CONTENT

There's a bit of a chicken-and-egg problem with how a Blueprint is created and used, but let's start with the `intro` namespace's functionality. In the `intro` subdirectory, create an `intro.py` file with this content:

```
from flask import render_template
from datetime import datetime
from random import sample
from . import intro_bp

class PageVisit:
    COUNT = 0

    def counts(self):
        PageVisit.COUNT += 1
        return PageVisit.COUNT

class BannerColors:
    COLORS = [
        "lightcoral", "salmon", "red", "firebrick", "pink",
        "gold", "yellow", "khaki", "darkkhaki", "violet",
        "blue", "purple", "indigo", "greenyellow", "lime",
        "green", "olive", "darkcyan", "aqua", "skyblue",
        "tan", "sienna", "gray", "silver"
    ]

    def get_colors(self):
        return sample(BannerColors.COLORS, 5)

@intro_bp.route("/")
def home():
    return render_template("index.html", data={
        "now": datetime.now(),
        "page_visit": PageVisit(),
        "banner_colors": BannerColors().get_colors()
    })
```

⊲— **Imports the as-yet-undefined intro Blueprint instance intro_bp**

⊲— **Notices how the home function is decorated with the intro_bp Blueprint instance route function rather than @app.route**

THE INTRO PACKAGE

The `intro.py` file contains Blueprint functionality and uses the as-yet-undefined `intro_bp` Blueprint instance. The `intro_bp` instance naming is a convention; adding _bp to the end of the instance name indicates a Flask Blueprint. The next step is to edit the empty `app/intro/__init__.py` file and create the `intro_bp` instance:

```
from flask import Blueprint

intro_bp = Blueprint('intro_bp', __name__,
    static_folder="static",
    static_url_path="/intro/static",
    template_folder="templates"
)

from app.intro import intro
```

⊲— **Imports the Blueprint class from the flask module**

Creates a Blueprint instance, initializing its name, filename, and paths to the static and template files

⊲— **Imports the intro module functionality**

Because the `__init__.py` file is inside a package, this code will be run every time anything within the package is imported, including the just-created `intro.py` module. The first thing the code does is import the Blueprint class from the flask module. It then creates the `intro_bp` instance by instantiating the Blueprint class with some parameters.

The parameters give the Blueprint a name, pass it the Python filename, and set the `static_folder` and `template_folder` parameters with path strings relative to the Blueprint location. This means the `intro_bp` Blueprint instance expects to find the templates it will render and the static assets those templates might require on a path relative to where the file containing the definition `intro_bp` Blueprint exists in the application file structure.

The `static_url_path` parameter is set to ensure that the Blueprint relative path doesn't conflict with the root `static` folder. The value assigned to the parameter is the relative path from the root directory to the Blueprint `static` directory.

This means that the `index.html` template that provides the home page's content needs to move somewhere the `intro_bp` Blueprint can find. It also means the static assets (CSS files, JavaScript, and images) need to move as well.

UPDATED MYBLOG DIRECTORY

The result of restructuring the directory to put all the files related to the intro Blueprint exists in the `examples/CH_07/examples/03` directory from the code repository:

```
├── app
│   ├── __init__.py
│   ├── intro
│   │   ├── __init__.py
│   │   ├── intro.py
│   │   ├── static
│   │   │   ├── css
│   │   │   │   └── index.css
│   │   │   ├── images
│   │   │   │   ├── myblog_banner.png
│   │   │   │   └── myblog_banner_50.png
│   │   │   └── js
│   │   │       └── index.js
│   │   └── templates
│   │       └── index.html
│   ├── static
│   │   ├── css
│   │   │   └── base.css
│   │   ├── images
│   │   │   ├── myblog_banner.png
│   │   │   └── myblog_banner_50.png
│   │   └── js
│   └── templates
│       └── base.html
└── myblog.py
```

In this directory structure, two pairs of `templates` and `static` directories exist, the first being the original at the project root from the previous example and the second being the set under the intro package. The second set is what the `intro_bp` Blueprint instance will use when looking for `templates` and `static` files because of the values passed to the `static_folder` and `template_folder` parameters when the instance was created.

If those two parameters had not been set, the `intro_bp` instance would have looked for `templates` and `static` assets in the app root `static` and `templates` directories under the `app` directory. Having the `templates` and `static` folders under the Blueprint packages you create makes the Blueprint more self-contained and portable to other projects.

One additional change needs to be made to the `index.html` file so it can access the static assets referenced by the HTML code. The `<script>`...`</script>` tags that reference the JavaScript that reacts to the button clicks on the home page need to be updated in this way:

```
<script src="{{ url_for('.static', filename='js/index.js') }}"></script>
```

The only change is the addition of the single character (`.`) in front of `static` in the `url_for(...)` statement. The `url_for(...)` statement will resolve this path to the `static` directory relative to the `intro_bp` Blueprint, and the `index.js` file will be pulled correctly.

APP PACKAGE CHANGES

Before you move on to create the new about page, take a look at the app/`__init__.py` file. All of the code related to the home page has just been moved to the `intro` module, so the file needs to be updated as follows:

```
from flask import Flask


def create_app():
    app = Flask(__name__)
    with app.app_context():                          Imports the intro module
        from . import intro          ◁──────         containing the intro Blueprint
        app.register_blueprint(intro.intro_bp)   ◁──┐  Registers the intro
        return app                                  │  Blueprint with the app
```

This code shows the application factory `create_app()` function simplified to remove the home page's code, which is now part of the `intro` Blueprint. This is all that's needed in the MyBlog application to get things rolling when the `flask run` command is called. By default, the `flask run` command looks in the application (which was in the `FLASK_ENV` environment variable) for a Flask instance named app. Finding the app instance will start to run the application, serving any URL endpoints that have been configured and registered with the app.

7.4.3 Create the about page

To demonstrate how the `intro_bp` Blueprint instance can contain features and functionality, you'll add an about page to the MyBlog application. To do so, add a new handler function to the `intro.py` file and register it with the instance by decorating it with a route as follows:

```
@intro_bp.route("/about")           ◁────────       Decorates the about() function and registers
def about():                                         it as the handler for the new route "/about"
    return render_template("about.html")             using the intro_bp Blueprint instance
```

Retrieves and renders the about.html template
file from the intro_bp relative templates directory

This code creates a URL endpoint route to "/about" and registers the about() function as the handler when that route is navigated to by a browser. To render an about HTML page, an about.html template is created in the app/intro/templates directory that's relative to the intro_bp Blueprint:

```
{% extends "base.html" %}          ◁ ─────

{% block content %}                ◁ ─────
    <div class="container-fluid mt-3">
        <div class="card">
            <div class="card-header">
                About
            </div>
            <div class="card-body">
                <h5 class="card-title">Information about this website</h5>
                <p class="card-text">
                    This is an implementation of the MyBlog blogging
                    web application. This web application is developed over
                    the course of multiple chapters from the book,
                    "The Well-Grounded Python Developer".
                </p>
                <p class="card-text">
                    The intent of the MyBlog application is not to create
                    a complete and fully feature blogging system, there are
                    many of those in existence already. The goal is to
                    progressively see and learn how to implement the big
                    picture that's necessary to implement a complex system
                    like this.
                </p>
            </div>
        </div>
    </div>
{% endblock %}
```

Like index.html, the about page inherits from base.html and gets the same features it provides.

The about page replaces the content block with Bootstrap-styled text information about the MyBlog application.

If you run the MyBlog application and navigate to 127.0.0.1:5000/about in a browser, the server will respond by rendering the about.html file to the display window. Figure 7.7 is a screenshot of the about page. The about page uses Bootstrap styles in the same manner as the home page.

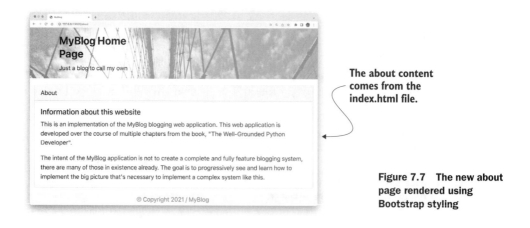

The about content comes from the index.html file.

Figure 7.7   The new about page rendered using Bootstrap styling

7.4.4   *Refactored app instance*

At this point, the MyBlog application—and Flask `app` instance in particular—has been refactored to better support a growing web application. Figure 7.8 shows how the `create_app()` function connects to the functionality contained in the external `intro` module, which has access to the `app` instance inside that function's scope. The `app` instance is returned by the `create_app` function imported inside the scope of the `myblog.py` code. The reference to the `app` instance is held by `myblog.py` for the life of the application.

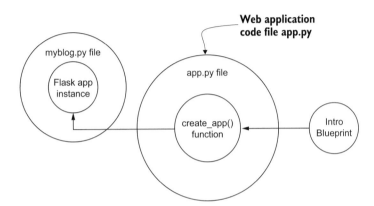

Figure 7.8
The visual structure of the refactored MyBlog `application`

7.5   *Navigation*

The MyBlog application now has two pages—the home and about pages. You can navigate to them directly by entering the URL into the browser, but that's not very convenient. Websites provide clickable links to navigate around the application; you'll add that navigation using Bootstrap.

The MyBlog site navigation is provided by a Bootstrap navbar added to the `base.html` template so it's rendered on any page inheriting from it, essentially site-wide. The Bootstrap navbar is visually attractive and responsive to device size. It contracts to be a drop-down menu for small devices.

You can also add some interactive touches by making the currently active page's menu item visibly highlighted. This means that if the about page is being viewed, the about menu item is highlighted. You'll add this by making use of features in Jinja2.

7.5.1   *Creating navigation information*

There are two parts to adding the navbar and making it interactive. The first thing to do is edit the `base.html` template file in the root templates folder and add this code at the top of the file:

```
{# configure the navigation items to build in the navbar #}
{% set
  nav_items = [
    {"name": "Home", "link": "intro_bp.home"},
```

This is a Jinja2 comment in the template.

Creates a variable named nav_items containing a list of dictionaries with navigation information in each dictionary item

```
      {"name": "About","link": "intro_bp.about"}
    ]
%}
```
△ **Creates a variable named nav_items containing a list of dictionaries with navigation information in each dictionary item**

The `{% set … %}` block allows you to create a variable just as you would in Python code used by other parts of the template. The `nav_items` list variable holds the navigation information necessary to build the Bootstrap navbar links.

Look at the link information in the `nav_items` structure. The home-page link is `'intro_bp.home'`, not just `home`. This would appear in an HTML link in a template like this:

```
<a href="{{url_for('intro_bp.home')}}">Home</a>
```

The `url_for` function knows how to find the page relative to the `intro` Blueprint and uses the `intro` Blueprint instance `intro_bp`. It then finds the URL endpoint `home` relative to that. You'll see how this is used when rendering the navbar next.

7.5.2   *Displaying navigation information*

The second part of creating the navbar is further down in the `base.html` template file. Just above the `{% block content %}{% endblock %}`, insert this code:

```
<nav class="navbar navbar-expand-lg
navbar-dark bg-primary">                          ◁──────  This begins the Bootstrap navbar
  <a                                                        styling section and sets the color
       class="navbar-brand ml-2"                            and style of the navbar.
       href="{{url_for('intro_bp.home')}}"
  >
    MyBlog                                          Creates the MyBlog brand icon as
  </a>                                              a clickable link to the home page
  <button class="navbar-toggler"
          type="button"
          data-bs-toggle="collapse"
          data-bs-target="#navbarSupportedContent"
          aria-controls="navbarSupportedContent"
          aria-expanded="false"
          aria-label="Toggle navigation">
    <span class="navbar-toggler-icon"></span>
  </button>
  <div class="collapse navbar-collapse"
       id="navbarSupportedContent">
    <div class="navbar-nav">                       Iterates over the
      {% for nav_item in nav_items %}    ◁──┘      nav_items variable
        {% if request.endpoint ==
             nav_item["link"] %}         ◁──────  Compares the current page
          <a class="nav-link ml-2 active"          to the current nav_item link
             aria-current="page"
             href="{{url_for(
                nav_item['link']                   Outputs a highlighted link
             )}}"                                  if the comparison was true
          >
             {{nav_item["name"]}}
          </a>
```

```
      {% else %}
        <a class="nav-link ml-2"
          href="{{url_for(
                nav_item['link']
          )}}"
          >
              {{nav_item["name"]}}
        </a>
      {% endif %}
    {% endfor %}
    </div>
  </div>
</nav>
```

**Outputs a normal link if
the comparison was false**

There's quite a bit going on here. Much of the code is about getting Bootstrap-style classes in the right places with the correct context and information. This is a lot of styling information to work with and learn when using Bootstrap. However, it's minuscule when compared to providing the same styling functionality with handwritten CSS code.

An interesting part of the template code is the for loop and the if statement within it. The for loop iterates over the previously created nav_items list, pulling out one nav_item at a time. The if statement uses the built-in object and attribute request.endpoint to determine if the page currently being built is the same as the nav_item["link"] value.

If the current page is equal to the nav_item link, the navbar menu item is an HTML link containing the class active and the HTML attribute aria-current= "page". The Bootstrap active class adds visual highlighting to the menu item. The HTML attribute aria-current="page" helps users navigating to the page that are using a screen reader for accessibility. If the current page is not equal to the nav_item link, the navbar menu item is rendered in its default state with no highlight applied.

7.5.3 *MyBlog's current look*

If you change your working directory to examples/CH_07/examples/04, there's a fully functional example program that implements what we've gone through. Use the following commands to run the application for Mac and Linux users:

```
export FLASK_ENV=development
export FLASK_APP=myblog.py
flask run
```

And these commands for Windows users:

```
set FLASK_ENV=development
set FLASK_APP=myblog.py
flask run
```

When the application is running, use your browser to navigate to 127.0.0.1:5000, and you'll see the application.

Newly added Bootstrap navigation bar

Figure 7.9 shows the current MyBlog application with the newly added Bootstrap navbar directly below the banner. This is the expanded view, with the home-page menu item highlighted by the `base.html` template code shown previously.

If you start to minimize the browser window horizontally, you'll see that the navbar navigation will be reduced to a dropdown button on the right side of the navbar (figure 7.10). If you click that button, the navigation menu items will appear, allowing access to the Home and About links. This shows the advantages of using Bootstrap's responsive design features.

Figure 7.9   The MyBlog application displaying a Bootstrap navbar

Making the browser window smaller adjusts the navigation bar for smaller devices. The menu is replaced by a button on the right. If clicked, the menu items are presented on the left in a list.

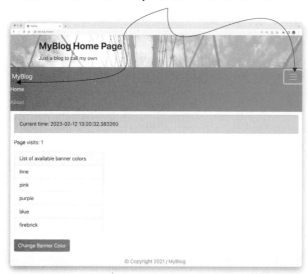

Figure 7.10   Bootstrap has its own media queries to manage smaller screens, adjusting the menu bar.

7.6   *Application configuration*

The MyBlog application has come a long way since its first incarnation, and there's work to do to improve it further. The development you're embarking on targets making the configuration, sustainability, and maintainability of the application better and easier.

7.6.1 Configuration files

The MyBlog application will eventually rely on functionality that needs configuration data—sending an email to an email service, accessing a database to store users and blog posts, and providing security data for the Flask application itself. In addition to the configuration data needed by the MyBlog feature set, you'll want to set up distinct data for development and production environments.

The configuration data creates an environment in which the MyBlog application will run. A development environment often provides additional debugging services and access to the inner workings of the application. If you develop an application in a team, different configuration data is needed to create a staging environment. A staging environment is where the team can test the various parts of the application before being pushed into production. A production environment removes the debug information and restricts access to only the feature set intended to be publicly available.

7.6.2 Private information

Any application whose feature set includes accessing systems or services requiring usernames, passwords, or API keys needs to keep that information private. For example, the MyBlog application will automatically send emails to users and administrators.

The MyBlog application won't handle sending an email directly but will instead use an external SMTP email server. The app will need to authenticate the email server with a username and password and possibly an API key. Although the MyBlog application will need access to this information, you don't want this information to become available in the public domain.

It would be easy to embed this information directly in the code, but that pretty much assures that it would become public. Unintentionally making private data public could happen as easily as embedding private information in the code and then checking that code into a publicly accessible repository like GitHub. Services like GitHub provide a valuable resource to developers, but they don't automatically protect you from publishing things you didn't intend to.

As a developer, you'll want to protect yourself and your employer so the services your application uses aren't abused. Besides being good practice, if the services cost money, failing to protect them could cost more than you expected.

One way to separate private information from an application but still have access to it is to store the information in separate files that the application can access at run-time. These files aren't checked into a repository, so they are at less risk of becoming public. Additionally, multiple versions can be maintained for the different environments in which the application can run, like development, staging, and production.

7.7 Flask Debug Toolbar

To make introducing configuration files more interesting, you'll be using them to add the Flask Debug Toolbar (https://github.com/pallets-eco/flask-debugtoolbar) to the MyBlog application when it's running in development mode. The toolbar is useful when developing a Flask application. It shows internal information right in the browser window that would otherwise only be available by debugging the application itself or by examining log information.

The configuration files you'll add will control information the Debug Toolbar requires to run and dynamically installs the toolbar only in development environments. The Debug Toolbar module needs to exist in the currently active Python virtual environment as follows:

```
pip install flask-debugtoolbar==0.11.0
```

7.7.1 FlaskDynaConf

The configuration information is stored in TOML files, which are human readable and support data types for the information contained within them. To gain access to the configuration TOML files, you'll need to install the dynaconf module into the current Python virtual environment as follows:

```
pip install dynaconf==3.1.2
```

The module contains a class specific to Flask that will automatically add configuration information to the Flask configuration system. The Flask Debug Toolbar requires the Flask app to have a SECRET_KEY value. The SECRET_KEY value is also used for security aspects of a Flask application used in later chapters. In the configuration file, it looks like this:

```
secret_key=" <random string of characters>"
```

> **TIP** Following my own advice, the actual secret key used during the example code development isn't revealed. The secret key's value should be a cryptographically strong string of characters that isn't publicly known.

You can generate a SECRET_KEY value with the following code:

```
python
>>> import secrets
>>> print(secrets.token_hex(24))
b3a40bcc3bcc5894c390681396ec04687ad869c6546cdff9
```
Sample output

The secrets module provides cryptographically strong random values better suited to manage private information. The printed results are copied between the quotes as the secret_key value in a file named .secrets.toml:

```
[default]
secret_key="<random string of characters>"
```

The file structure contains sections, indicated by the [default] line, and a set of key/value pairs of data. Because the secret_key is defined within the [default] section, that value is available in any other section unless it is overridden explicitly by another secret_key key/value pair. Completing the configuration to add the Flask Debug Toolbar requires the creation of another TOML file, settings.toml:

```
[default]
```
No default information
is currently defined.

Begins the definition of
configuration information for
development environments

**Enables
the Flask
debug
mode**

```
[development]
flask_debug = true
extensions = ["flask_debugtoolbar:DebugToolbarExtension"]
debug_tb_enabled = true

[production]
flask_debug = false
```

Begins the definition
of the configuration
for production
environments

Disables the Flask
debug mode

The configuration is separated into three sections—[default] (currently empty), [development], and [production]—and could be divided into as many as needed. Notice the listed values have data types, and the extension key's value is a list of strings. The flask_debug key/value pair has a value of true, which is a Boolean. Each section (aside from [default]) is keyed to the Flask environment variable initialized before running the application:

```
export FLASK_ENV=development
```

Only the information under the [default] and the indicated environment will be read from the settings.toml file at run time. The settings.toml files can be included in the repository, as it's useful to anyone wanting to work on the application and doesn't contain secret information. The secrets.toml file should be excluded from the project repository because it contains information that shouldn't be publicly available.

CONFIGURING MYBLOG

To use the configuration information, you need to make changes to the MyBlog application. Because the configuration is central to the application, make the following changes to the app/__init__.py file:

```
import os
import sys
from flask import Flask
from dynaconf import FlaskDynaconf
```
Imports the Flask-specific
dynaconf class

```
def create_app():
    app = Flask(__name__)
    dynaconf = FlaskDynaconf(extensions_list=True)
```
Creates an instance of the
FlaskDynaconf class, activating
the module loader feature

```
    with app.app_context():
        os.environ[
            "ROOT_PATH_FOR_DYNACONF"
        ] = app.root_path
        dynaconf.init_app(app)
        app.config["SECRET_KEY"] =
          bytearray(app.config["SECRET_KEY"], "UTF-8")
        from . import intro
        app.register_blueprint(intro.intro_bp)
        return app
```
Informs dynaconf where to look
for configuration *.toml files

Configures the Flask app based on the
dynaconf-read configuration files

Translates the SECRET_KEY string
into a bytearray as recommended
by the Flask documentation

The `FlaskDynaconf` class searches for configuration files based on file-naming patterns and directory structures and finds both the `.secrets.toml` and `settings.toml` files. It parses them and configures the Flask `app.config` object accordingly. Running the MyBlog application in `examples/CH_07/examples/05` in the development environment renders the home page in the browser and presents the Flask Debug Toolbar on the right side of the screen (figure 7.11).

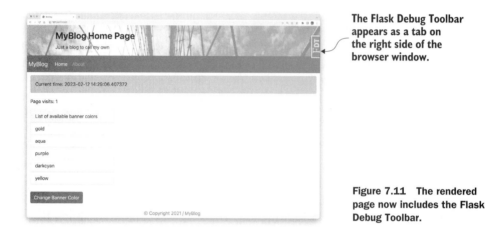

The Flask Debug Toolbar appears as a tab on the right side of the browser window.

Figure 7.11   The rendered page now includes the Flask Debug Toolbar.

The initial view doesn't show much difference except for the small tab in the upper right corner of the window labeled FDT for Flask Debug Toolbar. Clicking on this tab opens the toolbar and presents some information about the page as well as the tools it makes available. Figure 7.12 displays the expanded toolbar.

The Flask Debug Toolbar expanded into the browser display window and shows the information available to inspect

Figure 7.12   The Flask Debug Toolbar expanded view showing the tools available

Clicking on the Templates menu item loads the working area of the display with information about the home page template (figure 7.13). This includes the context variables used by the template, the URL that was requested, and the information about the session.

Selecting the Templates tool displays information about the currently rendered template.

Figure 7.13   The information about the current template is displayed after selecting the Templates tool.

Not all the menu options provide useful information. The Logging selection doesn't show anything currently but will after adding a logging configuration in the next section.

7.8   *Logging information*

Flask uses the Python logging module to log information to standard output (STDOUT), as you've seen when running the MyBlog application from the terminal command line. Almost any coding from a developer leads to inserting print statements into the code to get information out of a running application. A better approach to output this kind of information is to use the Python logging system.

Logging is a simple way to get a snapshot of what's happening at that point of execution in the application. The same facility is available when developing a web application through the logging system. Logging information to STDOUT is beneficial in a long-running server application.

The logging system has advantages over print statements; it supports severity levels for the logged information. The severity levels allow you to raise and lower the level of logs the application will produce. For example, you can output useful development information at the DEBUG level. The configuration of the application running in a production environment can be raised above the DEBUG level and none of the developer debug logs will be produced. The debug log statements can be left in place in the code.

It can also provide a standardized format that's chronologically arranged and useful when looking for events or the order of operations for a sequence of events. The Python logging system supports multiple paths, or handlers, for logged messages with different endpoints. These endpoints can be as simple as logging to STDOUT or more sophisticated, like sending an email or text message to a service in response to a logged message. For the MyBlog application, the logging configuration is relatively simple: sending logs to STDOUT with a particular message format.

7.8.1   *Configuration*

The Python logging module supports configuration from a dictionary, and that's what MyBlog will use. Configuring the logging system is another responsibility you'll add to the app package's create_app() function.

As mentioned, the logging system uses logging levels, ranging from NOTSET to CRITICAL, where NOTSET equals 0 and CRITICAL equals 50. In my experience, NOTSET is never used and is there to "round out the set." Besides providing some context about the logged message, the logging system's level acts as a simple filter. If the logging system's level is set to INFO for a particular logger, only messages with a level equal to INFO or higher will be logged.

The DEBUG (value 10) and INFO (value 20) levels are of interest for the development and production environments in which the MyBlog application runs. In development, the level can be set to DEBUG, and all logged messages with a level of DEBUG or higher will be logged. In a production environment, the level can be set to INFO, all log messages with a level of INFO or higher will be logged, and DEBUG-level messages will be ignored.

By differentiating the two environment's logging levels, you can add DEBUG-level messages into an application during development and leave them in place. In a production environment, those messages won't be logged. The Python dictionary to configure logging is created by reading a logging configuration YAML file with a support function in app/__init__.py:

```
def _configure_logging(app, dynaconf):
    logging_config_path = Path(app.root_path).parent / "logging_config.yaml"
    with open(logging_config_path, "r") as fh:
        logging_config = yaml.safe_load(fh.read())
```

```
      env_logging_level = dynaconf.settings.get(
➡          "logging_level", "INFO"
➡      ).upper()
      logging_level = logging.INFO
➡          if env_logging_level == "INFO"
➡          else logging.DEBUG
      logging_config["handlers"]["console"]["level"] = logging_level
      logging_config["loggers"][""]["level"] = logging_level
      logging.config.dictConfig(logging_config)
```

The _configure_logging() function has a leading underbar character, a convention indicating it's intended to be private to the module. The leading underbar is only a convention and does not add any privacy protections to the function.

   The function creates an env_logging_level variable based on the environment string passed to the function. The variable is used to create the configuration dictionary to control the logging level console STDOUT handler. The logging configuration information is in a file named logging_config.yaml at the project directory level:

```
version: 1
disable_existing_loggers: true          ◁──┐  Disables any existing
formatters:                                 │  loggers created by Flask
  default:
    format: '[%(asctime)s.%(msecs)03d]
➡      %(levelname)s in %(module)s: %(message)s'
    datefmt: '%Y-%m-%d %H:%M:%S'
handlers:
  console:
    level: DEBUG
    class: logging.StreamHandler          Configures only one handler
    formatter: default                    to send errors to STDOUT
    stream: ext://sys.stdout
loggers:
  '':
    level: DEBUG
    handlers: [console]
    propagate: false
```

The structure creates the formatters used by the handlers, which the loggers use. The formatters change the logging message default format used by the MyBlog application. Add a logging_level configuration key/value to the settings.toml file to both the development and production sections as follows:

```
[development]
...
logging_level = "DEBUG"

[production]
...
logging_level = "INFO"
```

Two changes need to be made to the create_app() function in app/__init__.py to use the dictionary returned by the _configure_logging() function. Add these two lines at the bottom of the import section

```
import logging
import logging.config
```

and add this line to the `create_app()` function immediately below the code that converts the `app.config[SECRET_KEY]` to a bytearray:

```
_configure_logging(app, dynaconf)
```
◁─┐ **Calling the function configures**
   logging for the MyBlog application

You can now add DEBUG-level log messages where needed to help develop the MyBlog application. The home and about pages can be modified as follows to demonstrate this:

```
logger = getLogger(__file__)

@intro_bp.route("/")
def home():
    logger.debug("rendering home page")
    return render_template("index.html", data={
        "now": datetime.now(),
        "page_visit": PageVisit(),
        "banner_colors": BannerColors().get_colors()
    })

@intro_bp.route("/about")
def about():
    logger.debug("rendering about page")
    return render_template("about.html")
```

Sends a DEBUG-level message to the logging system that the home page has been rendered

Sends a DEBUG-level message to the logging system that the home page has been rendered

When starting and running the MyBlog application, a DEBUG log message will be present in the logging output whenever the application home or about pages are accessed. If you run the code in `examples/CH_07/examples/06` and navigate to the about and home pages, the log output will look similar to this:

```
[2021-01-08 15:29:39,030] WARNING in _internal:  * Debugger is active!
[2021-01-08 15:29:39,055] INFO in _internal:  * Debugger PIN: 107-111-649
[2021-01-08 15:29:39,104] INFO in myblog: MyBlog is running
[2021-02-03 13:56:57.535] DEBUG in intro: rendering about page
[2021-01-08 15:29:55,707] DEBUG in intro: rendering home page
```

If you set the environment variable `FLASK_ENV=production` and run the MyBlog application, any DEBUG messages generated by the app won't be present in the logging output. Suppressing DEBUG messages is useful in production environments to keep from cluttering the logging output with development information.

7.9   *Adding a favicon*

A favicon is a graphic image used as a shortcut to represent a website. Supporting a favicon gives the MyBlog application some additional professionalism, so we'll add one.

The code in `examples/CH_07/examples/07` includes two versions of the MyBlog brand graphic; one in the .ico format (icon) and one in the .svg format (Scalable Vector Graphics). The first will give a browser window tab holding the MyBlog application the small brand icon. The second appears alongside the MyBlog text in the navigation bar. In this context, the brand icon is a visual shorthand associated with the MyBlog application.

The `favicon.ico` file has to be served from the MyBlog application when requested by the browser. The browser expects to find it in the root folder, which won't be part of any Flask Blueprint in MyBlog. The `favicon.ico` is made available by adding a route to it directly in the `app/__init__.py` file, inside the `app.app_context()` context manager:

```
@app.route('/favicon.ico')
def favicon():
    return send_from_directory(
        os.path.join(app.root_path, 'static'),
        'favicon.ico',
        mimetype="image/vnd.microsoft.icon"
    )
```

The code registers the URL route where the browser is looking for the `favicon()` function. Flask uses the `send_from_directory()` function to get the file's path, the filename, and the mime type and return it to the browser. The `send_from_directory()` function must be imported to make it available. The code in the repository does this.

You'll also add the MyBlog brand SVG image in the navigation bar built in the `base.html` template. The image is added immediately before the MyBlog text in the navbar brand section of the template:

```
<img src="{{url_for('static', filename='images/myblog_brand_icon.svg')}}"
    alt=""
    width="30"
    height="24">
```

This HTML code adds an image link that finds the `myblog_brand_icon.svg` file in the application root static folder and scales it appropriately for display in the navigation bar. Running the MyBlog application in `examples/CH_07/examples/07` presents a browser display that includes the `favicon.ico` and `myblog_brand_icon.svg` image files.

The `favicon.ico` file is displayed in the browser tab containing the MyBlog application. The `myblog_brand_icon.svg` file is displayed immediately to the left of the MyBlog text in the navigation bar. Both are shown in the figure 7.14 screenshot of the application. The brand graphic and name are clickable links returning the user to the application's home page.

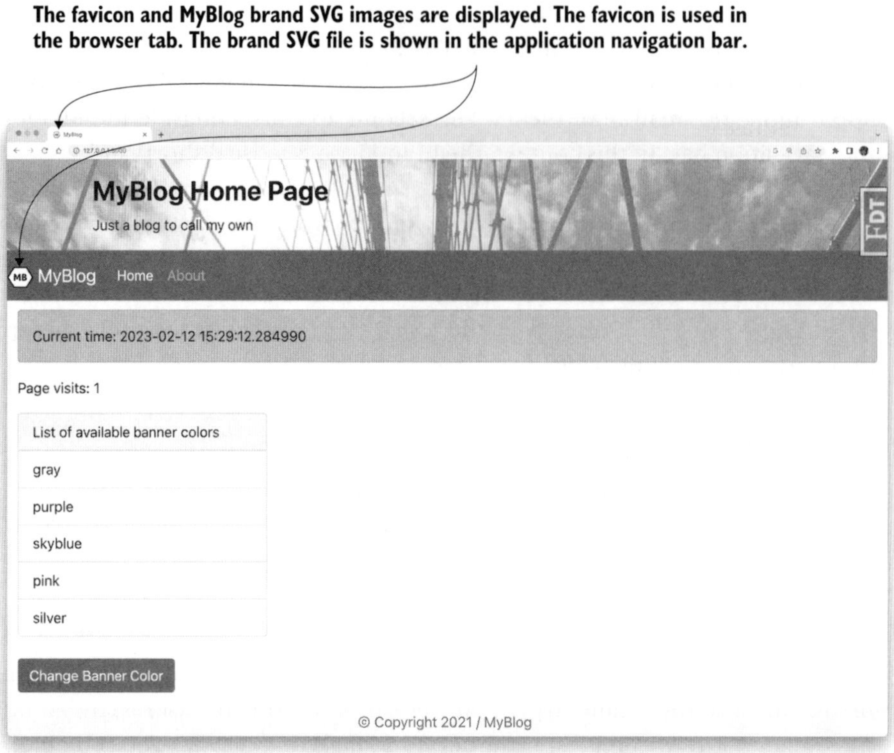

The favicon and MyBlog brand SVG images are displayed. The favicon is used in the browser tab. The brand SVG file is shown in the application navigation bar.

Figure 7.14   The browser display, including the favicon and MyBlog brand SVG images

7.10   Closing thoughts

Having Bootstrap integrated into the application goes a long way toward making MyBlog look polished and professional while at the same time reducing the development workload of creating that look and feel. The refactoring work done to MyBlog gives you a good foundation from which to grow the application further. Adding new features will be simpler because backtracking to address initial assumptions will be avoided.

By adding external configuration files to MyBlog, you've enabled the creation of multiple run-time environments and moved sensitive information to a more protected space. The use of configuration files also lets you add the Flask Debug Toolbar and logging levels to the MyBlog application.

You've taken some web development concepts and tools in hand where we can examine them with a magnifying glass to see their details and how they fit together. Being able to look closely at how modules work and connect will be key to adding new features. The next chapter will build on this excellent foundation by adding user authentication and creation, allowing the MyBlog application to secure pages to logged-in users only.

Summary

- By using the Bootstrap styling framework, we get good-looking and powerful styles and user interactions but keep the focus of our Python work. This helps to reduce technical domain switching between Python and CSS/JavaScript UI work.

- Moving from custom CSS to a framework like Bootstrap not only reduces styling workload but makes a website's look and feel more consistent across different browsers and operating systems.

- Restructuring the simple web application from the previous chapter allows us to keep complexity manageable and extensibility possible.

- Flask's Blueprint feature gives us a convenient way to structure the related web application URL endpoints into namespaces.

- Configuration files for an application should have public and private components. Public configuration information can be stored in repositories so others can work on the app and access the public configuration. Private or secret configuration information should never be present in a repository, as that risks exposure of the information.

- Logging information from a web application is useful to monitor the application's health and use. It also provides useful information about how to see and find problems that aid with debugging an application.

Do I know you?
Authentication

The MyBlog web application supports many users so they can post engaging content that the community will read. In addition, that community can read and comment on the content posted by other users. However, it's unlikely users want the content that they created edited or deleted by a user other than themselves.

To control who can access and use the MyBlog site, we'll need to identify users. Identifying users on a web application is called authenticating a user. This allows the application to ensure a user is who they claim to be.

Providing authentication to the MyBlog application is the intent of this chapter. However, doing so with a web application presents some unique challenges.

8.1   *The HTTP protocol is stateless*

The MyBlog web application follows the request/response model supported by HTTP. The user creates an HTTP GET request from the browser, and the server responds by sending the requested HTML, CSS, JavaScript, and image files back. Nothing in that transaction implies that the server has prior knowledge about the requests it received. The HTTP protocol is stateless, meaning each request is complete and independent from any previous request. The server maintains no memory of past, present, or future request/response transactions.

In this model, the request must contain all the necessary information so the server can build the appropriate response. Even if the same request is made to the server multiple times, the server will rebuild the same response each time.

If servers using the HTTP protocol have no memory, how do retail shopping sites know who you are when you purchase things? How does the web application running on that site remember the shopping cart you've created across multiple request/ response transactions? And most importantly, how does a shopping site ensure the credit card belongs to the user making the purchase request? The answers to these questions involve adding state information to the transactions between the client's browser and the web application server.

8.1.1   *Sessions*

A session allows the server to relate information about a user to incoming requests. The session commonly establishes the relationship with a cryptographically strong unique ID value generated by the server and saved as a cookie in the client's browser. This is known as a session cookie, though the client's actual cookie name can vary depending on the server framework in use.

The session usually contains a unique identifier the server encrypted when the session was created. To prevent the session from being modified on the client side, the unique identifier is encrypted before being passed to the client. Thereafter, every request the client makes includes the encrypted identifier.

When a request with a session arrives at the server, the server can decrypt the unique identifier and relate it to a specific user and any user information the server maintains—for example, a user's name, shopping cart, and more. The server can retain state information from one request to the next by layering a session on the HTTP protocol.

FLASK SESSIONS

Flask supports the use of sessions and makes them available to the MyBlog application. A session cookie doesn't exist between a client and the server until the server explicitly creates it. You can create a session by adding information to any URL route handler code you develop. The session is created and added to the client as a cookie in the response when that URL is accessed.

Flask uses the SECRET_KEY we created in the configuration from the previous chapter to sign the session cookie when created cryptographically. By doing this, the cookie can be viewed on the client side but can't be modified unless the SECRET_KEY is available. As mentioned in the previous chapter, when the SECRET_KEY is added to enable the Flask Debug Toolbar, it is essential that the SECRET_KEY be cryptographically strong and kept private.

By default, session cookies exist until the client browser is closed. This can be changed by modifying the session's permanent attribute, a Python datetime.timedelta() value. You can make a session exist for a year by adding the following in the server code:

```
                                            Marks the session
                                            as permanent
session.permanent = True          ⟵
app.permanent_session_lifetime =            Uses the Flask app instance to set the
➥datetime.timedelta(days=365)     ⟵         lifetime of the permanent session
```

Once a session exists, you can use it to maintain information across the request/ response transaction. Using a session cookie for information storage is convenient but has limitations. A cookie has a memory size limit imposed on it by the browser that can vary from browser to browser. The memory constraint on cookie size is one problem; another is the size of the data going across the internet for every request/ response message.

The information stored in a cookie is sent back and forth with every transaction between the client and the browser. Even in the age of widely available high-speed internet access, that's still a concern, especially for mobile devices. The solution to both these concerns is to use the session cookie to store the unique user identifier value and incorporate it on the server side to retrieve all the other information necessary to build the correct response to the request.

8.2   Remembering someone

Remembering the user gives the MyBlog application ways to control what features are available to users. For example, blog entries and comments are visible to anyone, but the ability to add a new blog entry or comment on an existing one is reserved for known users.

The user information described previously can be stored on the server and retrieved using the session cookie's unique user identifier. A unique user identifier value has to be created and stored and then used to authenticate that user. For a website, identifying a user happens when a user logs in through an authentication system.

8.2.1   Authentication

The MyBlog application uses the flask_login extension module from the Python Package Index (https://pypi.org/). The flask_login extension gives the MyBlog application session management abilities and tools to log users in and out and handle the somewhat difficult "remember me" functionality. It also adds protection to URL endpoints so only authenticated users can access the protected endpoints.

The login process follows the common email/password pattern to authenticate users. The process is illustrated in figure 8.1. The user's email address is a valid choice as a unique identifier because it is already unique and likely well remembered. From a high-level view, the login system you're going to create follows a stepwise workflow.

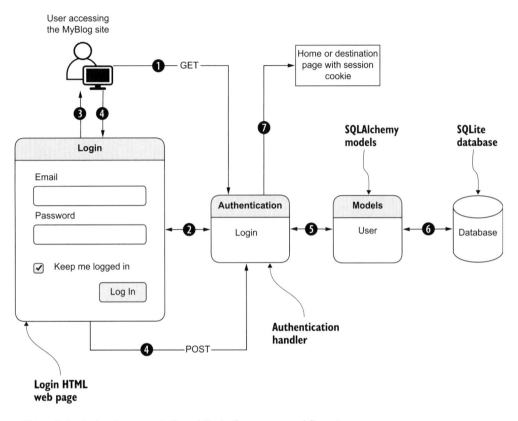

Figure 8.1 A visual representation of the login process workflow steps

The user login process follows this sequence of steps:

1 The user makes a GET request from their browser to the authentication login URL endpoint.
2 The authentication login handler responds to the GET request by returning the rendered login HTML page.
3 The user fills out the login page form fields and submits the form.
4 The form is submitted to the authentication login system using a POST request.
5 The login system tries to find a user with a matching email and password by using the models supported by the application.
6 The User model tries to find a user with a matching email and password in the application storage system.

7 If a matching user is found, the user is directed to the home page or the original destination page that the user wanted to view.

Because powerful computer CPU and GPU hardware are readily available, the ability
to crack user passwords is easier for hackers to implement. The MyBlog application
uses the `Flask_bcrypt` extension to hash the passwords stored on the server. The
`bcrypt` functionality creates a computationally expensive hash, making it resistant to
brute force attacks, even with increasing computer power.

> **TIP** Plain-text passwords should never be stored in a database and should
> always be cryptographically hashed first. This means your users will have to
> reset their passwords if they forget them. It also means the user accounts are
> protected if a hacker manages to gain access to your site's database, as the
> passwords are encrypted.

Figure 8.1 shows a storage mechanism accessed by step six. The `flask_login` extension requires this storage to persist users to retrieve and identify them later. To do this,
you'll use SQLAlchemy to manage the user data in an SQLite database. This chapter
focuses primarily on authenticating users and will defer more detailed information
about SQLAlchemy and utilizing a database until chapter 10.

To install all the modules necessary to run the example applications for this chapter, run the following command from within a Python virtual environment using the
`requirements.txt` file from the repository:

```
pip install -r requirements.txt
```

This makes the modules available in the code you create to add authentication.

LOGINMANAGER

First, add the modules necessary for authentication, password encryption, and user
persistence to the `app/__init__.py` module. Adding them to the import section at
the top of the module makes the functionality available to the `create_app()` application factory function:

```
import os
import yaml
from pathlib import Path
from flask import Flask, send_from_directory
from dynaconf import FlaskDynaconf
from Flask-sqlalchemy import SQLAlchemy          ⟵┐  Imports the SQLAlchemy
from flask_login import LoginManager        ⟵    │  functionality to manage
from Flask_bcrypt import Bcrypt   ⟵┐             ┘  the data persistence
import logging                     │       Imports the LoginManager to
import logging.config              │       handle user authentication
                             Imports the Bcrypt module
                             to cryptographically
                             encrypt user passwords
```

Then, right above the `create_app()` function, add new global instance variables for
the new functionality:

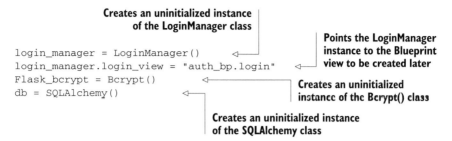

Inside the scope of the `create_app()` function in the initialize plugins section, initialize the new instance variables you just created with the app instance variable as follows:

```
os.environ["ROOT_PATH_FOR_DYNACONF"] = app.root_path
dynaconf.init_app(app)
login_manager.init_app(app)
flask_bcrypt.init_app(app)
db.init_app(app)
```

In the import routes section, import an `auth` module that you'll create shortly:

```
from . import intro
from . import auth
```

In the register blueprints section, register an `auth` Blueprint that will be created soon:

```
app.register_blueprint(intro.intro_bp)
app.register_blueprint(auth.auth_bp)
```

Add this new section just above the `return app` line at the bottom of the `create_app()` function:

```
db.create_all()
```
Creates the SQLite database if it doesn't already exist

The new code uses functionality that's defined in later sections of this chapter. This work initializes the authentication, encryption, and database systems whenever the app package is accessed or imported. The next step is to create the `auth` Blueprint that handles the user authentication functionality.

AUTH BLUEPRINT

Like the `intro` Blueprint, the `auth` Blueprint is a Python package containing distinct functionality. Create a directory named `auth` under the app package and then create an __init__.py file inside the `auth` directory. The __init__.py file generates and initializes the `auth_bp` Blueprint instance as we've done before:

```
from flask import Blueprint

auth_bp = Blueprint(
    "auth_bp", __name__,
    static_folder="static",
```

```
        static_url_path="/auth/static",
        template_folder="templates"
)

from . import auth
```

This code creates the `auth_bp` Blueprint instance whenever the `auth` package is accessed or imported. The actual authentication functionality is contained in the `auth.py` file also created in the `app/auth` directory:

```
from logging import getLogger
from flask import render_template, redirect, url_for, request
from . import auth_bp
from ..models import db_session_manager, User
from .. import login_manager
from .forms import LoginForm
from flask-login import login_user, logout_user, current_user
from werkzeug.urls import url_parse

logger = getLogger(__name__)


@login_manager.user_loader
def load_user(user_id):
    with db_session_manager() as db_session:
        return db_session.query(User).get(user_id)


@auth_bp.route("/login", methods=["GET", "POST"])
def login():
    form = LoginForm()
    if form.validate_on_submit():
        with db_session_manager() as db_session:
            user = db_session.query(User)
                .filter(User.email == form.email.data)
                .one_or_none()
            if user is None or not
            user.verify_password(form.password.data):
                flash("Invalid email or
                password", "warning")
                return redirect(
                    [url_for("auth_bp.login"))
            login_user(user,
            remember=form.remember_me.data)
            next = request.args.get("next")
            if not next or
            url_parse(next).netloc != "":
                next = url_for("intro_bp.home")
            return redirect(next)
    return render_template("login.html", form=form)
```

Annotations:
- Imports the auth_bp Blueprint instance from the package
- Imports the models, which will be created next
- Imports the login_manager instance from the package
- Imports the LoginForm, which will be created in the next section
- The function called every time the login_manager needs to determine if the user exists
- The login function registered with the auth_bp Blueprint for the "/login" route
- Begins a database session context manager scope to close the database session when the scope ends
- Gets a user from the database based on the form email value
- If no user is found, or the password doesn't verify, warn the user and redirect to the login.
- Sets the logged-in user and creates a session cookie

The `auth.py` module creates a route called `"/login"` associated with the `auth_bp` Blueprint instance and associates it with the `login()` handler function. The `login()` handler function has two purposes. When it is called because of an HTTP GET request, it returns the rendered `login.html` template, which will be created in the next section. If the function is called as the result of an HTTP `POST` request, it will process the contents of the form parameters in the `login.html` template.

The `if form.validate_on_submit()` code determines if the HTTP request method is a `GET` or a `POST` and branches accordingly. If the method is a `POST`, it will validate the form parameters against a set of rules configured in the `LoginForm` class. If the form parameters are valid, the function takes the following actions:

- Gets a user from the database using the form email parameter.
- If the user doesn't exist or the form password parameter is not valid:
  - Flashes a warning message to the user and re-renders the login screen. Flask uses the term *Flash* to mean presenting additional information to the user.
- If the user does exist and the form password parameter is valid:
  - Updates the login manager system about the user and creates a session cookie to remember them.
- Gets the page to which the user was trying to navigate when presented with the login action.
- Validates the request for that page if the `netloc` attribute is valid.
- Redirects the user to that page or the home page if `netloc` is empty.

USER MODELS

One of the goals of adding a login mechanism to the MyBlog application was to layer state information on top of the HTTP protocol to remember the user. Using the `flask_login` system, you're getting closer to that, but we need to have a unique identifier to save in the session cookie. The identifier can be used to retrieve information about the user.

Both require us to define and implement a user data structure. We will create a Python SQLAlchemy class—`User`—that will be stored in an SQLite database.

SQLite is a relational database system that Python can access via modules. An in-depth discussion about databases and accessing them with SQLAlchemy will be presented in chapter 10. Figure 8.2 shows all the information you'll be storing about logged-in users—their name, email, hashed password, and whether they are active. The created and

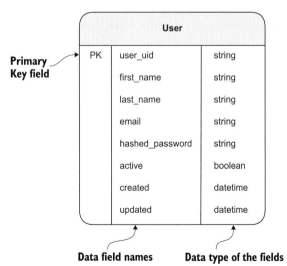

Figure 8.2   The ERD (entity relationship diagram) of the `User` table showing its fields and their data types

updated fields are simple audit information showing a timestamp when the record was created or updated.

The MyBlog application will store and present information it remembers, such as users, blog content, and comments. Each item will need to be defined and implemented as you create more features that the application supports. Because everything the MyBlog application can present is stored in a database, you'll start by using a database term—*models*.

The `app/models.py` module holds all database models that define and implement everything the MyBlog application stores. Because you need a `User` model to enable users to log into the system, let's create the `app/models.py` file now. The first thing to do in the `app/models.py` file is to import the modules needed:

```
from contextlib import contextmanager
from flask_bcrypt import (
    generate_password_hash,
    check_password_hash
)
from . import db
from flask_login import UserMixin
from uuid import uuid4
from datetime import datetime
```

The `import` statements give the `app/models.py` module access to the functionality needed to create the `User` class. The `User` class is employed with the `flask_login` extension to authenticate a user of the MyBlog application. Authenticating a user means identifying and verifying that the user is known to the MyBlog application and can access features available to those users.

We'll begin by creating the `User` class, which contains information about the user—their name, email address, and password, as well as the unique ID associated with the user that will be stored in the HTTP session cookie.

UUID DATABASE PRIMARY KEYS

When creating a database table, a common practice is to use an auto-incrementing integer value as the unique ID associated with each record in the table. Instead, the MyBlog application will use UUID values for this unique ID, called the *primary key*, for records in the table. A UUID is a long string of alphanumeric characters that is unique worldwide. The pros and cons of taking this approach are covered in chapter 10.

A small function is created to supply UUID string values when `User` records are created and inserted into the database:

```
def get_uuid():
    return uuid4().hex
```

The `get_uuid()` function uses the imported `uuid4()` function to create UUID values and then returns the `hex` string version of that value. Returning the `hex` string version makes the UUID value a little shorter.

Next, you must add the definition of the `User` class to `app/models.py`. This class uses multiple inheritances to obtain built-in functionality from the modules imported at the top of `app/models.py`.

The first is the `UserMixin` class, which presents the child class methods that the `flask_login` system expects to be available to access `User` information. The second is the `db.Model` class, which comes from the `db` instance variable created and initialized in the app module. The `db.Model` class gives a child class that inherits from it the SQLAlchemy functionality needed to interact with the database and define the columns in a table associated with the attributes of the class:

The User class multiply inherits from the UserMixin and db.Model classes.

Defines the unique ID value for User records using the get_uuid function

Defines the table name in the database where records of this class will be stored

Defines other User attributes

Defines record-auditing timestamp attributes

```python
class User(UserMixin, db.Model):
    __tablename__ = "user"
    user_uid = db.Column(db.String, primary_key=True, default=get_uuid)
    first_name = db.Column(db.String, nullable=False)
    last_name = db.Column(db.String, nullable=False)
    email = db.Column(db.String, nullable=False,
        unique=True, index=True)
    hashed_password = db.Column("password",
        db.String, nullable=False)
    active = db.Column(db.Boolean, nullable=False, default=False)
    created = db.Column(db.DateTime, nullable=False,
        default=datetime.utcnow)
    updated = db.Column(db.DateTime, nullable=False,
        default=datetime.utcnow, onupdate=datetime.utcnow)

    def get_id(self):
        return self.user_uid

    @property
    def password(self):
        raise AttributeError("user password can't be read")

    @password.setter
    def password(self, password):
        self.hashed_password = generate_password_hash(password)

    def verify_password(self, password):
        return check_password_hash(self.hashed_password, password)

    def __repr__(self):
        return f"""
        user_uid: {self.user_uid}
        name: {self.first_name} {self.last_name}
        email: {self.email}
        active: {'True' if self.active else 'False'}
        """
```

The `User` class inherits from the imported `UserMixin` and `db.Model` classes. This means the `User` class IS-A `UserMixin` class and IS-A `db.model` class and has access to both classes' methods and attributes.

By inheriting from the `UserMixin` class, the `User` class gets methods needed to function by the `LoginManager()` instance created in the app package. These methods use attributes defined in the `User` class to authenticate a user.

The `User` class also inherits from the `db.Model` and is how the SQLAlchemy functionality is added to the class, giving it access to the database. The `User` model defines the structure of a single row of data in a table named `"user"`, where each defined attribute is a column in a database table record.

The `get_id()` method overrides the method of the same name provided by the `UserMixin` class, replacing its functionality. The default `get_id()` method returns a `self.id` value, but because the `User` class defines the unique ID attribute name as `user_uid`, it's necessary to override the default behavior. The `get_id()` method is used whenever the `LoginManager` instance needs to determine if the unique identifier stored in the session cookie relates to a real user in the system.

Note the pair of `password()` methods that create a write-only attribute on the `User` class. Because it's not helpful (or even possible) to read the password because it's cryptographically hashed, the method decorated with `@property` raises an attribute error.

The `password()` method decorated with `@password.setter` creates the write behavior. The method intercepts setting the password attribute and generates a cryptographically strong hash of the password, which is stored in the `hashed_password` class attribute. Even though `hashed_password` is the attribute's name, the corresponding database column is named `"password"`. The `verify_password()` method is used in the `auth.py` module to determine if the password retrieved from the login form template matches the hashed version stored for the user.

8.2.2 Logging in

Coding up an HTML form to gather user input for the email and password is a straightforward process. With a submit button, the form contents can be sent to the MyBlog server as an HTTP `POST` request, and you can then process the form information.

Because users can make unintentional and intentional errors when entering form data, validating the form input information is necessary. For example, are the email and password within the required length restrictions? Are the email and password present at all? Does the email address conform to a standardized format? Implementing these validation steps is extra work that's difficult to get right. Fortunately, there's another Flask extension that dramatically simplifies form handling—`Flask-WTF`.

FLASK-WTF

The `Flask-WTF` extension integrates the more generalized WTForms package into Flask. Using the extension allows you to bind MyBlog server code to HTML form elements and automate handling those elements when the corresponding form is received by a handler using the HTTP `POST` method. To create the login form and its validation, add a new file to the `app/auth` package named `forms.py`:

```
from flask_wtf import FlaskForm
from wtforms import PasswordField,
➡BooleanField, SubmitField
from wtforms.fields.html5 import EmailField
from wtforms.validators import DataRequired,
➡Length, Email, EqualTo

class LoginForm(FlaskForm):
    email = EmailField(
        "Email",
        validators=[DataRequired(), Length(
            min=4,
            max=128,
            message="Email must be between 4
            ➡and 128 characters long"
        ), Email()],
        render_kw={"placeholder": " "}
    )
    password = PasswordField(
        "Password",
        validators=[DataRequired(), Length(
            min=3,
            max=64,
            message="Password must be between 3
            ➡and 64 characters long"
        )],
        render_kw={"placeholder": " "}
    )
    remember_me = BooleanField(" Keep me logged in")
cancel = SubmitField(
    label="Cancel",
    render_kw={"formnovalidate": True},
    )
    submit = SubmitField("Log In")
```

- Imports the FlaskForm class
- Imports the field type classes to create in the form
- Imports the field validation classes used to validate the form elements
- Creates the LoginForm, inheriting from the base FlaskForm class
- Creates the email form element and validators
- Creates the password form element and validators
- Creates the remember_me form element
- Creates the form cancel button
- Creates the form submit button

The LoginForm class defines an object to create when the form is rendered, containing all HTML elements in the form. The elements have a required first parameter—the name used for labels, the element form name, and the ID value. The validators parameter defines a list of validation steps that the element must pass for the form to be valid. The render_kw parameter is optional and defines additional HTML form attributes to be rendered with the element.

The email element is an instance of the EmailField class. The class constructor has a parameter "Email" used as is for any label rendered with the element and converted to lowercase when used for name and ID values in the HTML DOM (document object model). The validators define that an entry is required; the length must be between 4 and 128 characters long inclusive, and the element value must be in a valid email format.

The password element is an instance of the PasswordField class. The PasswordField renders the element as an HTML type of password, so the user-entered text is shown as a sequence of asterisk characters. The class constructor has a parameter `"Password"` used in the same manner as the email element. The `validators` define that a password is required, and the length must be between 3 and 64 characters long inclusive.

Notice the `render_kw={"placeholder": " "}` parameters on both the email and password attributes. These are necessary to make the Bootstrap styling input element's visual functionality work as intended.

The `remember_me` element is an instance of the `BooleanField` class. This will be rendered as an HTML checkbox with the label "Keep me logged in."

The `cancel` element is an instance of the `SubmitField` class and creates a cancel button that will take the user to the home screen when clicked. The `submit` element is also an instance of the `SubmitField` class and creates a submit button when the form is rendered. With the `forms.py` module in place, you'll need to create an HTML page where the `LoginForm` class will render the contained elements.

LOGIN FORM

The `login.html` file is created in the `app/auth/templates` directory, where the `auth_bp` Blueprint can access it.

```
{% extends "base.html" %}
{% import "macros.jinja" as macros %}

{% block content %}
<div class="login-wrapper mx-auto mt-3">
    <div class="container login">
        <form method="POST" novalidate>
            <div class="card">
                <h5 class="card-header">
                    User Login
                </h5>
                <div class="card-body">
                    <div class="card-text">
                        {{form.csrf_token}}
                        <div
                        class="form-floating mb-3">
                            {{form.email(
                            class_="form-control")}}
                            {{form.email.label(
                            class_="form-label")}}
                            {{macros.
                            validation_errors(form.email.errors)}}
                        </div>
                        <div class="mb-3">
                            {{form.password(
                            class_="form-control")}}
                            {{form.password.label(
                            class_="form-label")}}
                {{macros.validation_errors(form.password.errors)}}
                        </div>
```

Imports the macros.jinja macros file, which we'll discuss next

The login.html template inherits from base.html so it gets all the MyBlog page elements.

Cross-Site Request Forgery protection token reviewed at the end of this chapter

Creates the email element on the page, passing the element Bootstrap class information

Creates the password element on the page, passing the element Bootstrap class information

Creates the remember me element on the page, passing the element Bootstrap class information

```
                                    <div class="mb-3">
                                        {{form.remember_me}}
                                        {{form.remember_me.label(
                                        ➥class_="form-check-label")}}
                                    </div>
                                </div>
                            </div>
                        <div class="card-footer text-end">
                            {{form.cancel(
                            ➥class_="btn btn-warning me-2")}}
                            {{form.submit(
                            ➥class_="btn btn-primary")}}
                        </div>
                    </div>
    </form>
        </div>
    </div>
{% endblock %}

{% block styles %}
    {{ super() }}
    <link rel="stylesheet" type="text/css"
    ➥href="{{ url_for('.static',
    ➥filename='css/login.css') }}" />
{% endblock %}
```

Creates the cancel button, passing the element Bootstrap class information

Creates the submit button, passing the element Bootstrap class information

Remember back to the auth.py module and the login() handler assigned to the /login route. Two lines of code are of interest as related to rendering the login form and connecting it to the LoginForm instance created in forms.py:

```
form = LoginForm()
```

and

```
return render_template("login.html", form=form)
```

These two lines of code are important when the login() handler is invoked by an HTTP GET or POST request. The first creates the LoginForm class instance variable. The second passes that form instance to render_template as the second parameter, giving the Jinja template engine access to the form instance when rendering the login.html template elements. This is how the LoginForm definition instance is connected to the login.html template.

When a GET request is received, the template engine uses the form instance to help render it in the browser window. When a POST request is received, the body of the form contains the form data entered by the user, which populates the LoginForm attributes. The form validation methods for each attribute run to validate that the form data meets the validation requirements.

Running the code in examples/CH_08/examples/01 and navigating to 127.0.0.1:5000/login presents the login form shown in the figure 8.3 screenshot to the user. The login form presents input elements for the user to enter their email and password and whether they should be kept logged in.

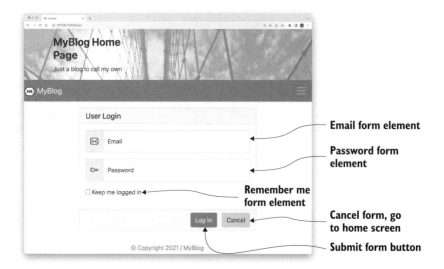

Figure 8.3   The MyBlog-generated login screen lets the user enter their email and password to access the site.

JINJA MACROS

Notice this line in the `login.html` template that's part of the email and password definition sections:

```
{{macros.validation_errors(form.email.errors)}}
```

This references a Jinja macro in the `app/templates/macros.jinja` file imported at the top of the `login.html` template. The `validation_errors()` macro handles displaying any `LoginForm` validation errors to the user so they can be corrected:

```
{% macro validation_errors(errors) %}
    {% if errors %}
        {% for error in errors %}
            <div class="text-danger small">{{error}}</div>
        {% endfor %}
    {% endif %}
{% endmacro %}
```

A macro is a function definition in the Jinja template engine, much like defining a Python function. The `validation_errors()` macro receives a list of `LoginForm` validation errors. It first checks if there are any errors and, if so, iterates over that list, displaying the error message in small red text below the form field that failed validation. The results of entering an invalid email address and a password of only two characters render the `login.html` template and include error messages indicating the problem to the user. Those errors are shown in the figure 8.4 screenshot.

You'll notice nothing happens if you enter a valid email address and password with an acceptable length and click the submit button. The `login.html` template is

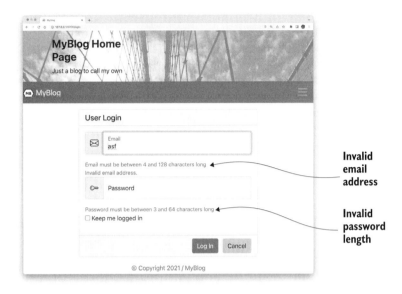

Figure 8.4   Errors presented if the email or password is invalid

rendered again, and there is no information presented to the user about what, if any-thing, happened. Looking back at the `login()` function in the `auth.py` file, there is a conditional check in the code right after trying to find a user by their email address:

```
user = db_session.query(User)
    .filter(User.email == form.email.data)
    .one_or_none()
if user is None or not user.verify_password(form.password.data):
    flash("Invalid email or password", "warning")
 return redirect(url_for("auth_bp.login"))
```

If the user is not found, it has a value of `None`, and the code executes the `flash()` message function and redirects to the login route; the `login.html` template is ren-dered again. No user was found because none had been created in the application yet. The intended code for this condition ran, and the user was redirected to the login screen. However, why isn't the `flash()` function doing anything to inform the user by displaying the invalid email or password message?

8.3   *News flash*

The Flask `flash()` function provides users feedback about events and activities in an application. When a message is created and sent to the `flash()` function, the mes-sage is appended to a list of messages available in the context of the next request and only the next request. This makes those flash messages available to the next rendered template.

The template has to access the message list and add the messages to the rendered HTML to display the flash messages. A direct way to do this is to iterate over the flash messages list using a Jinja `for` loop and create an HTML unordered list of the messages as part of the rendered HTML. We'll use Bootstrap to render the messages to display them temporarily and not disrupt the template style and presentation.

8.3.1 Improving the login form

The Bootstrap framework provides a component called toasts, which are lightweight alert messages that "float" above the content. Toasts have been made popular in both mobile and desktop operating systems. They are useful in the MyBlog application because they don't disrupt the template layout and are transient, and they disappear soon after the message is presented.

Because any URL endpoint handler can call the `flash()` function, it's useful to centralize where the flash messages are handled. The `base.html` template is ideal as it's intended to be inherited by every template in the MyBlog system.

Creating a Bootstrap toast involves a significant amount of HTML code that would need to be added to the `base.html` template file. A better option is to pull the flash message handling out of the `base.html` template and create a Jinja macro. The `flask_flash_messages()` macro function is added to the `app/templates/macros.jinja` file:

```
{% macro flask_flash_messages() %}                          ◁——  Begins the definition of the
    {% with messages = get_flashed_messages(                     flask_flash_messages() macro
    ➥with_categories=true) %}          ◁————————
        {% if messages %}                    Begins a with context block to
            <div aria-live="polite"          get the flash messages
                aria-atomic="true"
                class="position-relative">
             <div class="toast-container position-absolute top-0 end-0 p-3"
                    style="z-index: 2000; opacity: 1;">
                {% for category, message in messages %}   ◁————————
                    {% set category = "white" if                    Begins the for loop
                    ➥category == "message" else category %}        to iterate over the
                    {% set text_color = "text-dark" if category in [   list of flash messages
                      "warning",
                      "info",
                      "light",
                      "white",
                      ] else "text-white"
                    %}
                    <div class="toast bg-{{category}}"
                        role="alert"
                        aria-live="assertive"
                        aria-atomic="true">
                      <div class="toast-header bg-{{category}} {{text_color}}">
                        {% set toast_title = category if category in [
                          "success", "danger", "warning", "info"
                          ] else "message" %}
                        <strong class="me-auto">MyBlog: {{toast_title.title()}}</strong>
```

Are there any flash messages to process?

```
                    <button type="button"
                            class="btn-close"
                            data-bs-dismiss="toast"
                            aria-label="Close"></button>
                </div>
                <div class="toast-body {{text_color}}">
                    {{message}}
                </div>
            </div>
        {% endfor %}
        </div>
      </div>
    {% endif %}
  {% endwith %}
{% endmacro %}
```

Most of the flask_flash_messages() macro concerns itself with generating the Bootstrap styling required to present toast messages. The toast messages are added to the rendered template but aren't displayed to the user immediately. To do that requires JavaScript code to show the messages. The JavaScript code has to run every time a template that inherits from base.html is rendered, so create an app/static/js/base.js file as follows:

```
(function() {
    var option = {
        animation: true,
        delay: 3000
    }
    var toastElements = [].slice.call(document.querySelectorAll('.toast'))
    toastElements.map(function (toastElement) {
        toast = new bootstrap.Toast(toastElement, option)
        toast.show()
    })
}())
```

This code creates a self-invoking anonymous JavaScript function, meaning it runs as soon as the browser JavaScript engine parses the code. This kind of function is useful when you want to run some code immediately and keep variables out of the global JavaScript scope. Because base.js is included at the end of the base.html template, the function runs after the HTML DOM elements have been created, including the toast elements.

The option variable is a JavaScript object literal and is something like a Python dictionary. It contains configuration information passed to the Bootstrap Toast class to animate the toast message and remove it after 3000 milliseconds, or 3 seconds.

The function then creates the toastElements array variable containing all the toast HTML DOM elements on the page. An array in JavaScript is similar to a Python list. JavaScript arrays have a method called map that applies a function to each element in the array. The anonymous function passed to the map creates a new Toast instance passing the option object and then calls the show() method to display the toast message in the browser window.

Suppose you run the application in `examples/CH_08/examples/02` and enter a valid email address and password, but the values are unknown to the MyBlog application. In that case, the login page will be re-rendered with a toast message about the email or password being invalid. The screenshot in figure 8.5 shows the error produced.

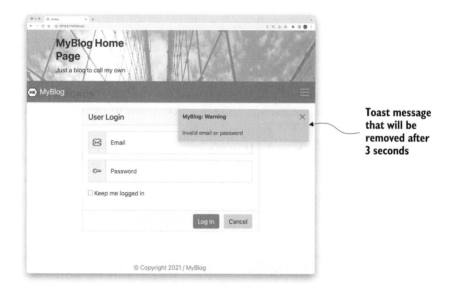

Figure 8.5   The rendered template presenting a Bootstrap toast message containing an error message

Now that users can theoretically log into the MyBlog application, it's time to allow a new user to register with the application, so they have an account to use when logging in!

8.4   *Making new friends*

Registering new users on the MyBlog application also uses the `flask_login` extension. The register-new-user process follows a pattern like the login process, as shown by figure 8.6. Instead of looking for a user, it creates and saves one to the database.

The register-new-user process is as follows:

1 The user makes a GET request from their browser to the authentication register-new-user URL endpoint.
2 The authentication register-new-user handler responds to the GET request by returning the rendered register-new-user HTML page.
3 The user fills out the register-new-user page form fields and submits the form.
4 The form is submitted to the authentication register-new-user system using a POST request.

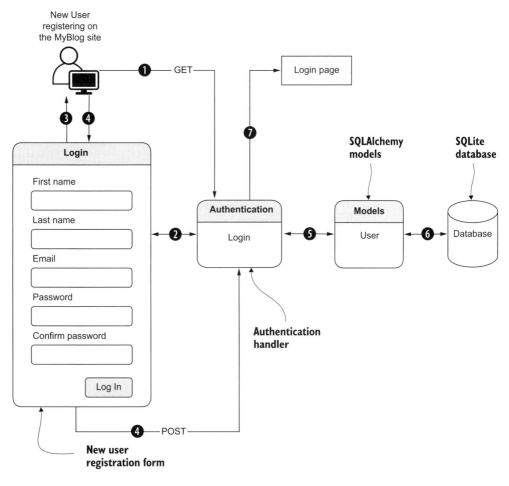

Figure 8.6 A visual representation of the register-new-user process workflow steps

5 The register-new-user system creates a user from the form data using the models supported by the application.

6 The `User` model saves the newly created user in the application storage system.

7 The user is directed to the authentication login page to enter their login credentials.

8.4.1 Auth Blueprint

The register-new-user handler is in the `app/auth/auth.py` file. Like the login handler, a form is derived from the `FlaskForm` class in the `forms.py` module called `RegisterNewUserForm`. Add this class instance to the line of code in `app/auth.py` that imports the `LoginForm` class:

```
from .forms import LoginForm, RegisterNewUserForm
```

Add a new handler to the module at the bottom of the file:

```
@auth_bp.route("/register_new_user",
    methods=["GET", "POST"])
def register_new_user():
    if current_user.is_authenticated:
        return redirect(url_for("intro_bp.home"))
    form = RegisterNewUserForm()
    if form.validate_on_submit():
        with db_session_manager() as db_session:
            user = User(
                first_name=form.first_name.data,
                last_name=form.last_name.data,
                email=form.email.data,
                password=form.password.data,
                active=True
            )
            db_session.add(user)
            db_session.commit()
            logger.debug(f"new user
                {form.email.data} added")
            return redirect(url_for("auth_bp.login"))
    return render_template("register_new_user.html",
        form=form)
```

Marks the register_new_user() function as the handler for the /register_new_user route for both GET and POST HTTP requests

Creates an instance of the RegisterNewUserForm()

If the HTTP request is a POST, validate the incoming form data.

If the user is already authenticated, redirect them to the home screen.

Creates a new user initializing the attributes with form data

Adds the newly created user to the database, logs that a new user was created, and redirects to the login page

If the HTTP request is a GET, render the empty register_new_user.html template, passing in the form instance for use in the template.

8.4.2   New user form

Repeating the pattern used for the login form, a Flask-WTForm and HTML template file were created to complete the register-new-user functionality. Add the Register-NewUserForm class definition to the app/auth/forms.py file:

```
from wtforms.validators import DataRequired, Length,
    Email, EqualTo
from wtforms import ValidationError
from ..models import User, db_session_manager

: intervening code

class RegisterNewUserForm(FlaskForm):
    first_name = StringField(
        "First Name",
        validators=[DataRequired()],
        render_kw={"placeholder": " ",
            "tabindex": 1, "autofocus": True}
    )
    last_name = StringField(
        "Last Name",
        validators=[DataRequired()],
        render_kw={"placeholder": " ",
            "tabindex": 2}
    )
    email = EmailField(
        "Email",
```

New items to add to the import section

Defines the RegisterNewUserForm class

Creates the first_name, last_name, email, password, and confirm_password form elements and validators

```
        validators=[DataRequired(), Length(
            min=4,
            max=128,
            message="Email must be between 4 and
            ➡128 characters long"
        ), Email()],
        render_kw={"placeholder": " ", "tabindex": 3}
    )
    password = PasswordField(
        "Password",
        validators=[DataRequired(), Length(
                min=3,
                max=64,
                message="Password must be between
                ➡3 and 64 characters long"
            ),
            EqualTo("confirm_password",
            ➡message="Passwords must match")
        ],
        render_kw={"placeholder": " ", "tabindex": 4}
    )
    confirm_password = PasswordField(
        "Confirm Password",
        validators=[DataRequired(), Length(
            min=3,
            max=64,
            message="Password must be between
            ➡3 and 64 characters long"
        )],
        render_kw={"placeholder": " ", "tabindex": 5}
    )
create_new_user = SubmitField("Create New User",
➡render_kw={"tabindex": 6})
    cancel = SubmitField("Cancel",
    ➡render_kw={"tabindex": 7})
```

> Creates the first_name, last_name, email, password, and confirm_password form elements and validators

> Creates the form submit buttons

This code creates the form passed to the register-new-user template to create the HTML DOM elements to render and apply validation rules when the form is submitted by a POST request. There is one additional method to add at the bottom of the RegisterNewUserForm class:

```
def validate_email(self, field):
    with db_session_manager() as db_session:
        user = db_session.query(User)
➡.filter(User.email == field.data)
➡.one_or_none()
        if user is not None:
            raise ValidationError("Email already registered")
```

The validate_email() method is a custom validation that ensures a new user isn't using an email address that already exists in the system. The FlaskForm class has the functionality to introspect classes that inherit from it. That introspection finds the validate_email() method and adds it to the validation for the email form field.

The `RegisterNewUserForm` class instance created in the handler is passed to the register_new_user.html template to render the user's form. This template is like the login.html template and isn't presented here. However, you can see the template by editing the examples/CH_08/examples/03/app/auth/templates/register_new_user.html file.

If you move to the examples/CH_08/examples/03 directory and run the MyBlog application and navigate to the 127.0.0.1:5000/register_new_user route, the form in figure 8.7 will be rendered in the browser. The form provides fields for new users to enter their first name, last name, email, and password and confirm the password. When the Create New User button is clicked, the form data is sent to the server, and the email address is checked to see if it already exists in the system. If the email is unknown in the MyBlog application, a new user is created and saved to the database.

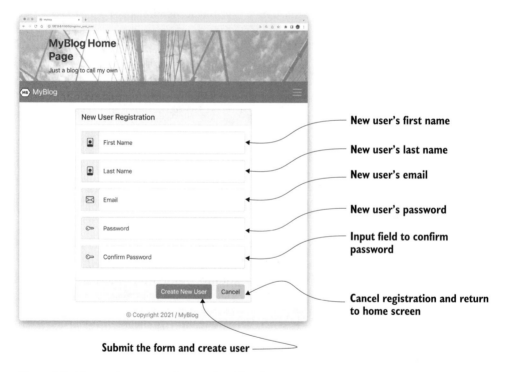

Figure 8.7   The create new user form rendered in a browser

8.4.3   *Oh yeah: logging out*

Now that users can log in to the MyBlog application, we also need to provide a way to log out. Besides nice symmetry, logging out of an authenticated application is vital so users have control over who can access the application with their credentials.

For the MyBlog application, the logout functionality is created by adding another URL route to the `auth` module. When a user navigates to the logout route, no template is presented. Instead, the route handler resets the session cookie and redirects the user to the application home page. Because the home page is available to any user, authenticated or not, this is a reasonable approach.

In the `app/auth/auth.py` module, modify the `from flask_login` line like this:

```
from flask_login import login_user, logout_user, current_user
```

And add this to the bottom of the `app/auth.py` module:

```
@auth_bp.route("/logout")
def logout():
    logout_user()
    flash("You've been logged out", "light")
    return redirect(url_for("intro_bp.home"))
```

Adds a new route and handler for logging a user out of the system

Calls the flask_login logout_user() function to log the user out

Flashes a message to inform the user they've been logged out

Redirects the user to the application home page

8.5   What's next

We've got the basics of our authentication system in place but need to add more functionality to make it fully useful. In the next chapter, you'll add the login capability to the navigation system so users can easily log in and out. We'll add the ability to confirm the user's email address, which will close the loop on authenticating that a user is who they say they are.

Users will need to reset their passwords if they've forgotten them and view and edit their profiles. We'll add these features to the MyBlog application as well.

We'll also add authorization roles to users to help the MyBlog application control what users can do when they're logged into the application. The roles will control who can create content, who can edit the content, and who can activate and deactivate that content. Once we have both authentication and authorization mechanisms in place, we can use those concepts to protect routes in the application so that only authenticated users with specific roles can navigate and see certain URL routes.

Summary

- Authentication is all about identifying who someone is in a consistent, reliable way. Doing so with the HTTP protocol takes some thought and code to make it happen.
- The Flask framework and third-party modules provide tools to aid you as a developer to manage users and the login and logout process.
- The Flask flash functionality combined with Bootstrap provides a good-looking and functional way to send messages to your users without disrupting the workflow or design of your site.

What can you do? Authorization

This chapter covers

- Adding login/logout to page navigation
- Confirming new users with email
- Allowing users to reset forgotten passwords
- Allowing existing users to change passwords
- Adding authorization roles to users
- Securing routes in the application

In the previous chapter, you created functionality to support users logging in and out of the MyBlog application. Logging in and out is essential functionality we need to make easily accessible to users. Therefore, you'll add this navigation functionality to the parent base.html template so that it's available everywhere on the MyBlog application.

9.1 Login/logout navigation

You've created a working authentication system, but, currently, it's accessible primarily by entering the URL into the browser navigation bar. Let's add the login/logout URL routes to the Bootstrap navigation system.

The authentication system has two mutually exclusive states as a user; you can only be logged in or logged out. Because of this, the authentication system is represented in the navigation menu as a single item that toggles between states depending on the user's current authentication status. Keeping with the idea of single responsibility and not overcomplicating the base.html template, the login/logout menu functionality will exist as a Jinja macro in the examples/CH_09/examples/01/app/templates/macros.jinja file:

```
{% macro build_login_logout_items(current_user) %}
    {% if not current_user.is_authenticated %}
        {% if request.endpoint == "auth_bp.login" %}
            <a class="nav-link ml-2 active"
               aria-current="page"
               href="{{url_for('auth_bp.login')}}">
        {% else %}
            <a class="nav-link ml-2"
               href="{{url_for('auth_bp.login')}}">
        {% endif %}
        Login
        </a>
    {% else %}
        <a class= "nav-link ml-2"
           href=" {{url_for('auth_bp.logout')}}">
        Logout
        </a>
    {% endif %}
{% endmacro %}
```

Begins the build_login_logout_items macro, passing in the current user from the base.html template

Is the current user unauthenticated?

Presents the login menu item and route as highlighted or not depending on the current route

Otherwise, if the current user is authenticated

Presents the logout menu item and route

The build_login_logout_items() macro will toggle the navigation display to show "login" or "logout," depending on the user's authentication state. The two menu items are tied to the login and logout URL endpoints.

The macro is added to the base.html template so the system can render it on any page the MyBlog application presents. Modify the section of code in the base.html template that creates the navigation menu to add this functionality:

```
<div class=" collapse navbar-collapse
     justify-content-between"
   id= "navbarSupportedContent">
     <div class=" navbar-nav mr-auto">
       {{ macros.build_nav_item(nav_item) }}
  </div>
  <div class="navbar-nav">
       {{ macros.build_login_logout_items(
          current_user) }}
  </div>
</div>
```

Right and left justify the two navbar-nav sections

Creates the second navbar-nav section and calls the macro to render the login/logout items

With the above changes in place, the MyBlog web application will display a highlighted login menu item when the login menu item is clicked and rendered. Run the application from the examples/CH_09/examples/01 directory and see the login menu item rendered. Figure 9.1 is a screenshot of the updated login page.

Figure 9.1 The user login registration form, including the newly added login menu item

9.2   Confirming new friends

When a potential user of the MyBlog application registers with the system, it's important to confirm who they are. This is often done by sending an email with a confirmation link to the email address they registered with. Since the MyBlog application uses the user's email address as a unique identifier, sending a confirmation email to that address closes the loop that the user intended to register with the MyBlog application. We'll add the ability to send emails from the MyBlog application so we can send the confirmation emails.

9.2.1   Sending email

Similar to using SQLite as the database, we'll implement a straightforward email system that works for MyBlog. To help keep things focused on MyBlog, I'm using an email service provider called SendInBlue (https://www.sendinblue.com/). I've set up a free account that lets the MyBlog application send 300 emails a month for free (300 is more than enough for this book).

SendInBlue provides an installable API module that lets Python applications send emails by making function calls. This module can be installed with this command:

```
pip install sib-api-v3-sdk
```

However, the module is included in the `requirements.txt` file for this chapter and was installed when you ran

```
pip install -r requirements.txt
```

at the time you built the Python virtual environment for this chapter. The SendInBlue service handles all the details of sending emails and simplifies the code we need to write for the MyBlog application.

> **TIP**   By using an external service like SendInBlue, we avoid having to set up an SMTP (Simple Mail Transfer Protocol) server. Not a small task, and outside the scope of this book.

When a new user registers with the MyBlog application on the New User Registration form, we want to add two things:

- A Boolean field called `confirmed` on the user database model, initially set to `False`
- The functionality to send an email with a confirmation link to the registering user's email address

Adding a `confirmed` field to the user model is simple enough and is shown in the `examples/CH_09/examples/02/app/models.py` code in the repository for this chapter.

EMAILER

We could send the email directly from the `auth.py` module's `register_new_user()` function, which would work fine. However, we'll likely want to send emails from elsewhere in the MyBlog application, so we'll embed the functionality into a new module that can be reused.

We'll create a new module as follows called `app/emailer.py` that has a single function, `send_mail()`:

```python
from logging import getLogger              # Imports the SendInBlue
import sib_api_v3_sdk                      # API module
from flask import current_app
from sib_api_v3_sdk.rest import ApiException

logger = getLogger(__name__)
configuration = sib_api_v3_sdk.Configuration()   # Configures the API
configuration.api_key['api-key'] =               # with your API key
    current_app.config.get("SIB_API_KEY")

def send_mail(to, subject, contents):
    api_instance = sib_api_v3_sdk.TransactionalEmailsApi(   # Creates an instance
        sib_api_v3_sdk.ApiClient(configuration))            # of the API
    smtp_email = sib_api_v3_sdk.SendSmtpEmail(
        to=[{"email": to}],
        html_content= contents,
        sender={"name": "MyBlog", "email":      # Creates the email object
        "no-reply@myblog.com"},
        subject=subject
    )
    try:
        api_instance.send_transac_email(smtp_email)   # Sends the email
        logger.debug(f"Confirmation email sent to {to}")   # object to be emailed
    except ApiException as e:
        logger.exception("Exception sending email", exc_info=e)
```

This code creates an instance of the SendInBlue API and configures it with the user's API key. I received the API key—which is in the `secrets.toml` file—when I created my account with SendInBlue.

The API instance variable `api_instance` is used to send the email object. The API expects the email contents to be in HTML, so the messages sent must include some basic HTML tags to render the email correctly.

CONFIRMATION EMAIL

Now that MyBlog can send emails, let's use it to send a confirmation email to newly registered users. The confirmation email will contain a link back to the MyBlog application. The link includes encrypted information sent along when the user clicks the link. When MyBlog handles a call to the link, it decrypts the information to determine if the request is valid. If it is, the user is confirmed in the database.

The encoded information also contains a current timestamp. When the link is clicked and the application handles that request, the timestamp is compared to the current time. The user has confirmed if the application handles the request within a timeout period. However, if the user waited longer than the defined timeout period, the confirmation link is considered expired, and the user isn't confirmed. The timeout value is set in the `settings.toml` file as 12 hours, which can be changed.

We'll add two function calls to the `register_new_user()` function handler to send the new user confirmation email. The first is a call to a new function, `send_confirmation_email(user)`, and the second is a call to the Flask `flash()` function, notifying the user with a toast message to check for the confirmation email:

```
@auth_bp.get("/register_new_user")
@auth_bp.post("/register_new_user")
def register_new_user():
    if current_user.is_authenticated:
        return redirect(url_for("intro_bp.home"))
    form = RegisterNewUserForm()
    if form.cancel.data:
        return redirect(url_for("intro_bp.home"))
    if form.validate_on_submit():
        with db_session_manager() as db_session:
            user = User(
                first_name=form.first_name.data,
                last_name=form.last_name.data,
                email=form.email.data,
                password=form.password.data,
                active=True
            )
            role_name = "admin" if user.email in
            ➥current_app.config.get("ADMIN_USERS") else "user"
            role = db_session.query(Role).filter(Role.name ==
            ➥role_name).one_or_none()
            role.users.append(user)
            db_session.add(user)
            db_session.commit()
            send_confirmation_email(user)        ◁──┐  Calls to new
            timeout = current_app.config.get(         send_confirmation_email(user)
            ➥"CONFIRMATION_LINK_TIMEOUT")             function to send email
            flash((
                "Please click the confirmation      Calls Flask flash()
                ➥link just sent "                   functionality to notify the
                f"to your email address within      user to check their email
                ➥{timeout} hours "                  within the confirmation
                "to complete your registration"     link timeout
                ➥))
```

```
                logger.debug(f"new user {form.email.data} added")
                return redirect(url_for("intro_bp.home"))
        return render_template("register_new_user.html", form=form)
```

Let's take a look at the `send_confirmation_email()` function:

```
def send_confirmation_email(user):                          Calls the new user method to
    confirmation_token = user.confirmation_token()    ◁──┐   construct a confirmation token
    confirmation_url = url_for(
        "auth_bp.confirm",                              Constructs a URL to insert in the
        confirmation_token=confirmation_token,          email that, when clicked, will inform
        _external=True                                  MyBlog that the user has confirmed
    )
    timeout = current_app.config.get(
  ➡ "CONFIRMATION_LINK_TIMEOUT")
    to = user.email
    subject = "Confirm Your Email"
    contents = (
        f"""Dear {user.first_name},<br /><br />
        Welcome to MyBlog, please click the link to    Constructs and sends an
      ➡confirm your email within {timeout} hours:       email with the confirmation
        {confirmation_url}<br /><br />                  URL to the user
        Thank you!
        """
    )
    send_mail(to=to, subject=subject,
  ➡contents=contents)
```

The `send_confirmation_email()` function calls a new method of the `User` model `confirmation_token()` to build a unique token with an expiration timeout. It then builds a URL to a new URL handler, `auth_bp.confirm`. Finally, the `_external =True` parameter causes `url_for()` to create a full URL that will work when a user clicks the link from their email client context.

Once the confirmation link is created, an email is created inline containing the confirmation link is sent to the new user. If the new user clicks the confirmation link within the 12-hour time limit, their account is confirmed.

Notice the `<br /><br />` HTML line-break elements in the email message. These HTML elements help format the message, so it's easily readable by the user.

USER CONFIRMATION TOKEN

Because the confirmation token is unique for each user, it's generated by a new method attached to the `User` model class:

```
def confirmation_token(self):
    serializer = URLSafeTimedSerializer(current_app.config["SECRET_KEY"])
    return serializer.dumps({"confirm": self.user_uid})
```

This method uses the `URLSafeTimedSerializer()` function to create a serializing instance based on the Flask `SECRET_KEY` and includes the current timestamp. Then, the serializer instance is used to create the unique token based on the new user's `user_id` value.

CONFIRM USER HANDLER

When a new user clicks the confirmation link in their email, this action makes a request to a new URL handler in the `auth` module to confirm that the token passed in the request is valid:

```
@auth_bp.get("/confirm/<confirmation_token>")          ⟵┐ Registers new/confirm
@login_required                                          │ URL route with Blueprint
def confirm(confirmation_token):              ⟵────────── Confirms a token, requires
    if current_user.confirmed:                             the user to log in
        return redirect(url_for("intro_bp.home"))  ┐ If the user is already
    try:                                            │ confirmed, redirect them
        # is the confirmation token confirmed?      ┘ to the home page.
        if current_user.confirm_token(
  ↦confirmation_token):
            with db_session_manager()
      ↦as db_session:                          If the token is valid, set the current
                current_user.confirmation = True   user's confirmation status to True
                db_session.add(current_user)       and save it in the database.
                db_session.commit()
                flash("Thank you for confirming your account")
    # confirmation token bad or expired
    except Exception as e:
        logger.exception(e)              If confirming the token raises an
        flash(e.message)                 exception, log it, inform the user,
        return redirect(url_for(         and redirect them to the resend
  ↦"auth_bp.resend_confirmation"))       confirmation page.
    return redirect(url_for("intro_bp.home"))
```

Confirms the token is valid points to the `if current_user.confirm_token(confirmation_token):` block.

USER CONFIRM TOKEN

The application needs to confirm a token received in response to clicking the link in the email is valid to verify that the user completed the registration process. This code acts as part of the confirmation process:

```
def confirm_token(self, token):
    serializer = URLSafeTimedSerializer(current_app.config["SECRET_KEY"])
    with db_session_manager() as session:
        confirmation_link_timeout = \
      current_app.config.get("CONFIRMATION_LINK_TIMEOUT")
        timeout = confirmation_link_timeout * 60 * 1000
        try:
            data = serializer.loads(token, max_age=timeout)
            if data.get("confirm") != self.user_uid:
                return False
            self.confirmed = True
            session.add(self)
            return True
        except (SignatureExpired, BadSignature) as e:
            return False
```

The `confirm_token()` URL handler creates a serializer instance just as the `confirmation_token()` creator method did. It then enters a database context manager and gets the confirmation timeout value and the confirmation data sent in the request.

The code then compares the "confirm" value of the data dictionary to the user's user_id value. If the values match, the user who clicked the link is the user who sent the confirmation link. The code to confirm the token is wrapped in an exception handler to return False if the token has expired or is invalid.

9.3   Resetting passwords

We're at a point where new users can register and confirm their email and existing users can log in to use the MyBlog application. We need to create a way for existing users to reset their password if they've forgotten it. In some ways, a password reset request is similar to confirming a new user; it sends a link to the user's email. A handler exists to present the user with the password reset form when the user clicks the associated link.

The link sent in the reset password email contains the encrypted user_uid value of the requesting user, along with an expiration timeout. The timeout value is set in the settings.toml file at 10 minutes and is configurable:

```
@auth_bp.get("/request_reset_password")          Registers the request_reset_password function
@auth_bp.post("/request_reset_password")         for both GET and POST HTTP methods
def request_reset_password():
    if current_user.is_authenticated:
        return redirect("intro_bp.home")         Creates an instance of the
    form = RequestResetPasswordForm()            request password form
    if form.cancel.data:
        return redirect(url_for("intro_bp.home"))
    if form.validate_on_submit():
        with db_session_manager() as db_session:
            user = (
                db_session.query(User)           Gets the user
                .filter(User.email ==            associated with the
                ➡form.email.data)               email from the form
                .one_or_none()
            )
            if user is not None:
                send_password_reset(user)
                timeout = current_app.config.get(  Sends the password
                ➡"PASSWORD_RESET_TIMEOUT")        reset email and
                flash(f"Check your email to reset   notifies the current
                ➡your password within {timeout} minutes")  user to check for it
                return redirect(url_for("intro_bp.home"))  within the timeout
    return render_template(
    ➡"request_reset_password.html", form=form)   #E
```

The application in the examples/CH_09/examples/03 directory presents the reset password form, as shown in figure 9.2 when it receives an HTTP GET request. The Password Reset form only presents a single field for the user's email that will be used to generate an email with the password reset link.

Email address
where reset
link should
be sent

Send reset password
link to the
entered email.

Cancel and return to the
home screen.

Figure 9.2   The form that allows registered users to reset their password

If a user is found for the email entered in the form, that user is passed as a parameter
to a new function, send_password_reset():

```python
def send_password_reset(user):
    timeout = current_app.config.get(
        "PASSWORD_RESET_TIMEOUT")
    token = user.get_reset_token(timeout)
    to = user.email
    subject = "Password Reset"
    contents = (
        f"""{user.first_name},<br /><br />
        Click the following link to reset
        your password within {timeout} minutes:
        {url_for('auth_bp.reset_password',
        token=token, _external=True)}
        If you haven't requested a password
        reset ignore this email.<br /><br />
        Sincerely,
        MyBlog
        """
    )
    send_mail(to=to, subject=subject, contents=contents)
```

**Creates the encrypted reset token
with the expiration timeout**

**Builds the
email content**

**Sends the email
to the passed-in
user's email address**

When the user clicks the link in the reset password email, a new URL endpoint function, reset_password(), is invoked:

```python
@auth_bp.get("/reset_password/<token>")
@auth_bp.post("/reset_password/<token>")
def reset_password(token):
    if current_user.is_authenticated:
        return redirect("intro_bp.home")
```

**Registers the request_reset_password function
for both GET and POST HTTP methods**

```
try:
    user_uid = User.verify_reset_token(token)
    with db_session_manager() as db_se
        user = (
            db_session
                .query(User)
                .filter(User.user_uid ==
                ➥user_uid)
                .one_or_none()
        )
        if user is None:
            flash("Reset token invalid")
            return redirect("intro_bp.home")
        form = ResetPasswordForm()
        if form.cancel.data:
            return redirect(url_for("intro_bp.home"))
        if form.validate_on_submit():
            user.password = form.password.data
            db_session.commit()
            flash("Your password has been reset")
            return redirect(url_for("intro_bp.home"))
except Exception as e:
    flash(str(e))
    logger.exception(e)
    return redirect("intro_bp.home")
return render_template("reset_password.html", form=form)
```

Gets the user_uid from the encrypted token passed with the URL

Finds a user matching the user_uid

Updates and saves the user's new password

The form shown in figure 9.3 lets the user enter and confirm a new password. When they click the Reset Password button, the handler is called with the HTTP POST method. The user_uid is decrypted from the token passed with the URL, and that user is searched for in the database. If the user is found and the form validates, the user's password is updated and saved in the database.

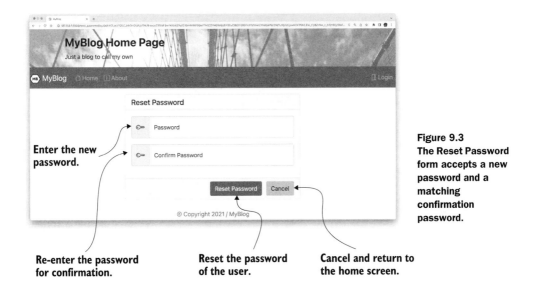

Enter the new password.

Re-enter the password for confirmation.

Reset the password of the user.

Cancel and return to the home screen.

Figure 9.3
The Reset Password form accepts a new password and a matching confirmation password.

9.4   *User profiles*

The MyBlog application currently saves only a few pieces of information about registered users: first name, last name, email, and password; whether they are confirmed; and if they are active. In addition to being able to reset their passwords if forgotten, users also want to change their passwords. So, we'll add a profile page that shows most of the user information and allows for password changes.

The profile is a form that presents and gathers information. It shows the user's name and email and has input fields to enter and confirm a new password. The form class that presents the profile information is added to the auth/forms.py file:

```python
class UserProfileForm(FlaskForm):
    first_name = StringField("First Name")
    last_name = StringField("Last Name")
    email = EmailField("Email")
    password = PasswordField(
        "Update Password",
        validators=[DataRequired(), Length(
                min=3,
                max=64,
                message= "Password must be between 3 and 64 characters long"
            ),
            EqualTo("confirm_password", message="Passwords must match")
        ]
    )
    confirm_password = PasswordField(
        "Confirm Updated Password",
        validators=[DataRequired(), Length(
            min=3,
            max=64,
            message= "Password must be between 3 and 64 characters long"
        )]
    )
    cancel = SubmitField(
        label= "Cancel",
        render_kw={"formnovalidate": True},
    )
    submit = SubmitField(label="Okay")
```

To generate the HTML to display on the browser requires a new URL handler in the auth/auth.py module:

```python
@auth_bp.get("/profile/<user_uid>")
@auth_bp.post("/profile/<user_uid>")
@login_required
def profile(user_uid):
    with db_session_manager() as db_session:
        user = (
            db_session
            .query(User)
            .filter(User.user_uid == user_uid)
            .one_or_none()
        )
```

Registers the profile function for both GET and POST HTTP methods

To view a profile, the user must be logged in (as discussed in the next section).

Gets the user associated with the user_uid in the URL path

```
    if user is None:
        flash("Unknown user")          If no user is found, this notifies the
        abort(404)                     user and aborts with a 404 error.
    if user.user_uid != current_user.user_uid:
        flash("Can't view profile      Prevents users from viewing
        ➥for other users")            profiles other than their own
        return redirect("intro_bp.home")
    form = UserProfileForm(obj=user)
    if form.cancel.data:
        return redirect(url_for("intro_bp.home"))
    if form.validate_on_submit():
        user.password = form.password.data    For a valid form submission, this
        db_session.commit()                    updates the user's password.
        flash("Your password has been updated")
        return redirect(url_for("intro_bp.home"))
return render_template("profile.html", form=form)
```

The HTML template to render the profile form isn't shown here but can be seen in the `examples/CH_09/examples/03/auth/templates/profile.html` template file. The rendered profile page, presented in figure 9.4, shows the user's information and provides a means to change the user's password.

The user information known to the MyBlog application, including the ability to change the password

Figure 9.4 The user profile page shows everything the MyBlog application knows about the user.

9.5   Security

The goal of building an authentication system is to provide security for an application's users, features, and functions. Security includes the features and functions that a user can perform when using the application. It also includes protecting the application by maintaining control and only allowing known users to access protected features and functions.

9.5.1   *Protecting routes*

Authenticated users have a cryptographically secure session cookie that the application identifies. In addition, we can use the session and `flask_login` module to protect routes in the application so that only users who are logged in and authenticated can navigate to those routes.

Currently, the MyBlog application only has two routes that aren't associated with authentication—the home page and the about page. Therefore, you'll temporarily create two new routes to demonstrate how to protect a route. Protecting a page is done by adding another decorator provided by the `flask_login` module to a URL route page handler. Add this to the import section of the `app/intro.py` module:

```
from flask_login import login_required          Imports the login_required decorator
                                                functionality from the flask_login module
```

Add a new route and handler to the `app/intro.py` module:

```
                                            Adds a new route
                                            for "/auth_required"
@intro_bp.route("/auth_required")
@login_required
def auth_required():                            Decorates the auth_required
    return render_template("auth_required.html")   handler with the
                                                login_required functionality
```

The `auth_required()` handler has two decorators: `@intro_bp.route()` and `@login_required`. Stacking decorators this way is absolutely fine. The decorator functionality wraps around other decorator functionality, working from the inner level outward. In this case, the `@login_required` decorator must be placed after the `@intro_bp.route()` (or any Blueprint instance routing) to make sure the `@login_required` functionality wraps the `auth_required()` handler functionality.

With the `auth_required()` handler protected by the `@login_required` decorator, an unauthenticated user will be redirected to the login page and unable to access the protected `auth_required` page. This is useful when you only allow authenticated users to see sensitive or private information or prevent access to forms that could change server data or functionality. An example use case for this security is allowing only authenticated users to create and post blog content to the MyBlog application.

9.6   *User authorization roles*

The other side of the authentication coin is authorization. Where authentication provides a mechanism to identify a user, authorization offers a way to control the user's capabilities.

One of the requirements of the MyBlog application is to give users roles in the application. A role would allow users with specific roles to perform actions not available to other users. For example, a user with an administrator role could update, activate, or deactivate any content in the system, not just content created by that user. Likewise, an administrator could also activate or deactivate a user.

A user with the editor role could update any content in the system, not just the content they created. However, an editor can't deactivate a user or their content.

A registered user can create content and activate or deactivate it but can't change the active state of another user or their content. We will add three roles to the MyBlog application: administrator, editor, and registered user.

9.6.1   Creating the roles

The roles will be initialized by the application and maintained in the database. The users in the database have a relationship to the defined roles. Because many users can have a certain role, but each user can only have one role, we have a one-to-many relationship concerning roles to users. The ERD shown in figure 9.5 illustrates this relationship.

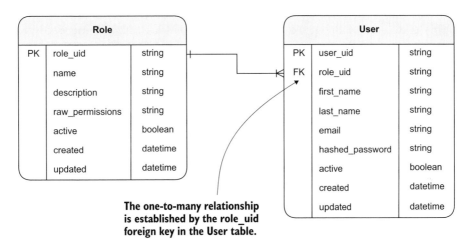

Figure 9.5   The new `Role` table and its relationship to the existing `User` table

The `Role` model is defined in the `examples/CH_09/examples/03/app/models.py` file:

```
class Role(db.Model):
    class Permissions(Flag):
        REGISTERED = auto()
        EDITOR = auto()
        ADMINISTRATOR = auto()

    __tablename__ = "role"
    role_uid = db.Column(db.String,
    ➥primary_key=True, default=get_uuid)
    name = db.Column(db.String, nullable=False,
    ➥unique=True)
```

Creates the Role class model

Creates the Permissions class internal to the Role class

Defines the table name for roles in the database

Creates the columns for a Role record

```
description = db.Column(db.String,
   nullable=False)
raw_permissions = db.Column(db.Integer)
users = db.relationship("User",
   backref=db.backref("role", lazy="joined"))
active = db.Column(db.Boolean, nullable=False, default=True)
created = db.Column(db.DateTime,
   nullable=False, default=datetime.now(
   tz=timezone.utc))
updated = db.Column(
    db.DateTime,
    nullable=False,
    default=datetime.now(tz=timezone.utc),
    onupdate=datetime.now(tz=timezone.utc)
)

@property
def permissions(self):
    return Role.Permissions(
       self.raw_permissions)
```

Creates the columns for a Role record

Establishes the one-to-many relationship with the User table

Creates a read property for a role's permissions

This code creates the `Role` database definition class. Notice the definition of the `Permissions` class inside the scope of the `Role` class definition. This is acceptable Python syntax and puts the `Permission` class inside the scope of the `Role` class.

The `Permissions` class is a `Flag` enum and gives the names `REGISTERED`, `EDITOR`, and `ADMINISTRATOR` automatically generated values. This class helps refer to the values by name, even though the `permission` value is stored as an integer in the `raw_permissions` column of the database.

The values in the roles database table need to exist for the life of the MyBlog application and act as a lookup table to constants. A method called `initialize_role_table()` in the `Role` class definition accomplishes this. This method is decorated with a `@staticmethod`, meaning it can be called without a `Role` instance variable. The method's purpose is to populate the `Roles` table at application startup. The method isn't included here but can be found in the `examples/CH_09/examples/03/app/models.py` file.

To initialize the `Roles` table, the following code is added to the `examples/CH_09/examples/03/app/__init__.py` file at the bottom of the `create_app()` function:

```
# initialize the role table
from .models import Role
Role.initialize_role_table()
```

These lines import the `Role` table class and then use it to call the `initialize_role_table()` static method to populate the `Roles` database table. In anticipation of upcoming functionality, the following code is also added to the end of the `create_app()` function:

```
# inject the role permissions class into all template contexts
@app.context_processor
def inject_permissions():
    return dict(Permissions=Role.Permissions)
```

These lines of code add the `Role.Permissions` property into the template context. This makes the `Role.Permissions` available for all templates as `Permissions`.

9.6.2   *Authorizing routes*

Besides protecting URL routes in the MyBlog application so only authenticated users can access them, you'll also want to protect URL routes so only authenticated users with specific permissions can access them. This will be useful in later chapters when forms are created that should only be accessed by editors or administrators.

To create this functionality, you'll need to create a decorator similar to `@login_required` but, instead, it should examine the user's authorization. To do this, create another module inside of the app directory, `app/decorators.py`:

```python
from functools import wraps
from flask import abort
from flask_login import current_user

def authorization_required(permissions):
    def wrapper(func):
        @wraps(func)
        def wrapped_function(*args, **kwargs):
            if not current_user.role.permissions
              & permissions:
                abort(403)
            return func(*args, **kwargs)
        return wrapped_function
    return wrapper
```

Creates the decorator function expecting to pass a permissions bitmask

Creates the wrapper to receive the wrapped function

Uses the @wraps(func) decorator to maintain the wrapped function signature

Creates the wrapper to receive the wrapped function's parameters

Aborts with an HTTP 403 error code if the user doesn't have the required permissions

Determines if the current user has the permissions necessary for this route

Let's demonstrate the `authorization_required()` decorator function. Update the `app/intro/intro.py` module and add this code to the bottom of the import section:

```python
from ..decorators import authorization_required
from ..models import Role
```

With these lines added, create a new URL route and handler:

```python
@intro_bp.route("/admin_required")
@login_required
@authorization_required(
    Role.Permissions.ADMINISTRATOR)
def admin_required():
    return render_template("admin_required.html")
```

Adds a new route for "/admin_required"

Decorates the admin_required handler with the login_required functionality

Decorates the admin_required handler with the authorization_required functionality

With this route in place, you can run the application and try to navigate to the URL http://127.0.0.1/admin_required. The system will generate a 403 error (`Forbidden`) for all users except those with administrator permissions. How to create an administrator will be covered next.

CREATING ADMINISTRATOR USERS

The MyBlog application has a relatively easy way to create an administrator user. In the `secrets.toml` file, there's a section of code like this:

```
admin_users = ["user's email you want to designate as an administrator"]
```

This creates a configuration variable `admin_users`, which is a list of email addresses. When a new user registers with an email in this list, they will have the administrator role assigned to them. By making the `admin_users` variable a list, you can have more than one administrator for the MyBlog application.

> **TIP** Creating the administrator(s) roles in the way described works well enough for the MyBlog application. It can also be used to create editors, though you'd have to know editor users ahead of time to put them in the `secrets.toml` file. Creating an admin interface to the application would create forms to allow for the creation and updating of additional roles. That's work for another day.

With the previous configuration in place, we can make this active by modifying the `examples/CH_09/examples/03/app/auth/auth.py` file and adding three lines to the `register_new_user()` function:

```python
@auth_bp.get("/register_new_user")
@auth_bp.post("/register_new_user")
def register_new_user():
    if current_user.is_authenticated:
        return redirect(url_for("intro_bp.home"))
    form = RegisterNewUserForm()
    if form.cancel.data:
        return redirect(url_for("intro_bp.home"))
    if form.validate_on_submit():
        with db_session_manager() as db_session:
            user = User(
                first_name=form.first_name.data,
                last_name=form.last_name.data,
                email=form.email.data,
                password=form.password.data,
            )
            role_name = "admin" if user.email
            in current_app.config.get("ADMIN_USERS") else
            "user"
            role = db_session.query(Role)
            .filter(Role.name == role_name).one_or_none()
            role.users.append(user)
            db_session.add(user)
            db_session.commit()
            send_confirmation_email(user)
            timeout = current_app.config.get("CONFIRMATION_LINK_TIMEOUT")
            flash((
                "Please click the confirmation link just sent"
                f" to your email address within {timeout} hours"
                "to complete your registration"
```

If the registered user's email is in the admin_users list, it gives them the administrator role.

Gets the assigned role from the roles table

Adds the registered user to the role collection, connecting the relationship

```
        ))
        logger.debug(f"new user {form.email.data} added")
        return redirect(url_for("intro_bp.home"))
return render_template("register_new_user.html", form=form)
```

The new code looks for the currently registering user in the `admin_user` configuration variable and creates the `role_name` variable with the appropriate value. It then uses the `role_name` variable to perform a lookup in the `Roles` table to obtain the designated `role`. The user is then added to the `role.users` collection to connect the role to the user, establishing the relationship. If you create a new user with the email in the `admin_users` list in the `secrets.toml` file and navigate to the `/admin_required` URL created earlier, you'll be able to navigate to that page successfully.

9.7 Protecting forms

There's another protection relevant to forms that we've glossed over. In both the `login.html` and `register_new_user.html` templates, there's a field within the form context that looks like this:

```
<form action="" method="POST" novalidate>
    {{form.csrf_token}}
    <!—rest of the form →
</form>
```

What is the `{{form.csrf_token}}` Jinja substitution element? If you view the source of either the `login` or `register_new_user` pages, you'll see an `<input…>` element that looks something like this:

```
<input id="csrf_token" name="csrf_token"
type="hidden"
value="IjE1NzU4NjE3OWNlMTUxYmM0Yzc3OTAyTOZiODk4N
jRmNTdmZGM5OGUi.
YEULPg.jVDKYLM3MMlpKK-BQSh2f1hWUfQ">
```

The element is a hidden input element (not shown on the browser page) with a strange-looking value. The MyBlog application server generates the value using the Flask `SECRET_KEY` configuration value and the user session unique identifier. This element aims to prevent cross-site request forgery (CSRF) attacks. The `form.csrf_token` is intended to protect a request that would take action (like an HTTP `POST`). When the server receives a protected form, it will validate both the session and `form.csrf_token` to ensure a malicious user hasn't altered it.

This protection is provided automatically by using the `Flask-WTF` module. You simply need to include the `{{form.csrf_token}}` in any form you want to protect.

9.8 Closing thoughts

You've created an effective authentication and authorization system by using the new modules you've learned about—`flask_login`, `Flask_bcrypt`, `Flask-WTF`, and `Flask-SQLAlchemy`. Ensuring user security is a decisive step toward having an application accepted by users. The authorization system you've created is functional and valuable to the MyBlog application. However, it is far from the last word in security. For example, suppose you need to secure a web application more tightly. You'll need to consider two-factor authentication or, more realistically, use a third-party service to host your authentication.

You've focused on authenticating/authorizing users of your application to an almost microscopic level. This level of detail helped create a useful and serviceable login/logout system to safeguard the users of MyBlog and the MyBlog system itself.

The next chapter will magnify your view of the database information introduced here. Then, you'll dive deeper into designing database tables and their relationships and how SQLAlchemy integrates the Python and database worlds.

Summary

- Taking advantage of the base.html template and inheritance allows us to add the login/logout functionality to every page in the MyBlog application.
- Interacting with an external service through their API lets us send emails to our users to confirm who they are and reset their passwords. Using such services helps scale the MyBlog application and eliminates the work of configuring, running, and maintaining an email server.
- A user's authorization is the other side of the coin to authenticating a user. The authorization information determines the user's role—what they can do while logged into a web application.
- Authentication and authorization can be used with Flask to only allow logged-in users with specific roles access to particular MyBlog pages. Pages that allow users to make system-wide changes, or changes created by other users, are usually protected in this way.

Persistence is good:
Databases

This chapter covers

- Persisting data
- Database systems
- Database structures
- Modeling data with SQLAlchemy

You've shown a great deal of persistence in getting this far, and I hope the journey has been rewarding and held your interest. As satisfying as sticking with something is, that kind of persistence isn't what this chapter covers.

This chapter is about persisting application data over time. You don't run the applications you use forever, and despite the stability of computer systems, they are shut down and restarted periodically.

Imagine using a complex spreadsheet and having to re-enter all the data every time you restarted the application or powered on the computer. Even with the enormous processing power of a computer, it would hardly be a helpful device if there was no way to save and restore the information entered into it.

10.1 The other half

As a developer, it's easy to think of the application code you're creating as the primary product of your efforts. But, in reality, your cool, essential application with all its well-thought-out features and functions is only half the story. The other, equally important half is the data that your application helps the user work with. Modifying, transforming, and providing insights into the data in which your users are interested is the raw material an application works with.

10.1.1 Maintaining information over time

A filesystem saves data to a storage medium independent of electrical power. Most personal computer systems maintain filesystems on either mechanical or solid-state drives. These storage devices have filesystem structures layered over them by the operating system of the computer.

The filesystem provides a hierarchically organized mechanism to save and retrieve files from the storage device. As far as the filesystem is concerned, a file is a sequence of data bytes connected to a file name existing somewhere in the hierarchy. In addition, the filesystem can create, modify, and delete files and maintains housekeeping metadata about the files, such as read, write, and executable status.

Application programs give meaning to the data in a file. For example, when a photo-viewing application opens a JPEG image file, the user sees a picture. The photo application can interpret the contents of the file and generate the expected visual results.

If a user were to open the same JPEG image file with a text editor, they would see a block of largely incomprehensible data. Most of the files in a filesystem are like this; their content makes sense only to the applications that can read and interpret them.

The MyBlog application needs to save, modify, and recall content to display to users. The content saved to the filesystem is in a format understood by the application. The MyBlog application already saves registered user information to the filesystem using a database. This chapter is a tangential topic away from the MyBlog application to take a closer look at databases.

10.2 Accessing data

Before diving directly into database systems, let's talk about storing data in general. To do so, we'll use customer orders for products, something everyone who's made online purchases is familiar with. Later, we'll use this idea to illustrate some issues when storing data in filesystems.

To begin with, imagine an online store that only sells a single product to many customers. Each customer might create multiple orders for that single product. To make the data relatively easy to present on the pages of this book, we'll keep the amount of information very low—the customer's name, their address, the product name, and the quantity in the order.

A common format for data in a filesystem is the comma-separated value format or CSV. A CSV file is easy to understand and has the advantage of being human-readable and accessible by computer systems.

A CSV file is a simple text file in which each line of text is a record of data ending in a newline character. A comma character separates the data elements in each line of text. The first line of text in a CSV file often contains the names of each comma-separated field in the remaining rows in the text file.

A CSV file contains no information about the data type for each element in a record, everything is just text. An application reads the CSV file and splits each comma-separated line of text into fields of text data. The imaginary company selling only one product to each customer could save all their customers' information and their orders in a single CSV file. Figure 10.1 shows one possible way the data could be saved.

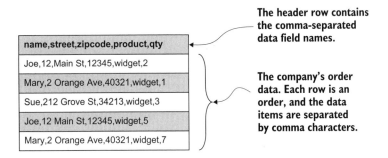

Figure 10.1   The CSV file structure containing all the company orders and the data for those orders

This CSV file is sufficient to represent the customers, their shipping address, and their orders. The first field contains the customer's name, the second their address, the third their zip code, the fourth field is the product name, and the last field is the number of products in the order. Because the company only sells a single product, this could work.

Even in this example, you might notice a potential problem. There's redundant data in the file. For example, customers and their addresses are represented multiple times for each separate order, as in the case of the orders for Joe and Mary.

The same data stored multiple times can be a problem if the customer Joe wants to start using his full name, Joseph. To accommodate this, the company would have to update all the records in the file related to Joe. This kind of update is prone to error, particularly if the file has become very large. Making a mistake and missing one or more of the Joe records would create two sets of customer records, one for Joe and another for Joseph.

We could resolve the problem by removing the redundancy and having only one record for each customer and representing multiple orders in that same record. You could create more comma-separated fields containing the quantities, but because there's no way to know how many orders a customer will create, it would be difficult for an application reading the CSV file to know how many order fields to expect.

We could pack multiple product and quantity fields into the single order field, but we'd need to use a delimiter distinct from a comma to separate the values. So, instead, we use the pipe character (vertical bar, |) to separate orders and the hyphen character (-) to separate the product from the quantity. Doing this allows you to maintain multiple orders per record so that an application can still parse the lines of text in the file.

Implementing this idea creates a CSV with all the data for multiple orders contained in one line of the file. Figure 10.2 shows the file with this structural change. The order information is still one comma-separated data item, but it will need to be parsed specifically to get the order data items.

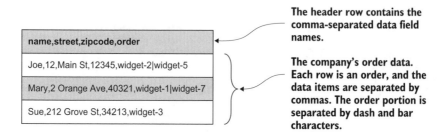

The header row contains the comma-separated data field names.

The company's order data. Each row is an order, and the data items are separated by commas. The order portion is separated by dash and bar characters.

Figure 10.2   The CSV file restructured to reduce data redundancy

This implementation reduces the redundancy in the file as well as its size. Reducing the redundancy comes at the cost of increased processing when reading and interpreting the data in this CSV file. The application will have to parse for the comma, the pipe, and the dash character delimiters in the order field.

Suppose our imaginary company decides to sell multiple products, and customers can ship an order to any address they want. Now customer orders need to contain the shipping address information, which needs its own delimiters within the field to stay distinct. Figure 10.3 illustrates this additional complication to the CSV file.

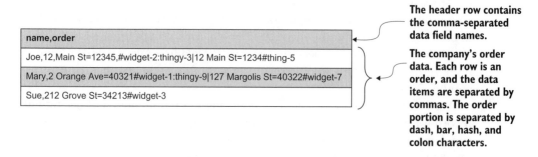

The header row contains the comma-separated data field names.

The company's order data. Each row is an order, and the data items are separated by commas. The order portion is separated by dash, bar, hash, and colon characters.

Figure 10.3   The CSV file restructured to accommodate multiple products and shipping addresses

Adding more delimiters could work, but it's getting silly with multiple data items to parse in the orders field. This approach also doesn't scale well, as adding more products makes the orders field even more complicated.

Resolving this problem means recognizing the logical divisions between the data elements to be stored. For example, a customer can ship multiple orders to different shipping addresses, and each order can contain multiple products and quantities.

Each customer can have multiple orders, but each order is related to only a single customer. Similarly, each address can be related to multiple orders, but each order will ship to only a single address.

Orders and products are a little more challenging. An order can contain multiple products, and a product can be part of multiple orders. To resolve this, we invent the concept of an order having an item. An item relates to an order and a product, providing this two-way connection. An item might also contain the quantity of products the item represents.

We can break the data into separate CSV files along these logical lines, essentially where we've added additional delimiters in the text. Taking this action creates five CSV files: customer, address, product, order, and item. The five CSV files separate the data along logical lines. Unfortunately, there's no way to connect a customer to an order, an order to an address, or an item to either an order or a product.

To connect the data, we need to create relationships between the rows of data in the files. We can do this by creating a unique identifying value for each row in every CSV file. At a minimum, the row identifier only needs to be unique across the rows in an individual CSV file.

We'll add another column at the beginning of each row and assign an integer value incremented for each row. The integer value uniquely identifies each row of data in a single CSV file, but there are still no relationships between CSV files.

To create relationships, we add the unique identifier from one record in a CSV file to another to indicate the relationship between the two. We'll add the unique identifier as a new value to all the rows in the order CSV file that relate to that customer to create this relationship. This kind of relationship is called one-to-many.

There's also another relationship we must establish. Each order can consist of multiple products, and each product can relate to multiple orders. A relationship like this is called a many-to-many. Conceptually, this is a many-to-one relationship combined with a one-to-many and is implemented by creating relationship associations. This is how the concept of an order item, as mentioned earlier, is implemented.

To do this, we'll create an item CSV file that contains the unique IDs from both the order and product CSV files for each item. In this way, an order can connect to multiple items and multiple products.

Figure 10.4 shows the five CSV files, their contents, and the relationships between them. Each file has a unique ID value as the first field in each row of data. The structure shows the `Customer`, `Product`, and `Address` files have no redundant data. It also shows the `Order` and `Item` files contain primarily relationship data, aside from the unique ID and the `qty` value in the `Item` file.

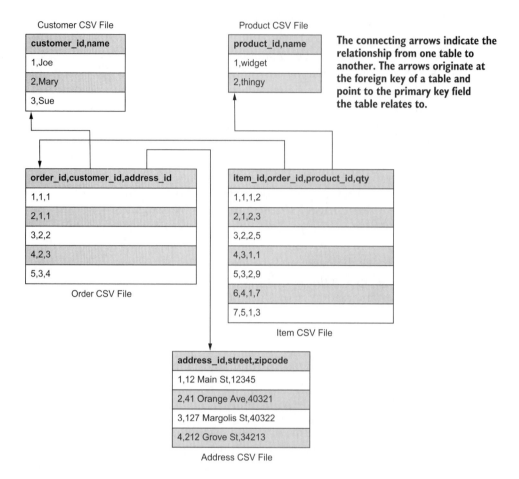

Figure 10.4   The CSV files eliminate data redundancy and allow for multiple products and addresses.

Because of the structure and contents of the CSV files, our imaginary company could continue to add new customers, new products to sell, and new shipping addresses, all without creating unsustainable redundant information. The program in `examples/CH_10/examples/01/main.py` uses this information to create simple invoice PDF files for all the orders in the system.

The program, available in the code repository, works by reading all the CSV files into memory and creating a `Transactions` container class to hold the information. Next, the orders in the `Transactions` class are inserted into the transaction information fields in a Jinja2 template. The resulting rendered HTML is converted to a PDF file, as shown in figure 10.5.

These ideas and their implementation work but have significant limitations. Because the CSV files are read into memory, the number of customers, products, and orders are limited to the amount of memory the application has available.

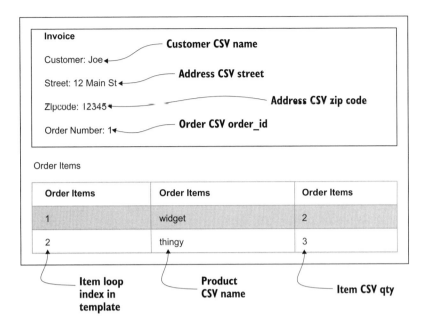

Figure 10.5   The PDF invoice generated by the `examples/CH_10/examples/01/main.py` program

The example program has only one use, to create a set of order invoices for all the orders in the system. There is no facility to search for an order, customer, or product. Any additional use cases our imaginary company might want, like searching or reporting, require more programming development.

Our imaginary company would likely want to have multiple users—both customers and employees—interacting with the data. Coordinating multiple access must be handled by the application so the data stays consistent and uncorrupted. If multiple applications access the CSV files, this presents another level of complexity to coordinate that access, keep the data synchronized and current in all applications, and prevent the files from becoming corrupted.

There's also no standardized way to use the CSV files. The CSV files are shared easily enough, but anyone wanting to use them would need detailed knowledge of the structure of the files and the relationships implied by that structure. They'd also have to maintain that structure if they wanted to modify the data contents.

For any application written in any language to work with the data, it would have to handle the intention of the CSV files specifically. In addition, any changes in the structure of the CSV files would necessitate changes to the software to be aware of those changes.

Many of our imaginary company's data shortcomings have to do with explicit management of the data and detailed programming to implement how to access and maintain the data. One solution to the problem is to move the data to a database system.

10.3   *Database systems*

Database systems allow you to persist data as well as the relationships between that data. One common type of database is the relational database management system, or RDBMS. RDBMS systems provide the functionality to create, read, update, and delete tables stored within them. These tables are analogous to the two-dimensional tables represented by the CSV files used in the previous example.

RDBMS systems also have the functionality to create and update the relationships between tables by connecting unique ID values across table boundaries. One of the advantages of a database system over using files to persist information is that creating, updating, and maintaining the data is handled by the database, not by your application code.

10.3.1   *Tables*

Tables represent the data that a database maintains. Conceptually, tables in a database are two-dimensional collections of rows and columns.

Like the CSV files presented previously, the rows are the individual records and the columns are the fields within a row. Unlike a CSV file where the columns are strings separated by a delimiter, the columns in database tables have defined data types. The data types supported depend on the particular database, but data types of text, integer, real (decimal numbers), and blob (binary objects) are generally supported.

Tables in a database can be represented graphically as part of an entity relationship diagram, or ERD. Rather than show the rows and columns that make up a table, the column and data-type information for a record are shown.

The ERD diagram header is the capitalized table name. The following rows contain specific information about each column, like the name of the column and its data type. The PK is shorthand for the primary key (the unique identifier for the table) and indicates that the customer_id is the primary key for the Customer table. Figure 10.6 shows a visual definition of the Customer database table.

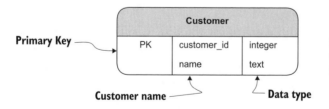

Figure 10.6   **The ERD diagram for the Customer table showing the field names and data types**

The order CSV file contained nothing but unique ID values—one for the row unique ID and two others to connect to the customer and address CSV file rows. The new FK abbreviation in figure 10.7 is shorthand for foreign key. A foreign key creates a relationship between two tables by referencing the primary key of another table.

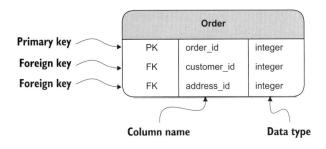

Figure 10.7   **The** Order **table contains a primary key and two foreign keys referencing other tables.**

10.3.2 *Relationships*

As important as storing and modifying data is to any application, the relationships between the data are just as important. The updated CSV files for our imaginary company enabled you to reduce the data redundancy of the original single CSV file. Reducing data redundancy is one important aspect of database normalization.

The separation of distinct data into multiple tables indicates the need to reconnect related data. RDBMS systems establish relationships between multiple tables with the use of primary and foreign keys.

The primary key in a database table is a column in a row (a record) whose value is unique across the entire table. It's often the case that the primary key column exists for the sole purpose of providing this unique ID value and contains no information about the record itself.

It's not always necessary to create a distinct primary key field. If a column of useful data is unique across a table, that column can be the primary key. For example, suppose a table containing information about people included their social security numbers. In this case, the social security number should be unique for every record in the table and could be the primary key.

> **TIP** Even if a column in a table contains data that's unique enough to be used as the primary key, it's often easier and more future-proof to create a distinct primary key column that's not dependent on the uniqueness of the data in the table.

Most RDBMS systems have the functionality to create auto-incrementing integer values when new rows are inserted into a table. These make convenient primary key values that are assured to be unique across the table as new records are inserted into the table and the value increments.

UUID PRIMARY KEYS

Another option to create primary key values is to use UUID (universally unique identifier) values. A primary key with a UUID value is not only unique across the table but unique across all tables in all databases. Having a universally unique primary key can be helpful as the structure and use of the database change.

As conditions and requirements change over time, database structures are updated to meet the needs of those requirements. One example might be merging two tables.

In this situation, all of the records from both should exist in the merged table, and each record still needs a unique primary key.

If both source tables were created with auto-incrementing integer primary key values, merging the tables likely creates primary key conflicts. If the primary key values are changed to resolve the conflict, any relationships depending on a foreign key that points to the original primary key value are broken. A considerable amount of effort is necessary to fix this kind of problem.

However, if the primary key values are UUID values, then merging the tables presents no conflicts because the definition of a UUID value is that it's unique everywhere. Any foreign key that references a UUID primary key still works with the merged table.

Another interesting, perhaps small advantage of using UUID-based primary keys is "security through obscurity." For example, in a web application for our imaginary company, they might have a URL like this:

```
https://imaginary_company.com/orders/2
```

Someone might guess that the last part of that URL is an auto-incrementing primary key for a particular order in a database. Therefore, they could change the last value in the URL and see every order in the system, which might reveal more information than you'd like.

However, if the database used UUID primary key values, the URL might look like this:

```
https://imaginary_company.com/orders/1a99289c9de5482b90c3b45e20a60c20
```

Now the last part of the URL that references a particular order in the orders collection is a UUID value with the hyphen (-) characters stripped out. Now it's essentially impossible for someone to guess an order primary key value that would work. It's not really a security step, just a side effect of using UUID primary keys.

Using a UUID as the primary key in database tables does increase the storage cost, as UUID values are larger than integers. They might also adversely affect the performance of the database in a small way. The cost versus value question needs to be considered when deciding whether to use UUID values as primary keys. The MyBlog application database uses UUID primary keys, not so much because of any requirements for MyBlog functionality but to present the implementation.

ONE-TO-MANY

In our imaginary company, a one-to-many relationship exists between customers and orders. To establish a one-to-many relationship, the unique `customer_id` value from the customer table is also present as a column of data in the order table as `customer_id`. The `customer_id` value is a foreign key relating to the customer table. Any number of order records can have the same `customer_id` foreign key value, creating the one-to-many relationship.

When creating a foreign key in a table, part of the definition given to the database engine is to what table the foreign key relates. The foreign key tells the database engine there's a relationship and helps it provide the functionality to use that relationship.

MANY-TO-MANY

Our imaginary company also establishes a many-to-many relationship. Establishing a many-to-many relationship is more involved and, in some ways, can be thought of as a one-to-many relationship connected to a many-to-one relationship. Creating this requires an association table that acts as the many parts between the two just mentioned.

The `Item` table creates the association between the `Order` and `Product` tables. The `Item` table has a foreign key to the `Order` table `order_id` field and a foreign key to the `Product` table `product_id` field.

10.3.3 *Transaction database*

The transaction database you'll create uses a naming convention for the tables and the columns within those tables. The tables are named using singular nouns for what they contain: customer, product, and so on.

The naming convention seems counterintuitive because a table has multiple records, and a plural version of the noun might seem more fitting. However, the table is defined in terms of one row of data and the data types and meanings of the record's columns. How the table is accessed can return one or more records, but the table itself is configured based on a single record.

Additionally, it can get surprisingly awkward to use plurals when naming tables. For example, try to define a person in a database table. The plural version would be a table named `people`, with possibly a primary key of `people_id`, which seems inelegant. Renaming the primary key to `person_id` works better, but now there is a cognitive disconnect between the table name and the primary key.

The primary key columns are named using a convention of the table name appended with `_id`. Although seemingly redundant and wordy as the primary key name, it's apparent that the column with such a name is a foreign key when used in another table.

> **TIP**   The naming convention used in this example database is by no means the definitive one to use. As has been mentioned, naming things is hard, and it's no different with databases. There are many conventions about how to name things in databases, and the right one comes down to comfort for you and your team.

Figure 10.8 represents the transaction database table's structure and the relationships between them using common database ERD notation and symbols. Notice how the connection between tables goes from primary key in one table to foreign key in another.

The connecting lines are all variations of one-to-many relationships. The existence of the `Item` table creates the one-to-many and many-to-many relationship between the `Order` ⟷ `Item` ⟷ `Product` tables. Figure 10.8 presents the complete ERD diagram for the company database. Creating, updating, and interacting with the data in an RDBMS system uses the Structured Query Language (SQL) that most RDBMS systems provide.

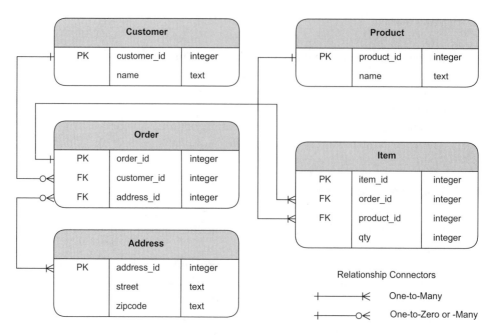

Figure 10.8   The complete ERD for the transaction database of our imaginary company

10.3.4 *Structured query language: SQL*

Accessing the functionality of a database is standardized so any programming language that has a library available to connect to the database can use it. This standardization makes the database much easier to share between applications than a proprietary system.

Much of the standardized functionality of RDBMS systems is exposed to the user by using Structured Query Language, or SQL. SQL interacts with an RDBMS system as a declarative programming language. A declarative language lets you express what you want a computer system to do and not explicitly instruct the system on how to do it.

One way to think about this would be to go to a bakery and ask for a cake. You expect the baker will hand you a cake, not ask for a recipe to make a cake.

GETTING DATA

You'll be creating the transaction database later in this chapter, but here I'll show some SQL queries to access data. This SQL statement

```
SELECT * FROM customer;
```

returns these results:

```
customer_id   name
-----------   ----------
1             Joe
2             Mary
3             Sue
```

The SQL command keywords are in uppercase, which is just a convention. The statement asks the database to return all rows from the customer table. The asterisk (*) character is a wildcard to get all columns for each row returned. The semicolon (;) character at the end of the SQL statement is the terminator for the command.

This SQL query asks for only the names in the customer database sorted in descending alphabetical order:

```
SELECT name FROM customer ORDER BY name DESC;


name
----------
Sue
Mary
Joe
```

SQL also provides functions that transform and act on the data. The statement below returns the number of customers:

```
SELECT COUNT(*) AS 'Total Customers' FROM customer;
Total Customers
---------------
3
```

The COUNT function returns the total number of results produced by the query and assigns that value to an alias—'Total Customers'—used as the column heading for the results output.

USING RELATIONSHIPS

Because the tables in the transaction database represent normalized data without redundancies, making interesting queries requires using relationships. In this SQL statement, the customers, all the addresses used for their orders, and the number of times they've used an address for an order are returned and sorted alphabetically by name:

```
SELECT c.name, a.street, a.zipcode, COUNT(c.name) AS 'Times Used'
FROM CUSTOMER c
JOIN 'order' o ON o.customer_id = c.customer_id
JOIN address a ON a.address_id = o.address_id
GROUP BY a.street
ORDER BY c.name;


name         street       zipcode      Times Used
----------   ----------   ----------   ----------
Joe          12 Main St   12345        2
Mary         127 Margol   40322        1
Mary         41 Orange    40321        1
Sue          212 Grove    34213        1
```

Here, the SQL statement spans multiple lines, which works fine as the statement isn't completed until the final termination character (;). As before, only some values from the tables are returned, but those values span multiple tables.

Initially, the query starts at the customer table and assigns it to an alias shorthand used in other parts of the query to reduce ambiguity. To get the customer address used with each order, the query needs to use the relationships between the customer, order, and address tables. Using the JOIN keyword achieves this. It tells the database how to connect one table to another using the primary key from one to the foreign key of another.

The primary key from one table must equal the foreign key of the other for that row to be part of the results. The code that follows the ON keyword provides the condition to be met to include the data.

Notice the 'order' table is in single quotes in the first JOIN statement. The single quotes are necessary because the word order is an SQL keyword; placing it in single quotes tells SQL to interpret 'order' as the table name rather than a keyword.

The text GROUP BY a.street tells SQL to aggregate the results based on identical street values. The results returned indicate this. For example, Joe has two orders but used the same address for both. Mary also has two orders but used a different address for each one.

The SQL used to build invoices for all the orders of our imaginary company is written like this:

```
SELECT
c.name, a.street, a.zipcode, o.order_id, p.name, i.qty
FROM 'order' o
JOIN customer c ON c.customer_id = o.customer_id
JOIN address a ON a.address_id = o.address_id
JOIN item i ON o.order_id = i.order_id
JOIN product p ON p.product_id = i.product_id
```

And returns these results:

name	street	zipcode	order_id	name	qty
Joe	12 Main St	12345	1	widget	2
Joe	12 Main St	12345	1	thingy	3
Joe	12 Main St	12345	2	thingy	5
Mary	41 Orange	40321	3	widget	1
Mary	41 Orange	40321	3	thingy	9
Mary	127 Margol	40322	4	widget	7
Sue	212 Grove	34213	5	widget	3

This SQL query joins all the tables in the transaction database to re-create the redundant data for customers, orders, addresses, products, and items.

10.4   SQLite as the database

Before we get to creating and using a database with SQLAlchemy, let's talk about the particular database we'll use for the transaction database and MyBlog in general. In chapter 8, we used SQLite to persist data. For the transaction database and the rest of the MyBlog development, we'll continue to use SQLite.

The decision to use SQLite was based on a few considerations. The SQLite website states that SQLite is likely one of the most widely used database systems globally if you look at the numbers and types of systems that use it. It's also small, fast, full-featured, and completely serves the needs of the MyBlog application.

The other, and probably more relevant consideration regarding this book, is that SQLite runs as an in-process database, which means that it runs as a module pulled into the application like any other Python module. There's no need to install, configure, and maintain a database server like MySQL, PostgreSQL, or SQL Server to build and learn with the MyBlog development process.

> **TIP** Database servers like MySQL, PostgreSQL, and SQL Server are powerful, capable systems that could easily handle the needs of the MyBlog application. However, it would take time and book real estate to help readers get those systems up and running.

Lastly, the use of SQLAlchemy helps to abstract away the underlying database and lets you focus on development and database concepts rather than a particular database implementation. Should your needs with MyBlog outgrow what SQLite can do for you, replacing it with another database system is easier because of the abstraction that SQLAlchemy provides.

10.5 SQLAlchemy

SQLAlchemy is a popular and powerful database access library for Python that provides an object-relational mapper (ORM). One of the benefits of working with Python is that it's an object-oriented language, and everything in Python is an object. Working with data as Python objects feels more natural and more Pythonic.

Python can access database systems using SQL directly, and this is a viable approach. Most Python database libraries that support SQL return lists of tuples or dictionaries containing the results of the SQL statement.

The SQL statement illustrating how to get the data to create invoices for orders shows the data, but all relationship information is lost. Using this data would require software to glean the hierarchal relationships in Order ⇔ Item ⇔ Product. The disconnect between objects and flat data is known as object-relational impedance mismatch, and it's a problem the SQLAlchemy ORM solves.

10.5.1 Benefits

Using SQLAlchemy to access a database allows you to think about objects and methods rather than SQL and result sets. For the most part, you don't need to know SQL to work with the underlying database. Instead, SQLAlchemy builds the necessary SQL statement to map the resulting data to Python objects and vice versa.

Most RDBMS databases support SQL; however, they often add proprietary functionality to their implementation. Aside from specific use cases, SQLAlchemy abstracts these differences away and works at a higher level.

Another advantage SQLAlchemy provides is protecting your application from SQL injection attacks. For example, if your application adds user-supplied information to use with database queries, your application is vulnerable to this kind of attack. The XKCD comic in figure 10.9 shows this nicely.

Figure 10.9 Exploits of a Mom (Source: xkcd.com. Licensed under CC BY-NC 2.5)

10.6 *Modeling the database*

Connecting the database to SQLAlchemy requires modeling the table structures with Python class definitions. The models map the table record structure, the field data types, and the relationships between tables to Python class definitions. Instances of these Python classes are created by calling methods on the classes, which SQLAlchemy translates to SQL statements.

Because the ultimate goal is to use SQLAlchemy with the MyBlog application, we'll use `Flask` and the `flask_sqlalchemy` modules to help define the classes. The `flask_sqlalchemy` module provides convenience features and definitions, but the classes defined here could just as easily have been defined with the SQLAlchemy module alone.

10.6.1 *Defining the classes*

The `examples/CH_10/examples/02/main.py` program imports a `models.py` module. The `models.py` module contains all of the code to create the database object, model the tables, and populate the database with data from the CSV files of `examples/01`.

THE DATABASE CONNECTION

All of the classes to be defined inherit from a common SQLAlchemy-provided database object. The database object is created in this way prior to defining the classes:

Creates the Flask instance

```
app = Flask(__name__)
app.config["SQLALCHEMY_DATABASE_URI"] =
    "sqlite:///transaction.sqlite"
app.config["SQLALCHEMY_TRACK_MODIFICATIONS"] = False
db = SQLAlchemy(app, session_options=
    {"autoflush": False})
```

Configures SQLAlchemy to use SQLite and where to create the database file

Turns off an unnecessary default configuration that generates a warning

Creates the SQLAlchemy database object, in this case with autoflush turned off, which helps make DB operations more atomic at the point of issuing a commit()

The intent of this code is to create the db object instance used to define the table models. The database itself is stored in the single `transaction.sqlite` file.

MODELING THE TABLES

The transaction database ERD shown previously is a good guide to creating the class definitions needed to access the database with SQLAlchemy. The class definitions define the database tables to be created, the column names within a record, and their data types.

There are also fields defined that don't exist in the database but are created and maintained by SQLAlchemy when instances of the models are created. These extra fields provide useful functionality when working with the model instances, particularly for relationships between tables—for example, the orders attribute defined next in the Customer model. SQLAlchemy maintains a Python list of all the orders associated with a Customer instance. Let's look at the Customer and Order class definitions:

```
class Customer(db.Model):        Creates the class, inheriting from     Associates the class
    __tablename__ = "customer"   the db instance Model class            definition with the
                                                                        customer database table
    customer_id = db.Column(db.Integer,   Creates the customer_id column as an
      primary_key=True)                   integer type and as the primary_key
    name = db.Column(db.String)
    orders = db.relationship("Order",     Creates the attribute orders, connecting
      backref=db.backref("customer"))     a customer to all their orders
```

Creates the name column as a string → (points to name line)

Creates the class, inheriting from the db instance Model class

Associates the class definition with the order database table

```
class Order(db.Model):
    __tablename__ = "order"
    order_id = db.Column(db.Integer,      Creates the order_id column as an
      primary_key=True)                   integer type and as the primary_key
    customer_id = db.Column(db.Integer,
      db.ForeignKey("customer.customer_id"))   Creates the customer_id as an
    address_id = db.Column(db.Integer,         integer and as the ForeignKey to the
      db.ForeignKey("address.address_id"))     customer table and customer_id field
```

Creates the address_id as an integer and as the ForeignKey to the address table and address_id field

Quite a lot is happening in these class definitions. By inheriting from the db.Model class, the Customer and Order classes get SQLAlchemy functionality, allowing the classes to interact with the underlying database.

The customer_id column is defined as an integer and as the primary key. By doing this, the customer_id field is initialized by an auto-incrementing function every time a new Customer instance is added to the database. The same happens for the order_id field in the Order class.

The name column is a simple string that maps to whatever database type best supports Python string-type variables. Because SQLite is the underlying database, that type is TEXT.

The Customer class attribute orders is interesting and useful. It does not define a column in the database customer table at all. Instead, it creates an attribute maintained by SQLAlchemy that is available to you as a developer.

The orders attribute uses the relationship established by the customer_id foreign key created in the Order class. A Customer instance has an orders attribute that is a Python list of the Order instances associated with the customer. The odd-looking backref parameter passed to db.relationship(...) creates a SQLAlchemy-maintained attribute named customer in the Order class definition that points back to the Customer instance to which the order relates. Figure 10.10 presents a visual representation of this SQLAlchemy-maintained list of orders in the customer instance.

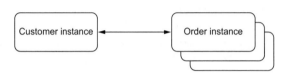

Figure 10.10 **The one-to-many relationship between a customer and their orders is a Python list.**

The backref parameter creates a SQLAlchemy-maintained Python list of orders in instances of the Customer model.

The orders attribute lets you write Python code like this when you have a Customer instance:

```
print(f"Customer {customer.name} has these order number")
for order in customer.orders:
    print(f"Order number: {order.order_id}")
```

The relationships and the attributes created and maintained by SQLAlchemy are very useful when printing out order invoices. The rest of the SQLAlchemy model definitions follow:

```
class Address(db.Model):
    __tablename__ = "address"
    address_id = db.Column(db.Integer, primary_key=True)
    street = db.Column(db.String)
    zipcode = db.Column(db.String)
    orders = db.relationship("Order", backref=db.backref("address"))

class Product(db.Model):
    __tablename__ = "product"
    product_id = db.Column(db.Integer, primary_key=True)
    name = db.Column(db.String)

class Item(db.Model):
    __tablename__ = "item"
    order_id = db.Column(db.Integer,
    ➥db.ForeignKey("order.order_id"),
```

Creates the class, inheriting from the db instance Model class

Associates the class with the item database table

```
primary_key=True)
product_id = db.Column(db.Integer,
    db.ForeignKey("product.product_id"),
    primary_key=True)
qty = db.Column(db.Integer)
order = db.relationship("Order",
    backref=db.backref("items"))
product = db.relationship("Product")
```

Creates the order_id as an integer and as the ForeignKey to the order table and order_id field

Creates the qty field to track the quantity of product for this item

Creates the instance-only attribute order, connecting an order to this item

Creates the product_id as an integer and as the ForeignKey to the product table and product_id field

Creates the instance-only attribute product, connecting a product to this item

The `Item` class definition creates the many-to-many association relationship between an order, the items in that order, and the products related to the items.

10.7 Creating and using the database

Once the SQLAlchemy models are defined, the database can be created. This line of Python code creates the database:

```
db.create_all()
```

If the `transaction.sqlite` SQLite database file defined earlier doesn't exist, it's created with table structures defined by the models, and those tables will be empty. However, if the `transaction.sqlite` database file does exist, the code won't re-create it; it will just connect to it.

It's essential to recognize that any changes made to the SQLAlchemy models won't appear in the database if the database already exists. You can delete and re-create the database, and it will match the updated models, which is fine in this case but an unreasonable action most of the time.

> **TIP** With an existing database, you'll need to use SQL statements, or other database migration tools, to modify the database to match the updated SQLAlchemy models. As a working developer, it's not common to create a database from scratch. The more frequent activity is modifying an existing database to add new features and functionality to it. Python tools like Alembic (https://pypi.org/project/alembic/) are useful for this kind of activity with SQLAlchemy.

10.7.1 Adding data

Even though creating and populating a database from scratch isn't an everyday activity for a developer, we'll look at it in the `examples/CH_10/examples/02/models.py` to see how SQLAlchemy creates and inserts database table records. The program's goal in `examples/CH_10/examples/02/main.py` is to replicate the behavior of `examples/CH_10/examples/01/main.py` but use a database instead of CSV tables. To do so means parsing the CSV files and inserting the data into the database using SQLAlchemy. The `models.py` module contains the SQLAlchemy models and the

statement to create the database. It also has a custom function to read the CSV files
and load them into the database tables as follows:

```
def load_database():
    customers = CsvData("customer.csv")
    addresses = CsvData("address.csv")          Loads all of the CSV files into variables
    orders = CsvData("order.csv")               that are rows of dictionaries
    products = CsvData("product.csv")
    items = CsvData("item.csv")

    with session_manager() as session:          Uses a context manager to control
        # create the customers                  when the objects are committed
        for customer in customers.data.values(): (or not) to the database
            session.add(Customer(
                name=customer.get("name")
            ))

        # create addresses
        for address in addresses.data.values():
            session.add(Address(
                street=address.get("street"),   Creates Address instances and adds
                zipcode=address.get("zipcode")  them to the database session
            ))
        # create products
        for product in products.data.values():
            session.add(Product(
                name=product.get("name")        Creates Product instances and adds
            ))                                  them to the database session
        # commit these items
        session.commit()                        Commits the session to the database,
                                                assigning unique IDs to all the objects in that
                                                session and persisting them in the database
        # build a map of orders
        orders_map = {str(index): Order()
        for index, order in enumerate(
        orders.data.values(), start=1)}         Creates an orders map to help connect
                                                orders, items, customers, and products
        # build the orders and items
        for item in items.data.values():        Iterates over
            # get the order_id and order associated  the items
            with this item
            order_id = item.get("order_id")     Finds the order to which the
            order = orders_map.get(order_id)    current item is related

            # get the customer, address and product associated with the item
            customer_id = orders.data
            .get(order_id)
            .get("customer_id")
            customer = session.query(Customer)
            .filter(Customer.customer_id == customer_id)
            .one_or_none()
            address_id = orders.data
            .get(order_id).get("address_id")
            address = session.query(Address)
            .filter(Address.address_id == address_id)
            .one_or_none()
```

Creates Customer instances and adds them to the database session

Finds the customer to which the found order is related. The second statement is an SQLAlchemy query to get the customer instance.

Finds the address to which the found order is related. The second statement is an SQLAlchemy query to get the address instance.

```
        if order.customer is None:
            order.customer = customer
        if order.address is None:
            order.address = address
```

> **Assigns the customer and address to the order only if they don't already exist**

```
        # create an item with it's many-to-many associations
        product_id = item.get("product_id")
        product = session.query(Product)
        ➥.filter(Product.product_id == product_id)
        ➥.one_or_none()
        new_item = Item(
            qty=item.get("qty")
        )
        new_item.product = product
        order.items.append(new_item)
```

> **Finds the product instance to relate to the item, assigns it to the item, and then appends the item to the order**

```
    # add the populated orders to the
    ➥session and database
    for order in orders_map.values():
        session.add(order)
    session.commit()
```

> **Adds all the initialized orders to the session and commits the session to the database, persisting the orders and items**

There is quite a lot happening in this code. The gist is to read the CSV files and use the data to create instances of the corresponding SQLAlchemy models. Then use the SQLAlchemy-maintained attributes to develop the relationships between the instances.

Creating the `customer`, `address`, and `product` instances and then persisting them to the database with the `session.commit()` statement generates the unique ID primary key value for each record. The primary key values are used later to establish relationships when creating the orders and their associated items.

10.7.2   Using the data

The `examples/CH_10/examples/02/main.py` program demonstrates using the `transaction.sqlite` database to generate the invoice PDF files for all the orders:

```
import os
import csv
import sqlite3
from pathlib import Path
from jinja2 import Environment, FileSystemLoader
from weasyprint import HTML
from models import load_database, Order,
➥session_manager
```

> **Imports functionality from the models.py module. Notice that only the SQLAlchemy Order definition is used.**

> **Passes a single Order instance to the create_invoice function**

```
def create_invoice(order):
    """Create the PDF invoice for the order

    Args:
        info (dict): The info information to generate the invoice with
    """
    invoice_filename = f"invoice_{order.order_id}.pdf"
```

```
    # delete existing order invoice file if exists
    if os.path.exists(invoice_filename):
        os.remove(invoice_filename)

    # set up Jinja2 to generate the HTML and then the PDF file
    path = Path(__file__).parent
    env = Environment(loader=FileSystemLoader(Path(path)))
    template = env.get_template("invoice_template.jinja")
    html_out = template.render(order=order)
    HTML(string=html_out).write_pdf(
        invoice_filename,
        stylesheets=[
            "page.css",
            "bootstrap.css",
        ]
    )
```

Passes the single order instance to the Jinja template as the context parameter

```
# load the database
load_database()
```

Calls the load_database function defined in the models.py module to populate the database

```
# generate an invoice file for all the orders
with session_manager() as session:
    for order in session.query(Order).all():
        create_invoice(order)
```

With a database session, queries the database for all orders, iterates over them, and passes the single instances to the create_invoice function

The bulk of this program creates the invoice PDF files from the single SQLAlchemy Order instance passed to it. Because of the relationships established by the models, everything necessary to print an invoice is connected to the Order instance. The Jinja template uses the order context parameter to fill in the dynamic parts of the template:

```
<html lang="en">
  <head>
    <title>Invoice</title>
  </head>
  <body>
    <div class="container border border-dark border-2 rounded-2">
      <div class="container border border-dark mt-3 mb-3">
        <h3>Invoice</h3>
        Customer: {{order.customer.name}}<br />
        Street: {{order.address.street}}<br />
        Zip Code: {{order.address.zipcode}}<br />
        Order Number: {{order.order_id}}<br />
      </div>
      <table class="table table-striped table-bordered caption-top">
        <caption>
            Order Items
        </caption>
        <thead>
          <tr>
            <th>Item Number</th>
            <th>Product Name</th>
            <th>Quantity</th>
          </tr>
        </thead>
        <tbody>
```

Uses the order instance customer attribute to get the customer's name

Uses the order instance address attribute to get the address to which the order was shipped

Prints out the order's unique ID value

```
        {% for item in order.items %}
        <tr>
          <td>{{loop.index}}
          <td>{{item.product.name}}
          <td>{{item.qty}}
        </tr>
        {% endfor %}
      </tbody>
    </table>
  </div>
  </body>
</html>
```

Uses the order instance items
collection to print out the item
information in a table

Creating models for the tables with one-to-many relationships between the tables, SQLAlchemy provides attributes to access the data hierarchically rather than in a flat, two-dimensional way. The models, and the object instances created from them, allow you to consider the data in Pythonic terms rather than manage relationships yourself and jump from list to dictionary and back.

Our imaginary company and its simple data requirements allowed us to see how databases can greatly enhance merely persisting data. By adding relationships to the data structure, the storage of interrelated data is greatly simplified and functionality is improved.

10.8   Closing thoughts

You've taken a microscopic view of database systems to gain knowledge about what they do, how they do it, and why they're useful. Database systems give you access to powerful functionality and using SQLAlchemy to interact with those systems lets you think about them in Pythonic terms. In addition, using tools like SQLAlchemy helps you stay in the single Python domain rather than make mental context switches between SQL and Python domains. It's certainly possible to work in the latter, but it's more productive to work in the former.

Summary

- Persisting data over time usually means saving it to a long-term storage device, like the hard- or solid-state drive system attached to a computer. Files provide a simple solution but present some disadvantages.
- Database systems give applications a way to persist data in a structured way and establish relationships between that data. Relational database management systems (RDBMS) are applications that provide storage for structured, related data.
- Data storage is important to any application, but the relationships between data groups are equally important. The support for one-to-many and many-to-many relationships (among others) dramatically increases the utility of modern database systems.
- The Python SQLAlchemy module bridges the gap between the tables with rows of data in a database system to a more object-oriented access method in a Python application.

I've got something to say

At long last, we're at the point of adding content to the MyBlog application. Everything we've done so far to build the application has been aimed at creating the infrastructure to enable posting content to the blog.

You've created a database to persist information the MyBlog application manages over time. In addition, you've created users with roles so those users can register with and use the application. You've also modularized the application using Flask Blueprints to help manage the app's growing complexity, which adds structure and control to the application to help you and your users create and manage content on the MyBlog application.

Let's establish a naming convention to help us discuss content. Content is the engaging information a user writes and other users read and comment on. Content has an author, a creation timestamp, an update timestamp, and a title. The author, timestamps, and title are all associated with the content and its metadata. We'll gather this information into what we'll call a *post*, like on a bulletin board, where a user "posts" information they want others to read.

11.1 MyBlog posts

A MyBlog `Post` object gathers the content and all the information associated with it in one place. The `Post` object is persisted in the database to be accessed, searched, and managed.

Before getting too far into creating content, I want to talk about one of the MyBlog design goals—the presentation of content. The content presented by the MyBlog application is stored as plain text. However, that text can contain markdown syntax to enhance the presentation of the content. Markdown is a way to include plain ASCII characters in text content used during presentation to render text in bold or italics, include header sections in the visually rendered content, and generate many other features.

To achieve this, we'll be using the `Flask-PageDown` module created by Miguel Grinberg. This module takes care of presenting MyBlog markdown content correctly. It also provides tools to use markdown text and preview how it will be rendered interactively. You can find information about the `Flask-PageDown` module here: https://blog .miguelgrinberg.com/post/flask-pagedown-markdown-editor-extension-for-flask-wtf.

> **TIP** Miguel Grinberg is a software engineer who writes about Python and Flask on his blog and publishes books and modules useful to a well-grounded Python developer. His work is well worth checking out.

11.1.1 Modeling the database

The `Post` object is another SQLAlchemy class defining the structure of the post database table where the information is persisted. Because users who register with the MyBlog application can create multiple posts, there is a one-to-many relationship between users and posts. Figure 11.1 is the ERD (entity relationship diagram) between the existing `User` and new `Post` tables. Next, we'll create the SQLAlchemy model the MyBlog Python application uses to communicate with the database and the `Post` table.

SQLALCHEMY POST CLASS

You'll create the `Post` class to model the `Post` table as you've done for other models in the MyBlog application. The `Post` class inherits from the `db.Model` class to give it SQLAlchemy functionality. It also uses the `get_uuid()` function to create UUID primary key values.

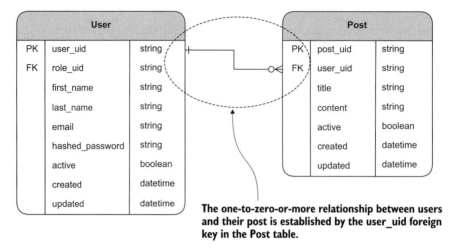

Figure 11.1   The ERD shows the one-to-zero or multiple relationships between users and their posts.

Here's the `Post` class definition from `examples/CH_11/examples/01/app/models.py`:

```
class Post(db.Model):
    __tablename__ = "post"
    post_uid = db.Column(db.String,
    ➥primary_key=True, default=get_uuid)
    user_uid = db.Column(db.String,
    ➥db.ForeignKey("user.user_uid"), nullable=False, index=True)
    title = db.Column(db.String)
    content = db.Column(db.String)
    active = db.Column(db.Boolean, nullable=False, default=True)
    created = db.Column(db.DateTime,
    ➥nullable=False, default=datetime.now(tz=timezone.utc))
    updated = db.Column(db.DateTime, nullable=False, default=datetime.now(
        tz=timezone.utc), onupdate=datetime.now(tz=timezone.utc))
```

Connects the model to the table named Post, as defined in the ERD diagram

Creates the primary key for the table using the get_uuid() function

Creates the foreign key relationship to the user table and user_uid value and indexes this column for faster querying

Marks the created field so the database will automatically add a UTC timestamp when the record is created

Marks the updated field so the database will automatically update the UTC timestamp when the record is updated

The `Post` class creates a structure to manage the content, user (author), title, and audit information. Because we've established a relationship between the `Post` class and the `User` class, we need to modify the `User` class to take advantage of this relationship:

```
class User(UserMixin, db.Model):
    __tablename__ = "user"
    user_uid = db.Column(db.String, primary_key=True, default=get_uuid)
```

```
role_uid = db.Column(db.String,
➥db.ForeignKey("role.role_uid"), index=True, nullable=False)
first_name = db.Column(db.String, nullable=False)
last_name = db.Column(db.String, nullable=False)
email = db.Column(db.String, nullable=False, unique=True, index=True)
hashed_password = db.Column("password", db.String, nullable=False)
posts = db.relationship("Post",
➥backref=db.backref("user", lazy="joined"))          ◄──────────────┐
active = db.Column(db.Boolean, nullable=False, default=True)          │
confirmed = db.Column(db.Boolean, default=False)      The new posts attribute,
created = db.Column(db.DateTime,                       which is a relationship
➥nullable=False,                                        to the Post class
➥default=datetime.now(tz=timezone.utc))
updated = db.Column(db.DateTime, nullable=False, default=datetime.now(
    tz=timezone.utc), onupdate=datetime.now(tz=timezone.utc))
```

The newly added `posts` attribute of the `User` class creates an association between the `User` and `Post` class. The `posts` attribute doesn't exist in the `User` table; it is created and managed by SQLAlchemy. The `posts` attribute is created when instances of the `User` class are created in response to database queries.

The use of *posts* plural is intentional, as the `db.relationship()` definition connects the single user to the many possible posts. The `posts` attribute is a Python list containing zero or more possible posts that the user can create.

The first parameter of the `db.relationship()` definition is `"Post"`. It is a string because the `Post` class is defined after the `User` class definition, and the use of a string causes SQLAlchemy to resolve the relationship at run time. It connects to the `Post` class using the `user_uid` attribute defined in the `Post` class as a `ForeignKey` to the `"user.user_uid"` attribute of the user table.

The second parameter to `db.relationship()` is `backref=db.backref ("user", lazy="joined")`, which handles two elements:

1 Creates an attribute named `"user"` on instances of `Post` classes that refer back to the parent user. SQLAlchemy maintains the `"user"` attribute.
2 Indicates that the relationship between `User` and `Posts` should use `"joined"` in the same select statement so the posts associated with a user are available immediately rather than requiring additional queries to retrieve them.

With the new `Post` and updated `User` class definitions, we can persist content and retrieve it in a consistent, structured way. Now we need to build a system to create and display that content.

11.2 Change of direction

Before proceeding much further, I should point out that the remainder of this book changes its presentation pattern. Previous chapters included extensive or complete code samples because I felt they were helpful to see the new concepts implemented. There are new concepts still to come, but they also include blocks of boilerplate code that you've seen before.

Presenting blocks of code in a book makes for dry reading and doesn't further the aims of the chapter, which are to introduce new ideas and how to implement them. So, rather than reviewing large code sections, we'll focus on what the code provides and refer to the specific code in the GitHub repository that accompanies this book.

11.3   Content Blueprint

At the beginning of this chapter, we discussed the benefits of having the infrastructure in place. We're going to take advantage of that infrastructure—in a cognitive sense because of what you know, and in an actual sense because of the structure you've built for the MyBlog application.

You're going to build a `Content` Blueprint to manage the MyBlog content. In every way, this is like the `Auth` Blueprint; it isolates functionality into a separate module, making it easier to think and work in the context of the content domain. Doing so puts into practice the idea of the separation of concerns.

As you did for the `auth` Blueprint, you'll add a new package directory named *content* under the app package. This directory has an __init__.py file containing the following code:

```
from flask import Blueprint

content_bp = Blueprint(
    "content_bp", __name__,
    static_folder="static",
    static_url_path="/content/static",
    template_folder="templates"
)

from . import content
```

This code is conceptually identical to what you've done previously for the `auth/` `.__init__.py` file. It creates a Blueprint instance called `content_bp` and configures it to have distinct `static` and `templates` folders. It also imports a module called `content` containing the handler for managing user content. Now that you've got a Blueprint namespace for MyBlog content posts, let's use it to present the content.

11.4   Displaying and creating posts

The MyBlog application needs a Python handler to intercept, as well as a function to process calls to the content URL to display the content. It also needs templates to render the posts as HTML pages in the browser.

11.4.1   Display handler

The content handler needs to access other parts of the MyBlog application, which it does by importing the required modules and instances in the `examples/CH_11/` `examples/01/app/content/content.py` module. The first handler in the content module is for the URL `"/blog_posts"`, and it deals with two functions:

- First, if the URL is invoked with a query string where `action` is `None`, it displays all the content posts in the MyBlog application.
- If the URL is invoked with a query string of `action=create`, it presents a logged-in user with a web page form where post content is created. That content can be saved to the database when the form is submitted.

The `blog_posts()` handler is a simple dispatch function to two other functions, depending on how the URL is invoked. Both actions could be handled in a single function, but that would have been more complex and harder to follow. The complexity is reduced by splitting the behavior into two functions.

The first dispatch function is `blog_posts_display()`, responsible for rendering all the MyBlog blog posts to a browser page. The `blog_posts_display()` function takes the following steps to display the list of blog posts:

1. Gets the search string from the request.
2. Begins a database session context manager.
3. Gets the current page from the request.
4. Creates a query to the database for content posts sorted in updated timestamp descending order.
5. Conditionally adds a filter to the query to control whether the user can see active posts or all posts. This allows users with editor or administrator permissions to see both active and inactive posts.
6. Conditionally adds a filter to the query to return posts only containing the search term.
7. Gets the relevant posts based on the query.
8. Renders the lists of posts to the browser display.

11.4.2 Display template

The content handler is responsible for gathering the intended data passed to the template. The template `examples/CH_11/examples/01/app/content/templates/posts.html` can then be rendered and sent to the browser.

Like the templates in the `auth` Blueprint, the content templates inherit from the system-wide `base.html` template file and build the content block from there. The template iterates over the list of posts, if any, passed by the content handler. The template code formats a one-hundred-character snippet of the content and renders it as a Bootstrap card. If you run the MyBlog application in `examples/CH_11/examples/01`, and you have sample content in the database, the system will render a content post page.

Notice the blog posts are displayed in order of the most recent first. This is because the query sorts the results in descending order using the updated timestamp. Because "The Second Post" was created after "This is the first post," it appears first in the rendered display.

Because there were only two posts in the database I used when the screenshot (shown in figure 11.2) was captured, there is no need to paginate the display, and only the single page link "1" is shown. The `render_pagination()` macro in the handler creates these page links. The number of blog posts to display per page is controlled by the configuration variable `blog_posts_per_page` in the `settings.toml` file.

The second blog post with its title and contents comes first because the posts are sorted by the updated date in descending order.

The first blog post with its title and contents comes after the second.

Figure 11.2   The browser page showing the rendered content for the first and second posts

11.5   *Creating posts*

Creating a MyBlog content post requires a URL handler, a form, and a template for the user to enter content and review it. Once users are satisfied with what they've created, they can save it to the database.

11.5.1   *Creation handler*

The second function in the `blog_posts()` dispatch handler is the `blog_posts _create()` function, which renders a form-based page with which a registered user can create and save blog post content. The `blog_posts_create()` handler function follows these steps to access the content from the form and save it to the database:

1 Creates an instance of the `PostForm` form handling class.
2 Checks if the form Cancel button was clicked and redirects to the home page if it was.
3 Validates the form if the Submit button was clicked and renders the empty form if it was not.
4 If the form was submitted and it passes validation, a database session context manager opens.
5 Creates an instance of the `Post` SQLAlchemy model class, passing in the form content.
6 Adds the `Post` instance to the database session.
7 Commits the session to the database.
8 Notifies the user that the post was created.
9 Redirects the user to the newly created post.

11.5.2 Creation form

Because the post is created using a form, the handler needs to have access to a class definition to manage that form. The `PostForm` class exists in the `examples/CH_11/examples/01/app/content/forms.py` file.

The `PostForm` class inherits from `FlaskForm`, just like the forms used in the `auth` Blueprint. The form to create post content has four elements:

- `title`—A `StringField` to contain the title text
- `content`—A `PageDownField` to contain the text, which can use markdown syntax for display when the content is rendered
- `post_create`—The `SubmitField` that submits the form to the handler
- `cancel`—Another `SubmitField` item that is intercepted by the handler to cancel any actions and return the user to the home screen

The `render_kw` parameter is added to all of the fields in the form. The `render_kw` parameter is a dictionary that adds extra HTML attributes to the elements when they are rendered to the browser display.

The `tabindex` key in the `render_kw` dictionary controls the order that the cursor will move from element to element when the TAB or ALT-TAB keys are pressed on the keyboard. The `autofocus` key in the `render_kw` dictionary controls which element has cursor focus when the form is rendered. The `tabindex` and `autofocus` keys add useability features to the form to help the user reduce the number of clicks necessary to navigate and use the form.

11.5.3 Creation template

The post-create template is connected to the `PostForm` class through the post-create handler. The handler uses the template file `examples/CH_11/examples/01/app/`

`content/templates/post_create.html` to render the form and send it to the browser. The interactive markdown behavior of the form is handled by creating a form field of type `PageDownField` and then rendering it on the page.

If you run the application from the `examples/CH_11/examples/01/` directory, log in, and navigate to create a post, you'll be presented with the post content creation form. The screenshot in figure 11.3 shows this display. The form has two text input fields, Title and Content. The bottom part of the screen interactively represents how the text in the Content field will be rendered by the browser. I've entered some text containing markdown for headers to show how the markdown is displayed by the `Flask-PageDown` module.

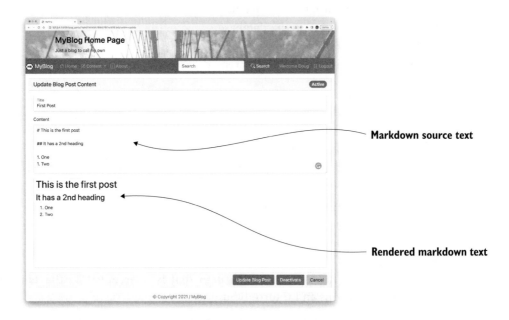

Figure 11.3   The blog post content-creation form uses markdown to style the content.

As the user types in the Content input field, the system will interactively update the lower part of the display to render that content. This is very useful when creating markdown content, and similar behavior is seen on sites like Stackoverflow and GitHub. Now that users can create MyBlog content, let's give them a way to edit that content to update their posts.

11.6   *Displaying and editing a post*

You've developed infrastructure to display multiple posts and create a new post. Now you need to build systems to display and edit a single post.

11.6.1 *Display handler*

In the previous section, you handled displaying multiple, abbreviated posts to the browser. You've also provided the ability to create new posts. Now we need to add support to display a single post. If you look back at the template to render the list of MyBlog posts, you'll see each post is wrapped in an HTML hyperlink anchor tag <a...> that generates a `"/blog_posts/{post_uid}"` URL. This link navigates the user to the single post using the unique `post_uid` value.

Like the initial handler for multiple posts, a single post is handled with a dispatch routine in anticipation of handling an HTTP `GET` request with or without a query string. The `blog_post()` handler is another such dispatch function, delegating to two other functions—one to display a single post and another to edit a single post.

The first function is the `blog_post_display(post_uid)`, which renders a single MyBlog post based on the `post_uid` parameter passed in the link. The function takes the following steps to get the post content from the database and display it in the browser:

1 Begins a database session context manager.
2 Creates the initial database query to get the post with the `post_uid` value. The query also performs a `JOIN` operation with the `user` table to get the user information related to the post.
3 Modifies the query based on the user permissions to see all posts or only active ones.
4 Executes the database query.
5 If no post was returned from the query, aborts with a `NOT FOUND` error.
6 Renders the post with the related single post template.

11.6.2 *Display template*

The `blog_post()` content handler gets the content post from the database using the `post_uid` value passed as a path parameter in the URL that invoked the dispatch function. Next, the `post` information is passed to the display template `examples/CH_11/examples/01/app/content/templates/post.html`. The template is responsible for rendering the data sent to it as an HTML page to display in the user's browser.

The template conditionally renders the Active badge in the upper right corner of the page to indicate the active/inactive state of the post. This is displayed for MyBlog administrators and editors as well as the author of the post. In addition, the template conditionally renders the Update button, anticipating navigation to the edit system. Figure 11.4 presents a screenshot of the rendered display.

The Created and Updated fields displayed a timestamp when the post's author created and last updated it. Both timestamps are presented in the logged-in user's local time zone. If you recall, all models of the tables in the MyBlog database have `created` and `updated` fields, and those fields are automatically populated with a UTC timestamp. So how is the system presenting local time zone timestamps when all it has

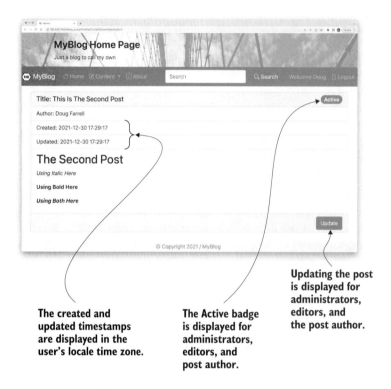

Updating the post is displayed for administrators, editors, and the post author.

The created and updated timestamps are displayed in the user's locale time zone.

The Active badge is displayed for administrators, editors, and post author.

Figure 11.4   A single-content post display as rendered for the post author

access to are UTC timestamps? Take a look at the `post.html` template, and you'll see this code snippet:

```
<li class="list-group-item">
    Created: {{ post.created | format_datetime | safe }}
</li>
<li class="list-group-item">
    Updated: {{ post.updated | format_datetime | safe }}
</li>
```

These few lines of code render the `created` and `updated` timestamps as HTML unordered list items. Notice that timestamp data is piped into `format_datetime` and then piped into `safe`. Previously, the `safe` filter has been used in MyBlog templates, but `format_datetime` is a new filter function that's added to the `app/__init__.py` module:

```
@app.template_filter()
def format_datetime(value, format="%Y-%m-%d %H:%M:%S"):
    value_with_timezone = value.replace(tzinfo=timezone.utc)
  tz = pytz.timezone(session.get("timezone_info", {}).get("timeZone", "US/
    Eastern"))
```

```
local_now = value_with_timezone.astimezone(tz)
return local_now.strftime(format)
```

The decorator adds the `format_datetime()` function as a filter to the template engine, making it available in the HTML template snippet shown previously. Because it's part of a filter pipeline, it accepts the value of whatever is before it in the template pipeline as a parameter—in this case, a UTC timestamp. It then uses `timezone_info` from the user's session to create a timestamp in the local time zone. That local timestamp is then formatted into a string and returned.

The `timezone_info` data comes from the user's session information. How does it get there? The `examples/CH_11/examples/01/app/auth/auth.py` module's `login()` function has been modified to add time zone information to the user's session. When a user logs in, the following line of code adds the time zone information to their session:

```
session["timezone_info"] = json.loads(form.timezone_info.data)
```

This line of code creates a dictionary of time zone information from a string stored in a form field called `timezone_info`. The `timezone_info` is a hidden field in the form populated by a small JavaScript function in the `login.js` file included in the login template:

```
(function() {
    let timezone_info = document.getElementById('timezone_info');
 timezone_info.value = JSON.stringify(Intl.DateTimeFormat().
 ➥resolvedOptions());
}())
```

The self-evaluating function runs when the browser has rendered the template. It finds the `timezone_info` hidden field element in the HTML page and populates it with the `JSON.stringify` results of calling the function `Intl.DateTimeFormat()` `.resolvedOptions()`. In the Chrome browser on my computer, this generates the JavaScript object:

```
{
    calendar: "gregory",
    day: "numeric",
    locale: "en-US",
    month: "numeric",
    numberingSystem: "latn",
    timeZone: "America/New_York",
    year: "numeric"
}
```

The previous object is useful information when presenting time and date information in a locale context. It's necessary to do this work in JavaScript because the functionality runs on the user's computer, which could be anywhere in the world. This makes the data returned relevant to the user, not the server where the MyBlog application could be running. The `format_datetime` filter function uses the `timeZone` field to determine how to create a local time zone value of the `created` and `updated` timestamps.

TIP When you're working on a web-based application, it's worth thinking about time zones when presenting data to your users. If you deploy your application to the internet, your users could be anywhere in the world. Presenting the UTC would be easy, but not very helpful to your user base.

11.6.3 Update handler

If a user decides to make changes to their blog content and clicks the Update button, they are directed to the dispatch function with the query string "action=update". The dispatch function handles the request and calls the blog_post_update() function. The function follows these steps to populate and present the page:

1 blog_post_update is decorated with @login_required, requiring a user to be logged in to update a post.
2 Begins a database context manager.
3 Creates a query to get the post based on the passed post_uid.
4 Modifies the query based on the user's role to get only active posts, or all posts.
5 Executes the query and gets the results.
6 Was no post found? Then the function aborts the request with NOT FOUND.
7 Gets the template form information and populates the fields with the post values.
8 Was the form Cancel button clicked? Then the function redirects the user to the home page.
9 Was the form submitted, and is it valid? Then it updates the post returned by the query with form data, saves the updated post to the database, and redirects the user to the post display page to show the updates.
10 Renders the post_update template using the form and the post returned by the query.

11.6.4 Update form

The data to update the post comes from the PostUpdateForm in the content/forms.py module. The form contains the field information used in the post_update.html template to build and render the HTML page to the browser.

The form provides the title, content, post_update, and cancel fields visible when the form is rendered. It also provides a hidden field called active_state, which holds the user's selected active state. The active state is controlled by the template conditionally rendering one of two other fields—activate and deactivate. The current user must be the author of the content or a MyBlog administrator for the activate and deactivate fields to be displayed.

Depending on the current active state of the post, one or the other of these fields are presented to the user as buttons. The form is submitted if the user clicks the button, and the active state value is toggled. The activate and deactivate buttons represent mutually exclusive actions to take, and only one is shown on the page at a time.

11.6.5   *Update template*

The `post_update.html` template is responsible for rendering the page to the browser where the logged-in user can modify the post's content. The template uses the form information and data passed to it to render the update-post display in the browser. Depending on the current user's role, they can toggle the active state of the post with the conditionally presented activate and deactivate buttons. The snippet of the template controlling this behavior is shown here:

```
{% if can_set_blog_post_active_state(post) %}
    {% if post.active == True %}
    {{form.deactivate(class_="btn btn-danger me-2")}}
 {% else %}
    {{form.activate(class_="btn btn-success me-2")}}
 {% endif %}
{% endif %}
```

The outer `if` statement calls the function `can_set_blog_post_active_state()`, which returns `True` or `False` if the currently logged-in user can change the active state of the post. The user must be an administrator or the post's author to do so.

The inner `if/else` conditional determines which field to render—`deactivate` or `activate`—depending on the current active state of the post.

The function `can_set_blog_post_active_state()` exists in the `content.py` handler module as part of two functions made available in the context of template processing:

```
@content_bp.context_processor            ◁──┐  Decorator to add template context
def utility_processor():                     │  functionality to the content Blueprint
    def can_update_blog_post(post):        ◁──┐
        if not current_user.is_anonymous:     │  Returns True if the currently logged-
            if current_user.role.permissions &│  in user is an ADMINISTRATOR or
            ➡(Role.Permissions.ADMINISTRATOR |│  EDITOR, otherwise returns False
            ➡Role.Permissions.EDITOR):
                return True
            if current_user.user_uid == post.user.user_uid:
                return True
        return False
                                          │  Returns True if the currently
                                          │  logged-in user is an ADMINISTRATOR
    def can_set_blog_post_active_state(post):  ◁──┘  or the author of the post content
        if current_user.is_anonymous:
            return False
        if current_user.role.permissions & (Role.Permissions.ADMINISTRATOR):
            return True
        else:
            if current_user.user_uid == post.user.user_uid:
                return True
        return False
                          │  Returns the two functions to
                          │  add to the template context
    return dict(          ◁──┘
        can_update_blog_post=can_update_blog_post,
        can_set_blog_post_active_state=can_set_blog_post_active_state,
    )
```

11.7   *Content to comment hierarchy*

The MyBlog application can have many content posts. Each post can have many comments associated with it. Each of those first-level comments can also have many comments associated with it. The MyBlog application will limit comment nesting to two levels to keep things reasonable.

The hierarchy in figure 11.5 shows two content posts, posts 0 and 1. Content post 0 has two level 1 comments associated with it, with the first comment having two level 2 comments and the second comment having one level 2 comment. Content post 1 has three level 1 comments, with only one having a level 2 comment.

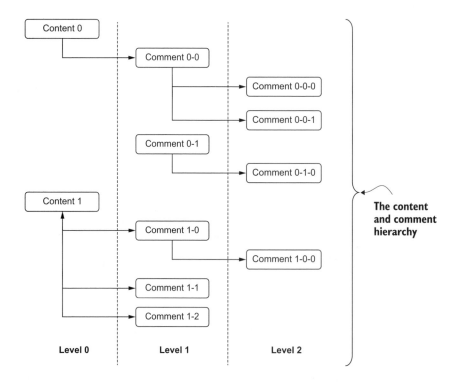

Figure 11.5   The content and comment relationship structure forms a hierarchy.

Post content can contain markdown syntax, used at display rendering time, but is otherwise stored in the database as text. Comments on content won't support markdown when displayed but are also stored as text. Aside from the title field associated with content, comments look very much like content when storing them in the database.

This suggests a relationship between content and comments that we can take advantage of in the application. Content is stored in the `post` table, and it wouldn't be unreasonable to store level 1 and 2 comments in separate tables based on the listed hierarchy. By creating separate tables, the `post` table could have a one-to-many relationship to level 1 comments, and level 1 comments could have a one-to-many relationship to level 2 comments.

A three-table database structure would work and provide the desired functionality. However, I think it has some drawbacks. First, content and comment posts are almost identical in structure. They both have content related to the user who posted them, and they have created and updated timestamps.

The primary difference between them is that comments don't have a title. The SQLite database engine doesn't allocate space in the database for text fields unless needed, so not using the title field doesn't cost anything in terms of disk space.

The second drawback is the arbitrary two-level nesting limit of comments. For MyBlog, the two-level limit helps keep examples in this chapter within reason. In a publicly available application, the requirements could easily change to three, four, or more levels of comments. Extending support for more levels by using a table for each level means adding new tables, where each new table essentially replicates its parent table.

We can overcome these drawbacks by being clever. For example, rather than having content—level 1 and level 2 comments—in separate, nearly identical tables, why not extend the existing `Post` table to support both content and comment posts? This is possible by adding a `parent_uid` field to the table, as illustrated in figure 11.6. In this way, a row can be the parent of another row while simultaneously being the child of some other parent row.

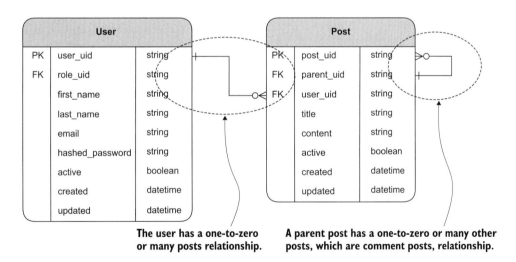

Figure 11.6 The self-referential `Post` table creates a hierarchal content/comment structure.

We've created a self-referential hierarchy by adding the `parent_uid` to the `Post` table and making it a foreign key to the `post_uid` of the same table. Any row with a `parent_uid` equal to NULL is the root of a hierarchy and a content post. Any row with a non-NULL `parent_uid` references another row in the table and is a child comment. The `parent_uid` that a child row references can be a content post or a comment post.

> **TIP**   Self-referential tables are very useful when you're trying to store hierarchical data. This is true if the nodes in the hierarchy are identical in structure, or close enough to identical.

Each row in the table can have a one-to-many relationship to a list of child rows within the same table. The top-level rows with no parent are content posts; others are comments. This structure has no inherent limit on the depth of comment nesting the table can support. With this self-referential structure, the two-level nesting constraint is a function of the application, not the database.

11.7.1 Modifying the post class

To implement the ERD diagram of the `Post` table, the `Post` class in the `models.py` module must be updated. You'll see the changes in `examples/CH_11/examples/02/app/models.py`:

```
class Post(db.Model):
    __tablename__ = "post"
    post_uid = db.Column(db.String, primary_key=True, default=get_uuid)
    parent_uid = db.Column(db.String,
        db.ForeignKey("post.post_uid"),          Adds the parent_uid foreign key
        default=None)                            to post_uid of the post table
    sort_key = db.Column(db.Integer,
        nullable=False, unique=True,
        default=get_next_sort_key)               Adds the sort_key, which is an
    user_uid = db.Column(db.String,              auto-incrementing value
        db.ForeignKey("user.user_uid"),          that's not a primary key
        nullable=False, index=True)
    title = db.Column(db.String)
    content = db.Column(db.String)               Adds the child relationship, creates
    children = db.relationship("Post",           the list of children associated with
        backref=db.backref("parent",             this post, and adds "parent" to each
        remote_side=[post_uid], lazy="joined"))  child, referencing the child's parent
    active = db.Column(db.Boolean, nullable=False, default=True)
    created = db.Column(db.DateTime,
        nullable=False,
        default=datetime.now(tz=timezone.utc))
    updated = db.Column(db.DateTime, nullable=False, default=datetime.now(
        tz=timezone.utc), onupdate=datetime.now(tz=timezone.utc))
```

The `parent_uid` value creates the one-to-many relationship between rows of the post table. The `children` attribute doesn't exist in the database but is created by SQLAlchemy when a `Post` object is returned by a query, adding a list of children associated with the post. It also adds a `parent` attribute to child rows referencing their parent row.

The `sort_key` attribute is used to keep the hierarchy in properly nested order when displaying a content post and its related comments. The default value of `sort_key` is a custom Python function called when a new row is created:

```
def get_next_sort_key() -> int:
    with db_session_manager(session_close=False) as db_session:
        retval = db_session.query(func.ifnull(
        ⇒func.max(Post.sort_key) + 1, 0)).scalar()
        if retval is None:
            raise RuntimeError("Failed to get new value for sort_key")
        return retval
```

The get_next_sort_key() function gets the current max sort_key value from the
post table, adds 1 to it, and returns that value. Having the function called as the default
value of sort_key creates an automatically incrementing unique sort_key value for
every row created in the post table. This behavior emulates the database's autoincre-
ment behavior for a primary key field. Unfortunately, SQLite doesn't allow this behavior for nonprimary key fields, which sort_key is not. The value is used when querying
the table to render a post and its hierarchy of comments, shown in another section.

11.7.2   Display handler

Comment posts are variations of content posts in the MyBlog application. Because of
this, displaying, creating, and updating them are handled by modifying the existing
handlers in content.py. Additional forms are added to get the user input to create
comments. These changes are in the examples/CH_11/examples/02/app directory.

The most significant change to the content.py module occurs in the blog_
post_display() function. Displaying a MyBlog content post requires rendering any
comments associated with the post in a meaningful hierarchical order. Structuring the
post table in a clever manner and making it self-referential means you have to be
clever with the query to get the post content and its comments.

Figure 11.5 indicates a treelike structure where one root node—a content post—
branches out to multiple comment post nodes. This kind of structure can be traversed
using recursion.

Because the content and comment posts are identical in definition, each one can
have zero or many children; the same functionality can be applied to each. The list of
associated children is iterated over at each node, and each child is descended into to
use the functionality again.

The same functionality is applied again until a node with no children is reached, at
which point the functionality ascends back to the child's parent, and the next child is
processed. This process continues until the entire tree attached to the content root
node has been traversed.

To create this kind of functionality with SQLAlchemy, and ultimately in SQL, we'll
use common table expressions (CTE) with recursion. A CTE is a temporary, named
result of an SQL query used within the context of a larger, enclosing query. A recursive CTE can traverse tree structures like the self-referential Post table.

The blog_post_display(post_uid) handler function has been simplified to:

```
def blog_post_display(post_uid):
    logger.debug("rendering blog post page")
    form = PostCommentForm()
```

```
with db_session_manager() as db_session:
    posts = _build_posts_hierarchy(db_session, post_uid)
    if posts is None:
        flash(f"Unknown post uid: {post_uid}")
        abort(HTTPStatus.NOT_FOUND)
    return render_template("post.html", form=form, posts=posts)
```

This handler function is passed the post_uid value as a parameter from the URL that invoked the handler and takes the following steps:

1 Gets the form associated with the display for user comment input.
2 Begins a database session context manager.
3 Gets the hierarchy of the posts related to the post_uid value.
4 Did we get any return posts? If not, it aborts the request.
5 Renders the post.html template, passing it the form, and posts data.

Getting the hierarchy of the posts results from calling the function _build_posts_hierarchy(db_session, post_uid). This function moves the relative complexity of the recursive query out of the display function for clarity. The leading _ character is just a convention to indicate the function is considered nonpublic. The _build_posts_hierarchy() function does the heavy lifting to get the hierarchy of the posts from the database starting from the root node (parent_uid equals NULL) and traverses the tree recursively to get all comments:

```
def _build_posts_hierarchy(db_session, post_uid):
    # build the list of filters here to use in the CTE
    filters = [
        Post.post_uid == post_uid,
        Post.parent_uid == None
    ]
    if current_user.is_anonymous or
    current_user.can_view_posts():
        filters.append(Post.active == True)

    # build the recursive CTE query
    hierarchy = (
        db_session
        .query(Post, Post.sort_key.label(
        "sorting_key"))
        .filter(*filters)
        .cte(name='hierarchy', recursive=True)
    )
    children = aliased(Post, name="c")
    hierarchy = hierarchy.union_all(
        db_session
        .query(
            children,
            (
                func.cast(hierarchy.c.sorting_key,
                String) +
                " " +
                func.cast(children.sort_key,
                String)
```

Creates filters used to get the post matching the passed post_uid and ensure it's a root (content) node

Adds a filter so only posts the user is allowed to view are returned by the query

Begins creating the recursive CTE

Creates an alias for the Post class

Completes the CTE

```
        ).label("sorting_key")
    )      #
    .filter(children.parent_uid ==
    ➡hierarchy.c.post_uid)
)
# query the hierarchy for the post
➡and it's comments
return (
    db_session
    .query(Post, func.cast(
    ➡hierarchy.c.sorting_key, String))
    .select_entity_from(hierarchy)
    .order_by(hierarchy.c.sorting_key)
    .all()
)
```

Completes the CTE

Queries the CTE for the hierarchical posts

This is the most complicated query in the MyBlog application and deserves an explanation. The `hierarchy` variable is set to the root node of the post based on the `post_uid` value. It's also declared as a recursive CTE. Remember, recursive behavior descends a tree with similar operations on similar objects. That recursive behavior is provided by the `hierarchy` query instance having a `union_all()` operation applied to it. This descends the tree by connecting `parent_uid` with `post_uid` values.

Notice what's going on with the `sort_key` value. The `sort_key` value is an auto-incrementing integer in the database, but the query casts it to a string labeled `sorting_key`. Comparing two posts by their `sort_key` values, the post with the higher `sort_key` value was inserted into the database after the post with the lower value. This is because the `sort_key` value auto-increments, so a new post inserted into the database gets a greater `sort_key` value than any other previous post.

The `sorting_key` value is a cumulative string of `sort_key` values, parent to child to child, separated by a space character. The `sorting_key` value provides the full path in descending chronological order to each post returned by the query. Because it is a string rather than a number, it sorts appropriately to display the post contents and its comments in order. The function returns the results of querying the recursive CTE and uses the `sorting_key` to apply an `order_by()` clause.

11.7.3 Display template

The `post.html` template is modified to display the post content and its comments. It has two phases: the first renders the content much as before; the second adds the hierarchy of related comments indented to indicate the hierarchy.

Because a content post can have many comments, the template iterates over the comment posts to render them to the HTML page. The rendering operation is almost identical for each comment, so the functionality is in a macro that is called during each iteration of the comment loop. The indent level of each comment is determined by splitting the `sorting_key` value of the post on space characters and using the length of the returned array to calculate the indent level.

The template also provides interface elements to create new comments and edit existing ones. This is done by using the Bootstrap modal functionality to open a dialog window over the current display to create and edit comments. A macro function provides the necessary modal HTML.

Both the comment and modal macros are in a new file. Keeping with the Blueprint namespacing, the template imports a content-specific macro file, `content_macros.jinja`. This file is located in the `content/templates` folder. Running the MyBlog application in `examples/CH_11/examples/02` and navigating to a post that contains content and related comments renders a page that displays both. Figure 11.7 is a screenshot of the rendered display.

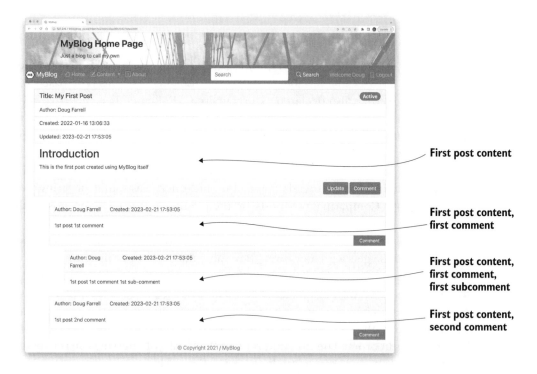

Figure 11.7   The content display will also show any related comments and subcomments.

11.8   Creating comments

The previous display shows user interface elements to create comments on the content and comment on an existing comment. Both behaviors depend on creating a post that references a parent post.

11.8.1   Creation template

We're changing the order of the presentation to talk about the comment creation template first because it exists in the `post.html` template already. Rather than navigate away from the currently displayed post to create a comment, MyBlog uses Bootstrap's ability to create modal windows.

Modal windows are subordinate to the main window but disable interaction and display as a child window over the main window. This is useful in UI design to help keep the user's frame of reference connected to the task at hand.

Bootstrap creates the HTML elements of a modal window in the HTML of the window the modal will appear over. The containing HTML DOM element of the modal window is set to invisible when the parent window is rendered and appears because of an action by the user.

At the end of the `post.html` template, a call to a content macro is made:

```
{{ content_macros.form_create_comment_modal() }}
```

The file `examples/CH_11/examples/02/app/content/template/content-macros.jinja` contains the macro code. The macro inserts the HTML elements necessary to build the modal window into the rendered post display.

Each of the comment buttons in the display activates the modal window, making it visible (figure 11.8). The modal window presents a form with an HTML text area to

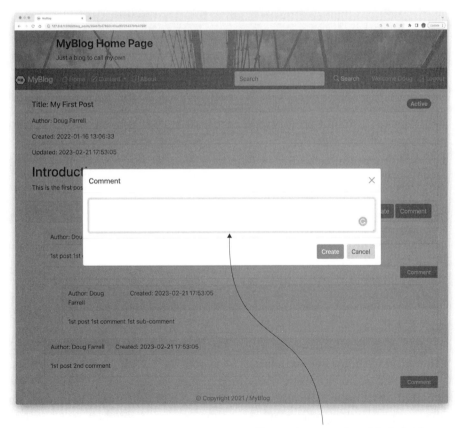

The create comment modal window is
displayed over the current content display.

Figure 11.8   Creating a comment happens in a modal window over the current content display.

enter the comment. It also has a hidden field populated with the `post_uid` value of
the parent post to which this comment relates. The hidden field was populated by the
Comment button when it was clicked. The Create button submits the form to be processed, and the Cancel button closes the modal window. Because the modal exists in
the `post.html` template, the parent form elements were available when the template
was rendered.

11.8.2 Creation form

The form to handle creating a comment exists in the `app/content/forms.py` module. This simple form creates the hidden field for the `parent_post_uid` of the parent post, the text area field for the comment, and the create submit button.

11.8.3 Creation handler

When a user has entered comment text and clicked the Create button, the form is
submitted to the handler as an HTTP `POST` request to the URL `"/blog_post_
create_comment"`:

```
@content_bp.post("/blog_post_create_comment")
def blog_post_create_comment():
form = PostCommentForm()
if form.validate_on_submit():
    with db_session_manager() as db_session:
        post = Post(
            user_uid=current_user.user_uid,
            parent_uid=form.parent_post_uid.data,
            content=form.comment.data.strip(),
        )
        db_session.add(post)
        db_session.commit()
        root_post = post.parent
        while root_post.parent is not None:
            root_post = root_post.parent
        flash("Comment created")
        return redirect(url_for("content_bp.blog_post",
    post_uid=root_post.post_uid))
else:
    flash("No comment to create")
return redirect(url_for("intro_bp.home"))
```

The handler is responsible for validating the submitted form and creating the new
comment post in the database. The created post has a `parent_uid` value that comes
from making this a child of that post.

After the comment post is committed to the database, the `while` loop exists to iterate up the hierarchy and get the root post. The root post is used to redirect the user to
the root post of the hierarchy where the newly created comment will be rendered and
displayed.

11.9   Notifying users

Another feature we'd like to add to the MyBlog application is notifying users when someone they're following creates a new content post. A user who comments on a post is automatically added as a follower of the post.

Implementing followers creates a many-to-many relationship between users and posts. A user can follow many posts, and many users can follow a single post. As was shown in chapter 10, a many-to-many relationship uses an association table to connect two other tables. The examples/CH_11/examples/03/app/models.py module is modified to add the association table:

```
user_post = db.Table(
"user_post",
db.Column("user_uid", db.String, db.ForeignKey("user.user_uid")),
db.Column("post_uid", db.String, db.ForeignKey("post.post_uid"))
)
```

Instead of a class to model the user_post table, it's created as an instance of the Table class of SQLAlchemy. The user_post table has just two fields—foreign keys to the primary keys of each of the associated tables. The user model class is also modified to add the many-to-many relationship connection between it and the Post model:

```
posts_followed = db.relationship(
    "Post",
    secondary=user_post,
    backref=db.backref(
        "users_following",
        lazy="dynamic"
    )
)
```

The user.posts_followed attribute doesn't exist in the database but is maintained by SQLAlchemy. An instance of the User class returned from a query will have the posts_followed attribute as a list of Post instances.

The secondary parameter connects a User instance with a Post instance through the user_post association table. The backref parameter creates a users_following attribute in the Post class. This also isn't in the database but is maintained by SQLAlchemy. For a Post instance, the attribute users_following is a list of User instances following the Post.

To populate the user_post association table and create the many-to-many relationship, the blog_post_create_comment() handler function is modified with the addition of the following lines of code:

```
root_post = post.parent
while root_post.parent is not None:
root_post = root_post.parent
follow_root_post(db_session, root_post)
notify_root_post_followers(db_session, root_post)
```

The while loop to traverse upward in the post hierarchy was created in the previous example to get the root_post value. The two new functions—follow_root_post() and notify_root_post_followers()—use the root_post value:

```
def follow_root_post(db_session, root_post):
user = (
    db_session.query(User)
    .filter(User.user_uid == current_user.user_uid)
    .one_or_none()
)
if user is not None and root_post not in
➥user.posts_followed:
    user.posts_followed.append(root_post)
```

The follow_root_post() function gets an instance of the current user. When the user is found, the root_post is added to the posts_followed list if the user isn't already following that post:

```
def notify_root_post_followers(db_session, root_post):
post_url = url_for(
    "content_bp.blog_post",
    post_uid=root_post.post_uid,
    _external=True
)
for user_following in root_post.users_following:
    to = user_following.email
    subject = "A post you're following has
➥been updated"
    contents = (
        f"""Hi {user_following.first_name},
        A blog post you're following has had a
    ➥comment update added to it. You can view
        that post here: {post_url}
        Thank you!
        """
    )
    send_mail(to=to, subject=subject,
➥contents=contents)
```

The notify_root_post_followers() function first sets the post_url variable to the URL of the newly created content post. It then iterates over the list of the users who follow the post's author. Inside the loop, it uses the emailer module created for authentication to send a short email containing the post_url to the user_following user.

11.10 *Handling site errors*

So far, the MyBlog application has tried to handle errors and exceptions gracefully and redirect the user to another place in the application. Where exceptions have been raised and caught in try/except blocks, the exception handling has consisted of either logging the error or raising another, more specific one.

Flask handles exceptions that bubble up by rendering very generic HTML to display the exception message. This is great because the exception was handled and reported and didn't crash the MyBlog application, but it's not a good user experience.

A better solution is for the exception to be reported within the context of the MyBlog application, with the navigation bar present and a quick way to get back to another part of the experience.

Flask provides mechanisms to register error-handling functions using the register_error_handler method that is part of the app instance. Looking at examples/CH_11/examples/04/app/__init__.py in the create_app() function, you'll see these lines of code:

```
app.register_error_handler(404, error_page)
app.register_error_handler(500, error_page)
```

These lines of code use the Flask app instance that the create_app() function generated to call the register_error_handler() method. The first parameter to the call is the HTTP error code for which an error handler function is registered, and the second is the name of the handler function.

The method is called twice, once for a 404 (Page Not Found) error and again for a 500 (Internal Server Error) error. Any number of other standard HTTP errors can be handled in this way. Both calls register the same error_page() function as the handler. The error_page() function is at the bottom of the __init__.py module:

```
def error_page(e):
    return render_template("error.html", e=e), e.code
```

This function is passed the exception that caused the error as a parameter. Inside the function, a new template, "error.html", is rendered and passed the exception value. The exception code value is used as the HTTP return value for the page. The examples/CH_11/examples/04/app/templates/error.html template file does a few simple things:

```
{% extends "base.html" %}

{% block title %}{{ e.name }}{% endblock %}

{% block content %}
<div class="error_page mx-auto mt-3" style="width: 50%;">
  <div class="container">
      <div class="card text-center">
          <h5 class="card-header">
              {{ e.code }} : {{ e.name }}
          </h5>
          <div class="card-body">
              <div class="card-text">
                  {{ e.description }}
              </div>
          </div>
      </div>
  </div>
</div>
{% endblock %}
```

In terms of user experience, the most important thing is the template inheriting from "base.html". This gives the page the style of the rest of the MyBlog application and its navigation bar. In addition, this gives users who find themselves on an error page a way to get back to another page in the application. The rest of the template styles the output of the exception code, name, and description as a Bootstrap card.

CROSS-SITE SCRIPTING

Another area of concern that the code in `examples/CH_11/examples/04` attempts to handle are cross-site scripting (XSS) injection attacks. This kind of attack occurs when JavaScript is injected into a site and later runs on another user's browser.

Because creating content and comments lets the user enter plain text, that text could contain embedded JavaScript code in this form:

```
"… some benign content
<script>malicious_function()</script>
more plain content…"
```

The text is then saved in the database. If another user views the post containing this JavaScript, their browser has no way of knowing the script could be dangerous and runs it.

To prevent this behavior, a new module called `Bleach` is used to sanitize the user input text. The `Bleach` module is part of the `requirements.txt` file for this chapter and is imported at the top of the `content/forms.py` module. The user-entered text is filtered by the `content/forms.py` module before being saved:

```
def remove_html_and_script_tags(
input_string: str) -> str:
    return bleach.clean(input_string)
if input_string is not None else input_string
```

This function uses the `bleach.clean` method to sanitize the `input_string` parameter if it is not `None`, otherwise it just returns `input_string`. The `remove_html_and_script_tags()` function is added to all of the form classes that contain `StringField` or `PageDownField` elements. As an example, the `PostForm` content field has been updated to this:

```
content = PageDownField(
    "Content",
    validators=[DataRequired()],
    filters=(remove_html_and_script_tags,),
    render_kw={"placeholder": " ", "tabindex": 2}
)
```

The `filters` parameter is passed a tuple, the first element being the `remove_html_and_script_tags` function. When the form is submitted to the server, the filter function will be executed before the form provides the data during calls like this in `blog_post_create()`:

```
content=form.content.data.strip()
```

In this way, any embedded HTML code/scripts are disabled before the content is saved to the database.

11.11 Closing thoughts

This was a lot of ground to cover, and even if it uses some patterns you've seen before in other parts of the application, it represents a significant milestone in developing your skill set. By developing the MyBlog application, you're now able to zoom out to see the big picture necessary to build a larger application. You're also able to zoom in to see the detailed view needed to implement the parts of a big application.

The MyBlog application is now complete, as it has met the book's stated goals. As a teaching tool, I hope it has served you well. The application offers many opportunities for addition, modification, and improvement. I also think it's a good reference if you tackle developing another web application. To adapt an old cliché, "That's left as an exercise for the developer."

Summary

- Python classes using SQLAlchemy generate the MyBlog API to create posts and the user's relation to those posts. Doing so models the database tables, making them available to your Python application.
- By capitalizing on the `Flask-PageDown` module, we've added useful functionality to the MyBlog application without having to code that functionality ourselves. This is a key feature of an evolved developer, being able to recognize the talents of others and incorporate it into our own work.
- Self-referential hierarchal data maintained in a single database table is a powerful concept and feature of which to take advantage. By using common table expressions (CTEs) and recursion, it's possible to achieve this with SQLAlchemy and Python.
- Bootstrap has useful capabilities to create modal dialog boxes. These are useful to produce a form to gather data and keep them in the context of their current workflow. Using a modal to create comments on user content posts takes advantage of this feature.

Are we there yet? 12

Are we there yet?

So help me, I will turn this book around!

Joking aside, reading this book provides a great leap forward for a Python developer. If you've worked through the examples and built the MyBlog code, you've created an interesting application and managed the complexity of doing so. You've pulled together tools and techniques from many software engineering domains to create a cohesive whole that delivers useful functionality.

What's more, you've followed good practices to manage the complexity of the application. Having managed that complexity means the MyBlog application is maintainable over time and can be expanded on without making the structure brittle.

To answer the question "Are we there yet?" elicits the age-old response, "Well, yes and no." Let's talk about why the answer isn't definitive and how that's an energizing and exciting invitation to an adventurous journey to expand your skills as a developer even further.

12.1 Testing

An important aspect of creating software applications is testing them. I purposefully haven't included any discussion, or examples, of testing the code presented in this book. I did this for a couple of reasons.

First, writing test code often creates as much, if not more, code than the application being tested. This isn't a reason to avoid it, but in the context of this book, it would have added another technical domain of work over the examples. It would have also detracted from the educational intent of those examples.

Second, software testing is a big subject and warrants its own book. Including a subset of what software testing means would have done the subject matter, and you, a disservice. A great book about testing in the Python world is Brian Okken's *Python Testing with pytest* (http://mng.bz/Zql9).

Testing software benefits from automation in every way. Using testing tools and frameworks (like pytest) to automate tests provides consistency and early warnings if conditions change during development.

Also, in most cases, it's better if people other than the developer of the application perform the testing. It's far too easy as a developer to unconsciously follow the "happy path" that produces the desired results. This is very different from what users of your software do. They will push your software to its limits with edge cases and unintended boundary conditions. That being said, there are many types of testing to consider that apply to the applications and code you develop.

12.1.1 Unit testing

Unit testing is one of the cases where the developer of an application creates the tests. A unit test isolates a function or component and validates that it handles the inputs passed to the function and produces the expected outputs. Besides testing that the expected inputs produce the expected outputs, the tests should exercise edge cases. The tests should determine if the function reasonably handles unexpected inputs and if the output is an expected error condition or exception.

Unit tests should only examine the function or component being tested and not dependencies on external resources outside the test framework's ability to control or predict. Accessing a database, a network, or some unpredictable timing operation can cause a test to fail because the resource failed. In those cases, the external resource must be "mocked" to make the test repeatable. Mocking an external resource replaces the actual resource object with something that simulates its behavior but in a repeatable, dependable way.

12.1.2 *Functional testing*

Functional testing builds on unit testing by examining the functionality of systems and subsystems, which are built on functions and components. The purpose of the tests is to compare the actual functionality of a system against the requirements of that system. This draws on the specification to guide the development of a system and its intended purpose.

12.1.3 *End-to-end testing*

End-to-end (e2e) testing determines if the workflows provided by an application behave as expected from beginning to end. Is a user able to start, continue, and complete the process that the application is intended to provide?

12.1.4 *Integration testing*

Integration testing is similar to end-to-end testing with the addition that a system is run on the target hardware and in the environment where the application will be deployed. This isn't always possible, but steps should be taken to get as close to the target hardware and environment as reasonably practical.

12.1.5 *Load testing*

Load testing determines if an application running on its target hardware in its expected environment can handle the workload for which it's designed. Unit tests often use small subsets of controlled data to exercise functionality. Load testing data sets can be much larger to simulate actual use case data-handling expectations. For multi-user systems, like web applications, load testing also examines whether a system can handle the number of simultaneous users expected to access the system and remain responsive enough to meet their needs.

12.1.6 *Performance testing*

Performance testing determines if a system meets the performance requirements. The requirements can be expressed in terms of speed of processing, handling a specified number of multiple requests, the throughput of data, and other metrics. This kind of testing is dependent on a clear understanding of what the performance metrics are, how they will be measured, and that users and developers understand and agree on both.

12.1.7 *Regression testing*

Regression testing helps developers discover if code modifications in a system break functionality, adversely affect resource consumption, or change performance characteristics. Regression testing can automate examining and reporting on the results of end-to-end tests.

12.1.8 Accessibility testing

Accessibility testing is very dependent on who the audience is for the software you develop. If you are creating library code for users who are other developers, accessibility problems might focus on the developer experience.

However, if you are creating mobile or web applications that will be generally available to anyone, you need to think about how users with disabilities will access your application. The relevant disabilities can include vision and hearing impairment and other physical and cognitive concerns.

12.1.9 Acceptance testing

Acceptance testing is focused on whether software, or an application, meets the requirements that initiated creating it. The requirements can be defined by yourself, your colleagues, your company, or your customers. These are the stakeholders who determine if an application meets the agreed-upon requirements and can be considered complete.

It's enticing to assume that a fully complete and clear specification document is a necessity for acceptance testing. In my experience, for the average software project, no such document exists. Requirements are often vague and open-ended, which can lead to wildly different assumptions and understandings between users and developers about an application's functionality. Misunderstandings like this can cause the relationship between the end user and the developer to become adversarial, especially in situations where the developer accepts the requirements, and the user isn't involved in acceptance testing until the end of the project.

A different approach can often create a better path toward acceptance, with agreement all around. Because requirements are often insufficiently defined, it's better if the developer involves the user in an iterative process. As features are developed, they are demonstrated to the user, and course corrections are addressed as the product and its requirements are better understood by both parties.

Iterative development and acceptance-testing practice can turn an adversarial relationship into a more collaborative one. The final acceptance testing is more likely to be successful because the project outcome has been participated in by both the user and developer.

12.2 Debugging

If you attempted any of the examples, modified them, or wrote programs of your own, you've run into bugs in the code. There are no perfect programs, and bugs are part of a developer's life. There are runtime errors such as trying to divide by zero, and there are logical errors where the results of a program are not what you want or expect. Growing as a developer includes being able to find and fix problems—our own or others'—in program code.

12.2.1 Reproducing bugs

Before diving in and reading thousands, perhaps tens of thousands, of lines of code, it's essential to determine if the bug can be reproduced. Is there a series of steps you can take to cause the bug to occur reliably? Is there a set of data you can feed to the program to cause the bug to appear?

It's far more difficult to find and fix a bug if you can't exercise the bug consistently. This can mean taking the time to write harness code, or unit tests, to isolate the problem and inform you when the problem is resolved.

12.2.2 Breakpoints

Using a debugger to set breakpoints as part of your toolset is very effective for finding bugs in applications. A breakpoint is a location that you set in your application that triggers the application to stop running and transfer control to the debugger.

When a debugger intercepts a breakpoint, you can examine the state of the running application at that time. You can view variables, evaluate statements, and single-step to the next line of code to see the results.

Many debuggers can set conditional breakpoints, which are only triggered if certain conditions are true. For example, you can reproduce a bug, but only after thousands of iterations through a large data set. A conditional breakpoint can be set to trigger when a counter is equal to the number of iterations needed to trigger the bug. Examining code at a breakpoint is a valuable tool to ascertain what's occurring in an application at that snapshot of time.

12.2.3 Logging

Being able to observe the state of an application at a breakpoint is valuable, but sometimes you'll need to see the history of events as well. Logging events over the runtime of an application gives you a view of the path an application has taken through the code.

Adding a timestamp to those logging events also gives you a chronology of those events, when they occurred, and how much time has transpired between them. You can add print statements for this, but Python provides a better tool—the logging system. The Python logger module adds a great deal of visibility to the inner workings of your applications.

If you add `logger.debug(...)` statements to your code, you can log as much information as you need to help debug an application. Then, when the application is deployed, the `logger.level` can be set to `INFO` and the debug statements are ignored. This means the `logger.debug(...)` statements can be left in the code, unlike print statements, which should usually be removed to declutter the application's log output. If another bug manifests, the `logger.level` can be set to `DEBUG` and your `logger.debug(...)` statements become active again to assist with finding and resolving a new bug.

12.2.4 Bad results

Is the bug an application crash or are bad results being produced? In this case, it's very useful to use a debugger (standalone or built into an IDE) to understand the state of the application at the point the bug occurs or is about to occur.

Looking for the computation that generated the bad results can mean moving back and forth in the call stack (order of operations and function calls) to observe the values that contribute to the results. A pad and pencil, or a text editor, are useful here to keep track of these intermediary values. If the computations look right, perhaps the data set being fed to the application contains bad data.

12.2.5   Process of elimination

Often, the search for a bug is a process of elimination, constantly narrowing down the domain where the bug lives until you find it. This process can be in the code or the data. Using debugger breakpoints or logging statements can help narrow the domain in the code.

If you suspect the input data set is the source of the problem, use a divide-and-conquer approach to narrow in on the problem data. Cut the data in half and feed one half at a time to the application. Continue to repeat this process with the half that exhibited the problem until you find the value(s) that are triggering the bad results. Even with huge datasets, this process takes relatively few iterations.

12.2.6   Rubber-ducking the problem

Perhaps the simplest, and sometimes most effective, path to a solution is to talk about the problem with a friend or colleague. The act of putting your thoughts into words that clarify the problem for your audience often presents the solution or a path to the solution.

12.3   Tools

Like any complex, interesting task, there are tools available to help you accomplish your goals. Learning about useful tools and becoming proficient with them makes you a much more powerful developer.

12.3.1   Source control

The example code accompanying this book resides in a Git repository hosted on GitHub. Git is one tool used to create repositories for the source-code files necessary to create applications. Repository tools help manage the history of a project's development and the documentation of that history.

If you're working as the sole developer of an application, it's still well worth learning how to use a source-code management tool. Being able to review and restore the history of your work can be invaluable while working on a complex application over time. If you're part of a team working on an application, source control is a necessity to help manage and prevent collisions while more than one person works on the same section of code.

Lastly, using a hosted solution like GitHub offers a stable and convenient backup solution, over and above any backup system you maintain locally. You do backup your hard disk, don't you?

12.3.2 *Optimization*

When I was first writing software, I had daydreams about creating games with moving images that reacted to the player's input. At that time, computers were 8-bit systems with some 16-bit functionality, very limited memory, and CPUs that ran in the single-digit megahertz range.

With those goals, under those conditions, optimizing code for performance was a necessity. It was also a lot of fun figuring out how to pull a little more speed out of a system by using code only.

The lure of optimization is a siren song drawing in many a developer. Software runs exceptionally fast on modern computers, and thinking about how you can make an application run faster by different implementations, data structures, caching, and a host of other techniques is tempting.

The first element to consider when optimizing an application is the performance target. A general statement such as "make it faster" is not a clear requirement. Any reasonably complex application provides many features; you must determine which of those features is important to make faster, and by how much.

The second element to consider is measuring the performance of an application. It's important to measure the current baseline performance to establish if changes in the application improve the performance at all.

While thinking about optimizing an application, it's useful to keep the 90/10 rule in mind. As a rule of thumb, many applications spend 90 percent of their time in 10 percent of the code. If you embark on an optimization journey, this rule implies that you spend 90 percent of your development time working on the 10 percent of code where the application spends the bulk of its time.

Keep in mind a relevant concept I discussed in Chapter 1—optimizing your time as a developer. Reaching a "fast enough" state of an application that delivers the intended features right away is often more desirable than a marginally faster application that you deliver later. Remember the adage, "Shipping is a feature."

Lastly, an application's performance can be enormously improved by running it on a faster computer, on a network with more bandwidth, using a database with more capacity, and other dependencies outside of the application. These kinds of changes are often much less expensive in terms of developer time.

Becoming proficient with a tool also means knowing when not to use it.

12.3.3 *Containers*

A container provides an environment configured by the developer for an application to run in. In this way, an application in a container can run on any computing resource that can host the container. No matter what host the container runs on, the application in the container always interacts with the same environment.

The application in the container runs on what is commonly called a "guest" operating system. The guest operating system is a subset of a full operating system and is much smaller than a traditional virtual machine (VM). The application in the container makes calls to the guest OS for services, and the guest OS, in turn, makes calls to the "host" OS for services of the computing resource on which it resides.

Applications can also be developed directly in containers running on your development computer, which acts as the host for the container. This has the advantage of developing the application in the same environment (the container) with which it will be deployed.

12.3.4 *Databases*

The MyBlog application uses an SQLite database to persist the content and relationships created by users of the application. RDBMSs are often much larger and more complex than what we've created here, with many more tables containing millions of rows of data.

In the past, I have worked with existing databases far more than I've created them. As a developer, it's useful to learn more about database structures, tools, and techniques to expand the features of a database and maintain its performance. The databases presented in this book have done this by eliminating redundant data and taking advantage of the relationships possible in an RDBMS. It's also important to learn when redundant data is acceptable to improve query performance for an application.

Some database systems are document based rather than table based. These are often called NoSQL databases, as they sometimes don't provide SQL access to the data. Instead, the data is accessed by making function calls against the database API and passing parameters.

The NoSQL document-oriented databases often store information in JavaScript Object Notation (JSON) structures. Instead of table structures with strict data typing, the stored JSON data can be dynamically changed at will.

Both database approaches have advantages and disadvantages, and it falls to the developer and application stakeholders to determine which would serve the needs of an application best. A NoSQL database can be faster to retrieve data for certain kinds of applications. An RDBMS database can offer more structure and consistency to the data.

An additional wrinkle when considering either type of database is that both are acquiring more and more features of the other. Modern RDBMS databases offer the ability to store JSON data as a column within tables and functions to interact with the data contained by JSON documents. By the same token, NoSQL databases are offering SQL interfaces that allow more traditional queries to access the managed data.

12.3.5 *Languages*

This is a Python book, and Python is a powerful general-purpose language that is the right choice for many technical domains that can benefit from computer applications. That doesn't mean Python is the only, or even the best, choice in every situation.

One of the goals of this book is to give you a well-stocked toolbelt when constructing a Python application. Sometimes, however, the problem at hand would benefit from another toolbelt entirely. Learning and knowing other programming languages will benefit a well-grounded developer in many ways throughout their career.

For example, JavaScript is essentially the standard language when working in a web browser. Its superset, TypeScript, is also gaining traction, not only in the browser but as a server-side language.

Rust, C#, Go, Java, Kotlin, and many others all have wide application and acceptance as tools used in various programming domains. Those domains overlap, and the decision about which to use can be based on what language is most appealing and comfortable to a software developer.

Throughout my career, I've worked in Fortran, Pascal, C/C++, Visual Basic, PHP, JavaScript, TypeScript, and, of course, Python. Some of them I'd gladly work in again, some I'd rather not, but they all served me and my career well at the time. Staying current is an interesting and challenging part of being a developer. Spending time learning new technology tools should benefit you and your life, so spend it wisely.

12.4   OS environments

Many of the applications running in the world are hosted on Windows, Linux, or Mac computers. As a developer, the computer you work on will also most likely be a Windows, Linux, or Mac system. You can spend a career working in a single environment to develop and deploy your applications, but doing so might shrink the domain of the kinds of applications you can write.

Programming in Python allows you to create applications that are unaware of what operating system the application runs on most of the time. It's that last part, "most of the time," that is worth keeping in mind.

Becoming familiar with developing for other operating systems is valuable because it puts another tool in your hands to reach a wider audience. With the growing adoption of cloud computing and the use of containers for applications, developing on one platform and targeting another for deployment is common.

12.5   Cloud computing

Cloud computing systems allow computing resources to be located elsewhere and accessed securely through the internet. Besides moving the responsibility of running and maintaining computing hardware for a service, it gives developers the ability to size the computing resources and capabilities appropriately for user requirements. The size and capabilities of the resource can also be changed dynamically up or down, depending on the workload on the system.

Applications rarely execute in isolation and have dependencies on networks, file storage, load balancers, databases, and more. These dependencies are also available from cloud service providers and can be scaled to meet the needs of an entire integrated system. Applications can run independently in a cloud provider's computing instance, but it's becoming more common for an application to exist in a container.

12.6   Networking

The world is a very connected place and becoming more so all the time. Connections and what they bring to conversations and the choices we make have changed the fabric of society in extraordinary ways. A software application working in isolation would be a rare exception, as almost all significant applications run and depend on environments connected to a network and often beyond to the internet.

While working on the MyBlog application—getting the server running and accessing it with a local browser—it can be easy to forget that it's a networked application. There's no reason the application couldn't run on a server located in one part of the world and be accessed by a web browser somewhere else in the world. Writing applications for computer systems connected to networks means your application can provide information and resources to other systems, as well as consume information and resources provided by other systems on the network.

All modern languages provide tools and libraries to interface with networks and communicate across them. The MyBlog application is an example that uses the HTTP protocol to connect the server to the browser. Learning how to use and develop networked applications can increase the power and feature sets of your applications by orders of magnitude.

12.7   Collaboration

Building relationships is an important aspect of being a well-grounded developer. Certainly, creating and maintaining relationships in a database is vital, but building and maintaining relationships with the people in your life is far more important.

Even as the sole developer on a personal project, you'll be reaching out to ask questions on sites, blogs, and user groups, and of colleagues and friends, seeking help with challenges you'll face. Remember the idiom "Good developers are lazy"? It doesn't mean well-grounded developers are slow to complete their projects; it means we take advantage of already-existing solutions to problems to implement elements faster.

Being part of a community is a two-way street. We should listen more than talk, strive to offer more help than we ask for, and work hard to build and maintain relationships so others in the community seek us out.

Being part of a diverse community of developers means encountering various perspectives. In my experience, this exposure presents approaches, ideas, and solutions that I wouldn't have established on my own.

Collaboration is a multiplier. Connecting and sharing with people multiplies your talents and abilities as a developer manyfold.

12.8   Closing thoughts

You've come a long way on your journey as a well-grounded Python developer—from the early chapters of observing through a telescope to the huge field of view of many possible destinations and the many small details of a fully realized and focused application. The characteristics of being a software developer are unique from any other engineering endeavor. The domains in which we work span the macroscopic view of the unfathomably huge to the microscopic details of the unimaginably small.

I've been developing software for nearly forty years and accept that there are so many things I still want to learn. The desire to learn and the fortunate ability to do so have been key for me.

My goal for this book was to help guide you along a path that leads to being a well-grounded Python developer. Yet, the answer to the question "Are we there yet?" is happily "no." You are at a way station that branches into many paths, and you can follow any of them. I hope that you find the journeys ahead as enlightening and enjoyable and just plain as much fun as possible.

Summary

- Application testing is an important aspect of developing useful and stable applications. Many facets exist to testing an application—some can be automated, and some can't. It's also a big topic worthy of its own book.
- Being able to reproduce, find, and fix bugs is an essential skill of the well-grounded developer. Good tools and the right mindset are the starting places to begin debugging an application.
- Code optimization is a double-edged sword. It can offer great improvements to an application's performance, and it can be a huge time sink. Having reasons to optimize an application, specific goals to achieve, and metrics to measure whether you've achieved those goals are essential first steps.
- We've only touched on what databases can do for you as a developer and for your applications as a resource. Learning more about their capabilities and constraints is time well spent.

appendix
Your development
environment

As a Python developer, you need a suitable environment on your computer. The developer environment must cover a lot of ground. In general, it should include a set of tools with which you're familiar and some ideas about how you will structure project directories. Depending on your computer, it might also include environment variables you've set up to help make things more automated and therefore useful.

You'll find that what you're about to create and configure is a good starting point on the way to building your own useful and powerful development environment. For those of you who already have a development environment you're comfortable with, feel free to skim over this. However, be aware of any differences presented here; you'll need to account for them in your environment.

A.1 Installing Python

First, you're going to need Python installed on your computer. This might seem obvious, but it's a little more involved than it might first appear. Not all operating systems come with Python installed, and sometimes when Python is installed it's older than currently available versions. Even if the version of Python installed on your computer is recent, it's still a good idea to install Python for your use while developing.

If Python is installed along with the operating system, there's a good chance it's being used for system-level functions by the operating system. If that's the case, there's also a good chance your operating system is dependent on the version of Python it came with and any modules that were installed for that version to use.

The programming examples in this book will ask you to install additional third-party libraries using the Python package management tool pip. It's a bad idea to install these additional libraries in your system Python because a newly installed version of a library might change the functionality of an existing system requirement and break it. You also don't want updates to the operating system to change the Python functionality on which you depend for your development efforts.

With that in mind, you'll install version 3.10.3 of Python, which will be distinct from any operating system–installed version. The newly installed version of Python is entirely under your control and independent of the operating system. This means you can add, remove, and update library modules as you see fit, and only your program code will be affected.

You'll need to install the stable 3.10.3 version of Python so you'll have the same Python version that the sample programs in this book were coded and tested against to minimize runtime problems.

A.1.1   Windows

Python may or may not be installed by default on your Windows operating system, which isn't known to use Python. So once Python is installed, it's available solely for your development work.

Recent Windows versions have Python available in the Microsoft Store, making installation very easy. The Microsoft Store version of Python at the time of this writing is being evaluated, and not all features are guaranteed to be stable. This doesn't mean you shouldn't use it, just that you should be aware of these issues.

If you prefer, use the stable 3.10.3 version of Python available for your version of Windows by navigating to http://www.python.org in your browser and following the download links. For most users, the right version to use is the executable installer suitable for your CPU and OS version.

During the installation process, the installer allows you to check a box that adds Python to your PATH environment variable. Check this box and save yourself some trouble later. If you miss this and Python doesn't run from within PowerShell at the command prompt, you can always rerun the installer and add Python to the path.

A.1.2   Mac

On Macs, an older version of Python is installed that you should avoid using for your development. Instead, install the 3.10.3 version of Python that's completely separate from the system. To perform this installation, use the pyenv utility program. This program lets you install as many versions of Python as you'd like and switch between them. For the examples in this book, install Python version 3.10.3.

You'll need to have the Homebrew program installed on your Mac to follow the next steps. Homebrew is a package manager for Mac OS that you can use to install many useful command-line tools, like pyenv. The Homebrew program and its installation instructions are available here: https://brew.sh. After installing the brew program, open your terminal program and follow these command-line steps to install pyenv:

1 To install the pyenv utility program on your Mac, run the command: brew install pyenv.

2 To add useful setup information to your terminal configuration file to make using pyenv easier, run the following command to add pyenv support to your configuration file (.zshrc for me, but could be .bash_profile for you):

```
echo -e 'if command -v pyenv 1>/dev/null 2>&1; then\n
➥eval "$(pyenv init -)"\nfi' >> ~/.zshrc
```

3 To rerun your shell initialization scripts and activate the previous commands, run the command exec "$SHELL".

4 To install Python v3.10.3 on your computer in your home folder, run the command pyenv install 3.10.3.

5 To verify the installation of Python and the version, run the command pyenv versions.

NOTE   If you have a recent Mac with an M1 or higher CPU, the previous steps may be somewhat different for you.

A.1.3   Linux

There are so many versions of Linux in general use, it would be awkward and outside the scope of this book to present pyenv installation instructions for all those versions. However, if you're using Linux as your development platform, you're probably already familiar with how to find what you need to install applications like pyenv on the Linux system you're using.

Even on Linux systems that have Python 3 installed, it's better to install and explicitly control the version of Python you're going to use for development. Once pyenv is installed, use it to install Python version 3.10.3 with the following command lines:

```
pyenv install 3.10.3
pyenv versions
```

The first command installed the version of Python you're going to use for the examples in this book in a directory controlled by pyenv. That version is kept separate from any other Python versions installed with pyenv and the system version of Python. The second will list the versions installed, which should show the version you just installed.

A.2   *Python virtual environment*

Now that you have Python 3.10.3 installed on your computer completely separate from any system-installed Python, you might think you're ready to go. Even with a version of Python installed using the pyenv utility, you'll want to use another level of abstraction from that version in your projects.

Python 3.10.3 provides the built-in ability to create virtual environments. Python virtual environments are *not* the virtual machines you might be familiar with, like VMWare, Parallels, or VirtualBox. These tools allow an entire OS to run as a guest inside a different OS. A Python virtual environment only creates a Python installation inside a project directory. This Python installation can have modules added to it with the pip command, and these modules are only installed and available for the project-specific Python.

You can have many projects that use the same version of Python installed by pyenv, but each Python virtual environment is separate from the others. This means you can have different versions of modules installed by the pip command without conflict in each virtual environment.

> **NOTE** The value of Python virtual environments can't be overstated. Being able to create, maintain, and work with stable and complete Python and library installations goes a long way toward eliminating future problems. You want to be a Python developer, not a system administrator after all.

The pip command-line tool that comes with Python is a fantastic utility. It is the package installer for Python that allows you to add additional modules from the Python Package Index (https://pypi.org/). The modules available from the Python Package Index provide functionality above and beyond what comes with the Python standard library. The code examples in this book use quite a few modules from that resource.

A.2.1 *Windows*

In a Windows system, you install Python directly rather than using pyenv, as Windows doesn't use Python as part of its operation. You'll still want to use a project-specific Python virtual environment to keep your system-level Python installation separated from any modules you're going to install with pip.

To run the Python virtual environment activation and deactivation scripts, you'll need to change the execution policy of your computer. To do this, you'll need to run the PowerShell program as an administrator. Follow these steps:

1 Click on the Windows Start icon.
2 Scroll down to the PowerShell menu selection and drop down the submenu.
3 Right-click on the PowerShell submenu item.
4 Select Run as Administrator from that context menu.
5 Once you're in PowerShell running as administrator, run this command:

```
Set ExecutionPolicy Unrestricted
```

The system will prompt you with a question, which you answer with y and then hit the return key. At this point, exit PowerShell so you're no longer in administrator mode. You only need to do this once as it's a system-wide setting.

Open the PowerShell program again—not as an administrator—to get to a command-line prompt and follow these steps to create a new Python virtual environment specific to the project directory:

1 Run the command mkdir <project directory name>.
2 Run the command cd <project directory name>.

3 Run the command `python -m venv .venv`.
4 Run the command `.venv/Scripts/activate`.
5 Run the command `python -m pip install --upgrade pip` [optional].

Line 1 creates a new project directory with whatever name you want to give it. Line 2 changes your current working context into the newly created directory. Line 3 uses Python to create the Python virtual environment. This might take a few moments to complete.

Line 4 activates the virtual environment, prepending the command prompt with (`.venv`), indicating the environment is active. Once the environment is active, any additional libraries installed will be installed in the `.venv` directory and won't affect the Python version you previously installed. To deactivate the virtual environment, just enter `deactivate` at the command prompt.

Line 5 is optional and upgrades the version of the `pip` command that exists within the Python virtual environment you've just set up. If `pip` detects you are running an older version, it will print out a message informing you that you're running an older version and that you should update that version. You can ignore the information and skip line 5 if you like. I included it because I ran the command to stop seeing that message.

A.2.2 *Mac and Linux*

Setting up a Python virtual environment on the Mac is straightforward if you've installed the Python 3.10.3 version using `pyenv`, as described previously. Open your terminal program and follow these steps to create a new Python virtual environment specific to the project directory:

1 Run the command `mkdir <project directory name>`.
2 Run the command `cd <project directory name>`.
3 Run the command `pyenv local 3.10.3`.
4 Run the command `python -m venv .venv`.
5 Run the command `source .venv/bin/activate`.
6 Run the command `pip install --upgrade pip` [optional].

Line 1 creates a new project directory with whatever name you want to give it. Line 2 changes your current working context into the newly created directory. Line 3 creates the local file `.python-version`, which `pyenv` uses to control what version of Python to run when you're working in this directory—in this case, version 3.10.3.

Line 4 uses the local Python version to create the Python virtual environment in the `.venv` directory. Line 5 activates the virtual environment, prepending the command prompt with (`.venv`), indicating the environment is active. Once the environment is active, any additional libraries will be installed in the `.venv` directory and won't affect the `pyenv` Python version previously installed. To deactivate the virtual environment, enter `deactivate` at the command prompt.

Line 6 is optional and upgrades the version of the `pip` command that exists within the Python virtual environment you've set up previously. If `pip` detects you are running an older version, it will print out a message that you're running an older version, and that you should update that version. You can ignore the information and skip line 6 if you like. I included it because I wanted to stop seeing that message.

A.3   *Setting up Visual Studio Code*

It's possible to write Python code using just a text editor. Within the context of writing Python program code, a text editor is precisely that—an editor that adds no more or less than what you type on the keyboard. The Notepad application on Windows and the Textedit application on Mac are both examples of simple, capable text editors.

Microsoft Word, while a powerful editor, is not a good choice to create plain text, as its default is to save what you type without a great deal of additional information about formatting, font choices, and so on, that has nothing to do with program code. Any word processor application makes writing plain Python code more complicated than using a text editor.

Python programs are just plain text files having the `.py` file extension. Many text editors understand that a file with the `.py` extension is a Python file. These editors will provide whitespace indenting automatically when you hit the enter key at the end of a line of code that includes the block indicator character (`` ` ``:`` ` ``). They will also syntax highlight your code, which means changing the color of the text to highlight Python keywords, strings, variables, and other visual cues about the program you're creating.

Microsoft provides a free code editor called Visual Studio Code (VSCode for short), and it is a great choice to use as a Python program editor. Besides being an excellent editor, it has many extensions available to make it an even better system to work with when developing Python applications. You'll install one of those extensions for Python that turns Visual Studio Code into a complete integrated development environment (IDE). This extension provides Python syntax highlighting and other language-specific features. The most powerful feature is the ability to run and debug your code interactively from within the editor.

A.3.1   *Installing Visual Studio Code*

At the time of this book's publication, you can download Visual Studio Code at https://code.visualstudio.com. This link takes you to the Microsoft web page, which has links to download VSCode for Windows, Mac, and Linux. Visual Studio Code is a separate application from Visual Studio, which is Microsoft's much larger commercial application development system.

For Windows and Mac installation, the process is relatively simple: click on the link to download the installation program, then double-click on the downloaded file to install the application. For Linux installations, click on the link and, depending on your Linux version, choose the package manager that will run the installation process. After installation, add the VSCode application icon to the Windows taskbar, Mac dock, or the Linux desktop/application menu to make it more readily accessible.

A.3.2   Installing the Python extension

Once VSCode is installed, you'll need to add the Python extension from Microsoft. This extension provides syntax highlighting, IntelliSense, debugging capabilities, and many other features. Follow these steps:

1 Open the VSCode application.
2 Within VSCode, open the Extensions.
   – Click on the Extensions icon.
   – Select View -> Extensions.
3 In the Search Extensions in the Marketplace text box, enter "python" and click the return key.
4 Make sure to use the Python extension from Microsoft.
5 On that first item, click the install button.

Create a new Python code file with the .py file extension and enter some Python code. Does VSCode syntax highlight the code? Are you able to save and run the code from within VSCode?

At this point, VSCode is configured to work with Python files. Take some time and read the documentation about the Python extension in the right-hand windowpane of the application.

A.3.3   Other useful extensions

Besides the Python extension provided by Microsoft, there are other useful extensions available:

- *Python Docstring Generator*—Automatically generates Python docstring comments when you enter triple quotes (""") immediately after a function or method definition and click the enter key. The docstring is a template containing all the parameters and return values in an easy-to-navigate manner, making documenting your code much simpler.
- *Code Runner*—Makes it easier to run Python code files from a right-click context menu within VSCode.
- *DotENV*—Adds syntax highlighting for .env files, which are local environment files useful to initialize environment variables outside of code files.
- *Better Jinja*—Adds syntax highlighting to the Jinja templating language, which is the default for Flask web applications.

A.3.4   Starting from the command line

VSCode is a powerful GUI application that can be started by double-clicking on its icon or by clicking on its name/icon from a visual menu. This is a common use case for visual tools on the desktop but isn't the most helpful way to start the application for your purposes. Because all of this book's example code will use a Python virtual environment, it's useful to create a virtual environment before starting VSCode. It's also helpful to be able to start VSCode from the command line within the project directory containing the virtual environment. Starting VSCode this way will help it "see" and use the virtual environment in the directory. To configure VSCode to start from the command line in the directory you're in, do the following:

- Windows:
  - After installing VSCode, the system is already configured to open VSCode in the current directory from the PowerShell command prompt by entering this command:

    ```
    code .
    ```

- Mac:
  - Start VSCode.
  - Navigate to the Command Palette (View -> Command Palette).
  - Enter `shell` command to find the Shell Command: Install "code" command in PATH command.
  - Click on the above.
- Linux:
  - After installing VSCode, the system is already configured to open VSCode in the current directory from a terminal by entering the command:

    ```
    code .
    ```

A.3.5   *Starting a project*

With VSCode installed and configured to start from the command line, you can go through the steps of creating a project directory and starting VSCode to use it. Starting VSCode this way is used for all the example projects in this book and, in general, is an excellent way to create projects of your own. Follow these steps to create a new project:

1 Open a terminal or PowerShell and get to a command prompt.
2 Change your directory to where you'd like to create your project.
3 In that directory, create a new directory `mkdir <project name>`.
4 Change your directory to the newly created `<project name>` directory.
5 For Mac and Linux, enter this command: `pyenv local 3.10.3`.
6 Enter this command: `python -m venv .venv`.

At this point, the project is set up to use the Python version 3.10.3 virtual environment installed in the `.venv` directory. The name `.venv` is commonly used as the directory name for a locally installed virtual environment. You can activate your local Python environment and see if it's working by following these steps:

1 Activate your Python virtual environment as follows:
   Mac and Linux, enter this command: `source .venv/bin/activate`
   Windows, enter this command: `.venv\Scripts\activate`

2 Your command prompt will be prepended with (.venv).

3 Enter this command: python --version.

4 The system will respond with Python 3.10.3.

Now that your Python virtual environment is created in your project directory, VSCode will discover it when you start from the command line. Entering code . from the command line will open VSCode in the project directory. Because you created a Python virtual environment in the directory, VSCode will prompt you if you want to use that environment, to which you should respond yes. Follow these steps to continue configuring VSCode to work with any Python code you create within your project:

1 Open the Command Palette (View -> Command Palette).

2 Type Select Interpreter in the text box and click Python: Select Interpreter.

3 In the popup menu that appears, select the virtual environment you created as follows:

Windows: .venv\Scripts\python.exe

Mac and Linux: .venv/bin/python

4 Create a new file (File -> New File).

5 In the file editor window that's generated, enter the following code:

```
print("hello world")
```

6 Save the file as a Python file (File -> Save -> test.py).

VSCode will show a prompt informing you, "Linter pylint is not installed." Click the Install button. VSCode will use the pip command from your virtual environment to install PyLinter. A linter is a pre-runtime tool that checks your code for syntax errors, bugs, unusual constructs, and more and is a useful tool to have installed for every project.

7 Right-click on the test.py editor window and select Run Python File in Terminal.

NOTE It might feel like a great deal of work to get VSCode up and running and that you've simply given yourself another tool to learn. That's all true, but I encourage you to use and learn the tool. An IDE is a great effort multiplier and gives you, as a developer, real advantages.

After the last step, you should see "hello world" printed in a terminal window opened within VSCode. Congratulations, you've just run your first Python program within your powerful project environment!

A.4 *Some advice*

One more concept to emphasize is the most useful tool available to you—yourself. Invest time to optimize how you work as a developer. Having a suitable development environment that you're familiar with is powerful, but setting up a productive personal working environment is time well spent. If you're going to develop software for yourself, professionally, or both, you're going to spend a considerable amount of time doing so. A reasonable desk, a comfortable chair, a good monitor, and a suitable keyboard are all part of that environment.

This last piece of advice is based on years of working as a developer, both singly and in teams. (If it doesn't apply to you, please feel free to disregard it.) Spend time making the interface between you and your code as fast and seamless as possible. Learn to touch type and make use of keyboard shortcuts instead of using the mouse. My mom made me take typing classes in junior high back in the days of the IBM Selectric typewriter. I can tell you I was not too happy about it and didn't appreciate it for many years. Now I consider it one of the many gifts she gave me that I am thankful for every day.

There are many things you'll write as a developer besides code: documents, wiki pages, web pages, presentations, notes, emails—the list is long and only getting longer. Sending your thoughts out through your hands and onto the screen quickly and accurately moves the mechanics out of the way and lets your thoughts and ideas flow.

index

RELATED MANNING TITLES

Fast Python
by Tiago Rodrigues Antão

ISBN 9781617297939
304 pages, $59.99
April 2023

Publishing Python Packages
by Dane Hillard
Foreword by David Beazley

ISBN 9781617299919
248 pages, $59.99
December 2022

Python Concurrency with asyncio
by Matthew Fowler

ISBN 9781617298660
376 pages, $59.99
February 2022

Full Stack Python Security
by Dennis Byrne

ISBN 9781617298820
304 pages, $59.99
July 2021

For ordering information, go to www.manning.com